Reading Contemporary Picturebooks

Reading Contemporary Picturebooks takes a close look at one of the most vibrant and exciting branches of children's literature – the modern picturebook. There has been an enormous increase in the quantity of high quality picturebooks published for children, yet our understanding of what it means to be visually literate and our knowledge of how readers negotiate such composite texts is limited. This book takes a sample of contemporary picturebooks and examines the features that make them unique, suggesting ways of studying and understanding the form.

Issues addressed include:

- the interaction of word and image in picturebooks
- the ecology of the picturebook
- the picturebook as process
- picturebooks at play
- postmodernism and the picturebook
- studying and understanding picturebooks

Reading Contemporary Picturebooks is both an introduction to a fascinating and innovative branch of children's literature and a detailed examination of how picturebooks work.

This book will be of interest to students, teachers and researchers interested in reading, children's literature and media studies.

David Lewis is one of the leading British specialists on picturebooks. He was formerly Lecturer in Primary Education at the University of Exeter.

Reading Contemporary Picturebooks

Picturing text

David Lewis

Routledge
Taylor & Francis Group

LONDON AND NEW YORK

First published 2001
by Routledge
2 Park Square, Milton Park, Abingdon, Oxon, OX14 4RN

Simultaneously published in the USA and Canada
by Routledge
270 Madison Ave, New York NY 10016

Routledge is an imprint of the Taylor & Francis Group

Transferred to Digital Printing 2006

© 2001 David Lewis

Typeset in Goudy by Bookcraft Ltd, Stroud, Gloucestershire

British Library Cataloguing in Publication Data
A catalogue record for this book is available from the British Library

Library of Congress Cataloging in Publication Data
Lewis, David, 1947 Oct. 1
  Reading contemporary picturebooks : picturing text/David Lewis.
    p. cm.
  Includes bibliographical references and index.
  1. Picture books for children. 2. Illustrated children's books.
  3. Children's literature. 4. History and criticism. 1. Title.

PN1009.AI L49 2001
809'.89282—dc21   00–051801

ISBN 0–415–20886–6 (hbk)
ISBN 0–415–20887–4 (pbk)

Publisher's Note
The publisher has gone to great lengths to ensure the quality of this reprint
but points out that some imperfections in the original may be apparent

Printed and bound by CPI Antony Rowe, Eastbourne

For Maureen, Simon and Claire

Contents

Figures

Acknowledgements

Many people have influenced the development and writing of this book, but in particular I am grateful to Margaret Spencer who first taught me how to look at and think about picturebooks, and to Geoff Fox for reading the first complete draft of this book and teaching me, in the nicest possible way, how to make it better. Thanks must also go to Leslie Cunliffe of Exeter University for reading the first draft of Chapter 8 and giving helpful advice. The boys and girls with whom I worked at Coopers Lane School in South-east London deserve my thanks too, as do their teachers. I am grateful to my colleagues at Exeter University's School of Education for taking over my responsibilities while I took a term's study leave to complete the PhD upon which much of the material in this book is based, and I thank Vanessa Burdon, an ex-student of the School of Education, for allowing me to use material from an unpublished case study. Last but certainly not least I am indebted to my wife Maureen for the support she provided in ways too numerous to mention, most importantly in helping me believe that writing this book was worthwhile, and I wish to thank my children, Simon and Claire, for acting as guinea pigs when they were too young to know better. It is to them, my family, that this book is dedicated.

I would also like to thank the following for permission to reproduce material in this book: Andersen Press for the illustrations from *Way Home*, text copyright © 1994 Libby Hathorn. Illustrations copyright © 1994 Gregory Rogers on page 73; Blackwell Publishers, copyright © 1958 Basil Blackwell & Mott Ltd., for the extracts from *Philosophical Investigations* by Ludwig Wittgenstein on pages 29, 124, 126 and 130; Jonathan Cape for the illustrations from *Drop Dead*, copyright © 1996 Babette Cole on pages 24 and 70; Jonathan Cape for the illustrations from *All Join In*, copyright © 1990 Quentin Blake on pages 16 and 108; Jonathan Cape for the illustrations from *Granpa*, copyright © 1984 John Burningham on pages 6 and 121; Jonathan Cape for the illustrations from *Time to Get Out of the Bath, Shirley*, copyright © 1978 John Burningham on pages 56 and 57; Julia MacRae for the illustrations from *The Man*, copyright © 1992 Raymond Briggs on pages 8 and 51; Lemniscaat b.v., for the illustrations from *Where is Monkey?* copyright © 1986 Dieter Schubert on pages 106, 107 and 111; Martin Secker & Warburg for the extract from *How Far Can You Go?*,

Introduction

Although books have always been illustrated, the special form of text that we now call the picturebook is a relatively recent invention. Its emergence from other forms of printed matter such as chapbooks, toy books and comics has been gradual and rather uneven so that the first examples that looked anything like the ones examined in this book began to appear towards the end of the nineteenth century and it was not until the second half of the twentieth century that the picturebook was fully formed.[1] Since the 1960s more and more picturebooks have been published every year so that now, in the early years of the twenty-first century, it is beginning to feel as if they have always been here. The form has its grand masters and living legends in figures like Maurice Sendak, its canonical texts which are studied in universities around the world, and its devoted readers in classrooms and homes everywhere.

And yet the workings of the picturebook are still rather poorly understood. This is hardly surprising as the serious study of any new cultural form is bound to lag behind its appearance and its adoption by the populace. In the case of picturebooks, it was only in the 1980s that the form began to be taken seriously as an object of academic study. Perry Nodelman's *Words About Pictures*, published in 1988, was one of the first attempts to analyse the workings of the picturebook and it has since become something of a standard work on the subject. However, as we shall see, there is still a good deal of disagreement over how we might best understand the picturebook. There has long been a broad consensus about the basic characteristics of the form, its combining of two distinct modes of representation – pictures and words – into a composite text, but it is precisely this doubleness, this two-sided quality, which has led to much confusion and disagreement. For example, are picturebooks first and foremost books – that is, stories that just happen to be 'told' in pictures as well as words – or are they better thought of as a kind of narrative visual art that happens to be annotated or captioned with words? Is it really the pictures that lie at the heart of picturebooks, or do we need to look for ways in which the pictures and the words interact and work upon each other? Further disagreements revolve around the fact that the vast majority of picturebooks are created for children. If we wish to be clearer about the nature of the picturebook should we attend to what children make of them or will our own close reading of individual texts be sufficient? And how relevant is it to our attempts to understand picturebooks that they are often used for teaching children to read?

This indecisiveness can even be sensed in the way that the metalanguage – the language we use to talk and write about the subject – is still relatively unstable. How should you spell 'picturebook', for example? Is it a compound word (picturebook), a hyphenated word (picture-book), or two distinct words (picture book)? Perry Nodelman has it as two words while Peter Hunt's *Children's Literature: an Illustrated History* has it hyphenated. Victor Watson's *Cambridge Guide to Children's Literature* makes it a compound and I have chosen to use this latter form here the better to reflect the compound nature of the artefact itself for I shall be arguing in these pages that the first step we should take in examining the picturebook is to look at it whole.

In the chapters that follow I shall be picking my way through the uncertainties and confusions mentioned above. Although I have not attempted to provide a simple answer to each individual question – indeed, I do not think we should expect simple answers – I hope that I have managed to articulate a more or less coherent vision. I have drawn upon a range of sources and precursors and can claim only modest originality but I have not attempted to summarize previous work in the field, nor have I tried to write a picturebook 'primer' or introductory text. The book is the fruit of my own reflections upon a form of text that I first became fond of when my children were very young and just discovering the world of books and print and pictures. As a result, it is undoubtedly eclectic in its approach to its subject and possibly (some readers may think positively) eccentric. Be that as it may, I hope it might serve to introduce the delights of the picturebook to those who are studying it for the first time, prove just disturbing enough to unsettle those who have some familiarity with the subject, and prompt as many as are interested to undertake their own investigations.

In writing the book I had to settle to my own satisfaction the question of how best to deal with another oddity about its subject, and that is the way in which the terminology we normally apply to books, texts and reading do not seem to attach to the picturebook so readily. For example, if we speak of 'the text' of a picturebook, do we mean the words or the words-and-pictures together? In almost all other contexts 'text' means words, so there is some risk of confusion here. And when we say we 'read' a picturebook does the word – and the process – apply equally well to the visual images and to the sentences and paragraphs alongside, or do we need another term that better represents the special relationship of picture and beholder? In order to reduce confusion to a minimum I have stuck as closely as possible to the following conventions. Picturebooks are *read* by *readers* and the combination of words and images working together in a picturebook I refer to as *picturebook text*. When the context makes it clear that the words are being referred to I use the term *text* (for example, 'the text alongside the image is as follows ...'). At all other times, when there is any risk of confusion, I refer to *the written text*, *the printed text* or *the words*. The pictures are *images*, *visual images*, *pictures* or *illustrations*. In a similar fashion, a *writer* or *author* creates the written text and an *illustrator* or *artist* creates the pictures. The term *picturebook maker* is used when writer and illustrator are one and the same person. At times it may be necessary to employ a more technical vocabulary and I have supplied a glossary at the end of the book to assist with any unfamiliar terms.

The first four chapters are largely, but not solely, concerned with the picturebook's formal features. I describe in Chapter 1 a sample of contemporary picturebooks and look for similarities and differences amongst them. I have begun in this way because I believe we will learn best, and learn most, by starting with an open mind about what picturebooks look like and by examining closely a more or less random sample. In Chapter 2 I take a critical look at some of the ways in which the interaction of pictures and words in picturebooks has been described and then, in Chapter 3, suggest an alternative way of approaching this task. I also make a case here for the importance of including the readings and responses of both adults and children in our thinking about picturebooks. Chapter 4 attempts to account for the flexibility and adaptability of the form by showing how the picturebook's capacity to co-opt, ingest and adapt to pre-existent forms keeps it perpetually open-ended and developing. In the final four chapters the emphasis shifts towards an examination of the ways in which readers and contexts influence the picturebook's shape and form. Chapter 5 looks at the association between young children, picturebooks and play and suggests that the picturebook's open-endedness, its capacity to constantly re-shape itself, is to some extent a response to the gradual emergence of children's understanding of books and reading. Chapter 6 looks critically at recent claims that many picturebooks betray a leaning towards the postmodern in their predilection for rule breaking. Chapter 7 reviews some of the main ways in which pictures come to have meaning for us, focusing especially upon the grammar of visual design recently devised and elaborated by Gunther Kress and Theo van Leeuwen. In Chapter 8 I explore, in a rather tentative fashion, how insights derived from the work of the philosopher Ludwig Wittgenstein might open up perspectives upon how the pictures in picturebooks come to have meaning for readers. This final chapter also leads me to my conclusions about how best to study and understand picturebooks.

Writing about picturebooks always involves trying to find ways around the fact that it is necessary to *see* the subject under discussion as well as read about it. There is something unsatisfying about being faced with pages of print when what you really want to do is examine the image that is being described in words. I have tried to deal with this difficulty in several ways. A small number of illustrations are distributed throughout the book, most of them placed in Chapter 1 where the sample is first described, and I have referred to these as often as I can. At other times – especially when I wish to make a narrowly focused or specific point about an image – I have attempted to describe illustrations in ways that, I hope, will allow readers to conjure up in imagination whatever is necessary to make sense of my arguments. I have also tried, outside of the basic sample, to allude only to books that are reasonably popular and well known.

At numerous points throughout the book I have drawn upon conversations with children about picturebooks. Most of these were carried out in a Southeast London primary school. They usually took place while a particular picturebook was being read so that we were able to talk about puzzles, immediate impressions and misunderstandings the moment they occurred. In every case I was far more interested in what the children had to say about what they were reading than in attempting to teach them anything. As a result, we developed a relationship that allowed the children to talk freely and openly about anything that seemed relevant to them. Over the last few years these conversations have been enormously helpful to me in my attempts to understand more fully what it means to read a picturebook, and two conversations in particular, each one about the same book, have been particularly revealing. The book is John Burningham's *Time to Get Out of the Bath, Shirley* and the readers, Nathan and Jane. Burningham has always been extremely skilful at teasing and provoking his readers as well as engrossing them, and this makes him especially useful to anyone attempting to investigate what it is we do when we try to make sense of combinations of words and pictures that purport to tell a story. Other conversations are reported from time to time, but Jane and Nathan's grapplings with Burningham's odd little story have taught me as much about picturebooks, if not more, than anything I have read or heard elsewhere (with one or two notable exceptions: see Acknowledgements). In reporting our conversations I have smoothed out some of the more awkward gaps and hesitations but have tried not to distort the sense of what was being said. It is never easy interpreting what children say about what they are reading but I believe the task has to be undertaken and I hope I have not done too much violence to their attempts to say what must at times have seemed almost unsayable. Nathan and Jane were six when we first met and will now be quite a few years older. I do hope they are still reading picturebooks.

Notes

1   It is difficult to be precise about when the modern picturebook first made its appearance but most authorities seem to be agreed that during the late nineteenth century picturebook makers such as Randolph Caldecott played a decisive role in transforming the Victorian toy book into something much more like the modern picturebook. Similarly, although many fine picturebooks were published prior to the 1960s, a number of factors converged around that time to enable publishers to produce and sell high quality picturebooks in larger numbers than ever before.

Chapter 1

Modern picturebooks
The state of the art

A picturebook is text, illustrations, total design; an item of manufacture and a commercial product; a social, cultural, historical document; and, foremost, an experience for a child.

As an art form it hinges on the interdependence of pictures and words, on the simultaneous display of two facing pages, and on the drama of the turning of the page.

On its own terms its possibilities are limitless.

(Prefatory note to Bader 1976:1)

Introduction

The purpose of this book is to explore both the nature of the picturebook and what it means to read one. Books and reading have always seemed to me to be inseparable so I have taken an uncompromising view of the picturebook as first and foremost a kind of text, a quasi-literary artefact more closely allied to other kinds of texts than to works of visual art.[1] I shall not ignore the pictures but I think it is unwise to make a beginning by disconnecting the several parts of something that is clearly a complex whole so that they can be examined separately. Far better to keep the complete object in view and see what kind of sense can be made of it in its completeness, however difficult that may be.

Barbara Bader had the measure of the picturebook, I believe, when she prefaced her influential study *American Picturebooks from Noah's Ark to the Beast Within*, with the words that I have placed at the head of this chapter. She offers us a working definition (' ... text, illustration ... the interdependence of pictures and words'), reminds us who picturebooks are for (' ... an experience for a child') and also hints at the picturebook's extraordinary potential. ('On its own terms its possibilities are limitless'). Much of what follows in this book is an exploration of that vision.[2]

This first chapter is largely descriptive. I have taken a number of picturebooks and given a brief account of each one. There are a number of reasons for beginning this way. First, I want to provide a sense of what the picturebook can be like, to conjure up an image of the form that we can work with. But I do not want this picture to be biased in any way towards picturebooks of my choice. It is always possible to influence an argument by selecting examples to fit a preferred view or theory but I would much rather start from a more or less random sample and see what that can show us.

On the other hand, I do want to use the opportunity of describing such a sample to exercise some influence upon how we look at picturebooks. Let me explain. Description is usually considered to be a fairly low-level kind of approach to a topic, less interesting and influential – less potent – than, say, argument or analysis. Description, if done well, seems to bring an object into focus before us but not much more than that. However, in describing something we inevitably call upon a favoured vocabulary, look at it from a particular perspective, throw a certain light upon it. Describing can therefore be a way of influencing how we see an object, and re-describing a familiar object is one of the ways that we attempt to change how we understand it.[3] So in describing a selection of picturebooks I am not just offering up a representative sample, I am already starting to make a case. It is only a start, of course, for there is much to follow: much that will be qualified and much that must be explained.

Put simply, I have a view of the nature of the picturebook but I do not wish to 'massage the data' to make it fit what I think. I need a sample that, if not wholly random, at least has not been the product of some one individual's preferences. Where might such a sample be found? I could begin by looking at what bookshops sell and purchasers buy, but such a survey would yield numbers of books that would be unwieldy for my purposes here.[4] What I have done is base my descriptions upon, and later drawn many of my examples from, the fairly short list of books that during the last two decades of the twentieth century were winners, in the UK, of the Kurt Maschler 'Emil Award'. The award was established in 1982 in memory of the author and illustrator of the children's novel *Emil and the Detectives*, Erich Kästner and Walter Trier, and is made annually for 'a work of imagination in the children's field in which text and illustration are of excellence and so presented that each enhances and yet balances the other'. The criteria thus correspond in a rudimentary way to the minimal working definition that I have borrowed from Barbara Bader, and that most students of the picturebook would recognize. The fact that the books on the list are award winners does not exactly guarantee their quality, but it does suggest that they are amongst the best of their kind, and the fact that they were selected one at a time, year by year, by a changing panel of three judges, removes some of the worry that they are simply the favourite books of a particular reader. It is not perfect, but I think it is a reasonable start.

Here, then, is the list of Emil Award winners from 1982 to 1999:

1982   *Sleeping Beauty and Other Favourite Fairy Tales* retold by Angela Carter, illustrated by Michael Foreman

1983   *Gorilla* by Anthony Browne

1984   *Granpa* by John Burningham
1985   *The Iron Man* by Ted Hughes, illustrated by Andrew Davidson
1986   *The Jolly Postman or Other People's Letters* by Janet and Allan Ahlberg
1987   *Jack the Treacle Eater* by Charles Causley, illustrated by Charles Keeping
1988   *Alice's Adventures in Wonderland* by Lewis Carroll, illustrated by Anthony Browne
1989   *The Park in the Dark* by Martin Waddell, illustrated by Barbara Firth
1990   *All Join In* by Quentin Blake
1991   *Have You Seen Who's Just Moved in Next Door to Us?* by Colin McNaughton
1992   *The Man* by Raymond Briggs
1993   *Think of an Eel* by Karen Wallace, illustrated by Mike Bostock
1994   *So Much* by Trish Cooke, illustrated by Helen Oxenbury
1995   *The Little Boat* by Kathy Henderson, illustrated by Patrick Benson
1996   *Drop Dead* by Babette Cole
1997   *Lady Muck* by William Mayne, illustrated by Jonathan Heale
1998   *Voices in the Park*, by Anthony Browne
1999   *Alice's Adventures in Wonderland*, illustrated by Helen Oxenbury

The first thing we might note about the list is that it contains a number of titles that do not seem to be picturebooks at all, despite the fact that they are finely, and at least in three cases copiously, illustrated. *Sleeping Beauty and Other Favourite Fairy Tales*, *The Iron Man*, *Jack the Treacle Eater* and *Alice's Adventures in Wonderland* are all much lengthier than the average picturebook with a far smaller picture-to-word ratio than we would normally expect. Also, apart from *Jack the Treacle Eater*, they are all volumes, or texts, that have been illustrated before, some of the stories many times, so that there is not the same close bond between picture and word that we find in most picturebooks. In principle any text in words could be illustrated by any artist but we expect the pictures and words in picturebooks to be woven together to create a single text composed of two distinct media, rather than have text in one medium (words) illustrated with designs in another (pictures). Does all this mean there are problems with the simple definition with which I began? I think the answer is 'Yes', for it is clear that pictures and words can 'enhance' and 'balance' each other without thereby creating a picturebook. But we need not abandon the criterion just yet. We have simply been alerted to the fact that the picturebook is unlikely to yield up its secrets willingly.

In the remainder of this chapter I provide a descriptive account of the picturebooks on the Emil list omitting those titles, mentioned above, that seem to me to be more like illustrated books. I hope to provide a sketch of what the modern picturebook looks like; to provide an introduction to the corpus of works that is to serve as our sample throughout the rest of the book; to introduce some of the themes that will be examined in more detail later; to suggest some of the relationships that exist between words and images in picturebooks and, most importantly, to indicate the extraordinary diversity of the picturebook.

A sample of modern picturebooks

Anthony Browne's *Gorilla*, a book that has retained its popularity with both adults and children and has come to be seen as an exemplary modern picturebook, won the award in 1983. It possesses the relative brevity which seems to be one of the hallmarks of the form (something *not* hinted at in Bader's definition) and it does appear to be genuinely composite: a single fabric woven from two different materials. We read the words and we follow the pictures and both seem to have roughly equal shares in the generation of the story. Both are necessary and neither, on its own, is sufficient. This much is true, but if we look closely we can find a number of different ways in which the words and pictures work together. The relationship that appears to be most straightforward is a simple kind of illustration: the pictures showing the reader (with varying degrees of specificity) what it is that the words tell us. Thus on the very first page we read of the heroine, Hannah, that, 'She read books about gorillas,' and there, right alongside the sentence is a picture of Hannah sitting cross-legged on the floor reading what appears to be a large picturebook about her favourite animal. However, some parts of the narrative are less easy to illustrate in this way – for example, states of affairs rather than actions – so a little further on we read that Hannah's father 'didn't have time to take her to see one [a gorilla] at the zoo.' and on the opposite page the state of 'not having time ... ' is coolly 'illustrated' with a picture of Hannah's father, separated from his daughter by the newspaper that he is holding up and reading at the breakfast table. The former is often referred to as *narrative* illustration – a simple echoing of the words – and many pictures in picturebooks perform this function, but we can see already that it is not quite as straightforward as it seems at first.[5]

For most of the book Browne's words are relatively simple and unadorned. They tell a plain tale of a lonely girl neglected by a father too busy to spend time with her. Many of the pictures, on the other hand, are rich in detail and significance, and embellish this narrative framework, taking us into both Hannah's home and her psyche. Browne uses point of view, framing, colour, visual distortions and illusions, embedded imagery and a host of other design features to give Hannah's story depth and weight. In fact, it is these pictures that keep drawing us back to the book to look more closely and to ponder the significance of newly discovered details. It is for the pictures that we re-read *Gorilla* because it is through the pictures that the story is opened up for *interpretation* while the function of the words is to link events together to make a coherent narrative.

Not surprisingly, many books on the Emil list resemble *Gorilla* in one way or

Figure 1 From *Gorilla* by Anthony Browne.

another. All of them, for example, exhibit some degree of narrative illustration, but it is the ways in which the other award winners differ from Browne's book that makes the exercise of comparison so interesting. *Granpa*, for example, is another title that has become very popular, especially with students of the picturebook, but it achieves its effects in quite a different manner from our first example. Instead of the plain narrative voice that we find in *Gorilla*, *Granpa* has no narration at all, the written text consisting of decontextualized fragments of conversation, the voices of the little girl and her Granpa distinguished only by the typeface. The pictures help to integrate these snatches of talk, for Burningham is very skilful at using his images for different purposes and investing them with different kinds of meaning.

In a development of a technique first tried out in *Mr Gumpy's Outing* and then in *Come Away From the Water, Shirley*, Burningham gives his monochrome line drawings and his coloured illustrations different functions. Each

One man went to mow
Went to mow a meadow...

Little ducks, soup and sheep, sunshine in the trees...

Figure 2 From *Granpa* by John Burningham.

moment within *Granpa* is represented on a double page spread. The coloured pictures, usually placed on the right-hand page, seem to represent the real world here and now, so that we seem to see the two protagonists at the moment of utterance or shortly thereafter. 'I didn't know Teddy was another little girl' says Granpa from his armchair, a faint expression of dismay on his face. The line drawings, on the other hand, are always placed to the left and seem to depict mental events rather than physical ones: memories, imaginings and hoped-for treats such as tea-time at four o'clock (the pattern is broken once with two all-colour double page spreads representing a moment of crisis and resolution at the heart of the book). The snatches of conversation are thus embedded in a picture sequence that has a distinct beginning: the little girl hurling herself into her Granpa's arms in welcome; a development of their relationship in the body of the book; and an ending suggesting the death of the beloved old man. Nevertheless, the fragmentary nature of the verbal text combined with the lack of a narrative voice means that there is no story here at

all in the conventional sense other than one that the reader might wish to tell on the basis of the sequence of words and pictures. The reader experiences much of *Granpa* as a series of glimpses into the lives of the little girl and her grandfather with more than the usual amount of space in between each scene.

The Man by Raymond Briggs also puts conversational exchanges alongside picture sequences but the effect here is far from minimal. For a start the book is much longer than the average picturebook (sixty-four pages rather than the more conventional twenty-four or thirty-two) and there is plenty of detail in the written text despite the absence of an overarching narrative voice. *The Man* betrays its formal origins on the first page where a sequence of comic strip images, not unlike those at the beginning of *The Snowman*, depicts a young boy in bed waking up to an adventure. The first words to be spoken are framed in speech bubbles but once the story gets under way the comic strip frames disappear and the storytelling centre of gravity shifts from the pictures to the words. Briggs retains the speech bubble for occasional use but largely relies, as

Figure 3 From *The Man* by Raymond Briggs.

Burningham does in *Granpa*, on different typefaces to distinguish the voices of his two protagonists. The body of the book, therefore, except for a brief return to the format of the comic strip part way through, reads rather like a screenplay, the pictures turning the book into something resembling the storyboard of a film (see Figure 17).

Figure 4 From *Voices in the Park* by Anthony Browne.

Anthony Browne's *Voices in the Park* places different voices alongside one another too, but here they are sequenced into four short sections – First Voice, Second Voice, Third Voice and Fourth Voice. Charles and his mother, and Smudge and her father each tell of the same events that took place on a trip to the park. Charles – a repressed little boy gorilla – is escorted by his mother and their dog, Victoria, to a bench where they sit in silence. Smudge – a cheerful little girl gorilla – sits on the same bench with her depressed and out-of-work dad. Victoria and Smudge's dog, Albert, strike up the usual kind of doggy relationship and rush away chasing each other about the park. Smudge invites Charles to play too and for a brief while both have fun away from their parents. Eventually Charles' mother decides it is time to go home and the two pairs, parents and children, go their separate ways.

Not a great deal happens, therefore, but the fascination of the book lies in the four different perspectives upon what happens. The voices themselves are carefully distinguished from one another. Each is represented by a different typeface in much the same way that the voices in *Granpa* and *The Man* are, but they also each possess a distinctive tenor and tone – stiff and formal for Charles' mother and carefree and casual for Smudge. Not surprisingly the pictures too play a major role in shaping our impressions of the characters, but they also shape our view of the kind of world each one inhabits. Charles' first view of the park, which we share by looking over his shoulder, is rather grey and wintry; but once he begins playing with Smudge the trees burst into blossom and the sky turns blue. Smudge and her oppressed father make their way to the park through a dismal urban twilight but they return beneath the cheerful glow of a street-lamp that has metamorphosed into a huge snowdrop – the flower that breaks the ice of winter and looks forward to the spring.

Like *The Man*, Colin McNaughton's *Have You Seen Who's Just Moved in Next Door to Us?* also draws upon comic strip conventions but unlike Briggs he completely does away with the sequence of frames, retaining only the graphic style and sensibility of the comic strip artist. Moreover, McNaughton's imaginative project is wholly different in kind to Briggs'. Here, as in the majority of his books, he seems to be far more interested in the ephemeral, idle nonsense that enraptures the minds of the young than in anything that might resemble real life: visual and verbal puns, jokes, Chinese whispers, misunderstandings and sidelong allusions to popular culture. However, despite the surface triviality, the work possesses a deeper significance. For a start, it requires a very active and alert reader. The written text comes in two basic forms. Running along the top of each double page spread is a series of simple rhyming couplets with refrain which comment upon, and direct our attention towards, the strange characters that appear in the pictures below. In addition, a host of verbal fragments in the form of questions, answers, exclamations and so on, along with a few shop signs and labels, are scattered throughout the scenes at the bottom of each page. At each page-opening, the pictures depict in elevation the façades of a bizarre street of houses and shops, some of them in cutaway form so that we can witness the activities of the inhabitants. The reader needs to scan each page carefully on the lookout for intertextual allusion and visual and verbal play. The relationship of word to picture is therefore not at all straightforward. The verse appears to annotate the pictures beneath, gesturing towards what we should look for, but the snippets of speech (what we 'hear' by virtue of the speech bubbles) are much more intimately tied up with what we see; the jokes require simultaneous attention to both.

As we move through the book each page is visually married up with the next so that at every page turn we seem to be seeing a further extension of the street. Thus apart from gradually moving along the pavement the reader goes nowhere in particular narratively speaking. Except, of course, to the end of the street where finally we meet just who it is who has moved in next door. The

An old lady with a broom,
    At number forty rents a room.
(Has she seen who's just moved in
    Next door to us?)

And living down below,
    We have Michelangelo.
(Has he seen who's just moved in
    Next door to us?)

Figure 5 From *Have You Seen Who's Just Moved in Next Door to Us?* by Colin McNaughton.

final pages open out into a panorama the size of two double page spreads and it is here at last that the reader discovers what everyone in the street is so concerned about: Mr and Mrs Average with their two children and cats. *Have You Seen Who's Just Moved in Next Door to Us?* is thus a modern reworking of that venerable and playful form, the topsy turvy. It is a vision of the world turned upside down wherein Hell's Angels do embroidery at home and Frankenstein's monster finds ordinary humans unnatural!

There are at least two other books on our list that make use of different text types and forms and which therefore complicate the relationship between words and pictures: *The Jolly Postman* and *Think of an Eel*. The former is super-ficially most like *Have You Seen Who's Just Moved in Next Door to Us?* because the story, such as it is, is told in verse. Here, however, the pictures are anchored to the words fairly tightly in much the same way that they are in *Gorilla*. They appear to visually echo whatever it is the words tell us. Thus, when we read:

> Once upon a bicycle,
> So they say,
> A Jolly Postman came one day
> From over the hills
> And far away ...

we have as an accompaniment a picture of the postman himself on his little red bicycle passing a signpost marked 'FARAWAY 4 MILES'. This, however, is as far as the parallel between *The Jolly Postman* and *Gorilla* can go, for although Janet Ahlberg's pictures are crammed with the most engaging detail, they do not invite interpretation in quite the way Browne's do. The meanings of these images are transparent, so that what you see is what you get. For example, in the witch's kitchen a bat hangs upside down on the clothes horse and a cat in a frilly apron, or 'pinny', is doing the washing up, but neither bat nor cat are metaphors for something else, or points of entry into a sub-text. The witch's household is simply organized that way. There is *ambiguity* in these pictures, however, for the Ahlbergs, like McNaughton, cannot resist puns, allusions and jokes, so while the witch reads her letter 'With a cackle of glee', the postman reads the *Mirror Mirror* newspaper in which there is an article about a stolen pig and, in a foreshadowing of events later in the book, a reference to the return home of a royal honeymoon couple.

All this, of course, is merely the frame or background for the letters them-selves which are the whole point and purpose of this remarkable book. Inter-spersed between the scenes of the postman delivering his mail are pages that double up as envelopes with the address on the recto and on the verso, the opening from out of which the letters can be drawn. There are birthday cards, letters of apology, junk mail, and even a letter from a solicitor. *The Jolly Postman* is by now probably famous enough not to need too much by way of further description here, but it does need to be stressed just how ingenious and innovative the Ahlbergs were in embedding a whole world of text and illustra-tion within such a small space. We shall look at *The Jolly Postman* in more detail in Chapter 5.

Think of an Eel, written by Karen Wallace and illustrated by Mike Bostock, is innovative too, but although it incorporates different text types within one book as do *The Jolly Postman* and *Have You Seen Who's Just Moved in Next Door*

So the Witch read the letter
With a cackle of glee
While the Postman read the paper
But *left* his tea. (It was green!)

Figure 6 From *The Jolly Postman* by Janet and Allan Ahlberg.

to Us?, it is wholly different in kind. It tells the tale of some fairly grotesque and fabulous creatures but is nonetheless rooted firmly in the natural world. It belongs to a series of books published by Walker Books – Read and Wonder – that are ostensibly non-fiction texts, dealing with everything from mushrooms to a piece of string, but they are written in such a way as to foreground narrative and evocative language while at the same time maintaining a strictly factual commentary. *Think of an Eel* tells of the eel's birth in the mysterious Sargasso Sea, its journey across the Atlantic Ocean to the rivers of America and Europe and back again to breed and die in the weedy Sargasso. The story is told in a poetic voice that employs the traditional devices of imaginative literature and deliberately emphasizes the mystery of the eel's epic journey. Beside a one-and-a-half page spread watercolour illustration of a dying eel drifting downwards through the brown weeds lies the following block of text:

There's eel-tomb and eel-cradle
in the weedy Sargasso.
After eighty days' swimming,
not eating, not sleeping,
eel's long, winding body

There's eel-tomb and eel-cradle
in the weedy Sargasso.
After eighty days' swimming,
not eating, not sleeping,
eel's long, winding body
is worn out and wasted.
He spills the new life
carried deep in his belly,
then sinks through the sea
like a used silver wrapper.

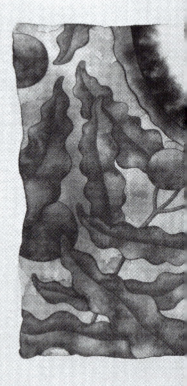

26

Figure 7 From *Think of an Eel* by Karen Wallace and Mike Bostock.

is worn out and wasted.
He spills the new life
carried deep in his belly,
then sinks through the sea
like a used silver wrapper.

Underneath is a tiny illustration of two eels in a spiralling embrace captioned – in a different typeface mimicking a handwritten cursive script, and in a wholly different register – with the words, 'The male eel's sperm fertilizes the female's eggs in the water'.

Think of an Eel is thus a curious book for it does not seem to fit comfortably within any of the conventional publishing and bibliographic categories. It certainly conforms to the basic criteria for a picturebook that we have been employing so far, and employs many of the literary devices traditionally employed

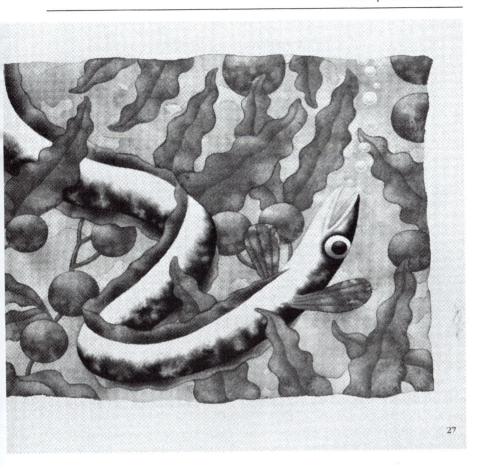

27

by poets and authors but, on the other hand, it is certainly not a work of imaginative fiction. The reader is clearly expected to read and learn about eels but the explicit invitation is also to Read and Wonder. *Think of an Eel* is thus a good example of how picturebooks frequently slip through the nets that publishers prepare for them by merging, or hybridizing, two or more genres or text-types.

So far in our examination of the list of Emil Award winners poetry and verse have featured in a number of works: *Have You Seen Who's Just Moved in Next Door to Us?*, *The Jolly Postman*, and *Think of an Eel* all employ poetic devices for a number of different purposes. There are three more books on the list, however, that have verse right at their hearts – albeit in very different guises: *All Join In* by Quentin Blake, *The Little Boat* by Kathy Henderson and Patrick Benson, and *The Park in the Dark* by Martin Waddell and Barbara Firth. In Blake's book, the verse comes in the form of short rhymes that are, from an adult point of view, extremely light and inconsequential, but they have been

Figure 8 From *All Join In* by Quentin Blake.

written to entrap a much younger audience. The rhymes are an incitement to give voice to the printed word, hence the invitation in the book's title.

The poems have strong rhymes, two or three verses for repetition and a bold, noisy chorus for emergent readers to chant. Each also comes with its set of busy but clear pictures that fill out the skimpy information provided by the rhymes in the narrative manner described above. 'Nice Weather for Ducks', for example, begins on a page which shows a file of slightly rumpled children, clad in wellington boots and raincoats and carrying rolled umbrellas, making their way down a muddy path accompanied by a straggling flock of ducks, every mouth and beak open in song. The verse begins:

> We're all off to the river
> along the muddy track
> And we're joining in the Duck Song
> QUACK QUACK QUACK.

With this book we can see clearly how the words seduce the listening child to join in the game of reading while the pictures add a density and a visual rhythm – a particularity – to the experience.

The verse in Kathy Henderson and Patrick Benson's *The Little Boat* is much more freely rhymed and is set alongside huge, landscape format illustrations that are bled to the edges of the page and spread across five-sixths of each page-opening. The words tell how a tiny boat, made from a scrap of polystyrene and a stick by a child on holiday at the edge of the ocean, is caught up by the tides and the wind and blown to a distant shore where it is found by another child playing beneath palm trees on a golden beach. The tale, then, is fairly slender inasmuch as it recounts the fortunes of what is in effect little more than a tiny piece of flotsam. However, it gains a certain lyrical quality through Henderson's carefully turned, unpunctuated text that scrolls down the left-hand margin of each page-opening as well as an attention-grabbing immediacy from Benson's bold images with their startling shifts in perspective, point of view and mood. The story begins with the following words placed alongside a beach scene which cleverly positions the viewer beside some adults sitting in the foreground beneath a pair of parasols looking out towards the open sea.

Down by the shore
where the sea meets the land
licking at the pebbles
sucking at the sand
and the wind flaps
the sunshades
and the ice-cream man
out-shouts the seagulls
and the people come
with buckets and spades
and suntan lotion
to play on the shore
by the edge of the ocean

There is little in the pictures to encourage interpretation for they illustrate fairly straightforwardly the scenes and events described in the words. They are thus *narrative* illustrations but they have an impact and effect within the book as a whole far in excess of what one might suspect of such a relatively undemanding relationship. They are large and bold and they dizzyingly switch point of view and perspective as the pages are turned. The second and third page-openings place the viewer so close to the children on the beach that only legs, feet and odd chunks of body are visible. We bend down with the little ship-maker as he pats his boat along the water-filled channels in the sand. Later, far out at sea, Benson places us down in the water, inches from the becalmed boat, our eyes just above the surface on a level with the lumpy polystyrene. Turn the page, and we are even closer to the jaws of a huge fish that bursts out of the water and seizes the boat in its teeth. A little later, we sit at the bottom of the ocean looking up as the tiny scrap lurches towards the sunlit surface.

The Little Boat is thus not lacking in drama despite its uncomplicated theme. *The Park in the Dark* is dramatic too, but here the shocks and surprises are

a little boy
made himself a boat
from an old piece
of polystyrene plastic
with a stick for a mast
and a string tail sail
and he splashed
and he played
with the boat he'd made
digging it a harbour
scooping it a creek
all day long by the edge
of the sea
singing
'We are unsinkable
my boat and me!'

Figure 9 From *The Little Boat* by Kathy Henderson and Patrick Benson

located within the familiar literary fantasy of the stuffed toys who escape from the toy drawer for a nocturnal adventure. 'Me, Loopy and Little Gee' – a monkey, an elephant and a little dog in a frock – forsake the quiet of their sleeping owner's bedroom and make for the park where they swing and slide in the playground until they are eventually driven home by the THING that roars after them: a late-evening commuter train.

In terms of its design, *The Park in the Dark* is not so different from *The Little Boat* inasmuch as it relies upon large, double page bleeds, this time extending across the whole of the available space, the words being contained in tall, narrow, rectangular boxes, or windows, over towards the left-hand edge. Waddell's text is, however, even more loosely structured than Henderson's and is a lot less clear in its forward narrative movement and descriptive content. This means that Barbara Firth has had a great deal of freedom to create the landscape of the park and its environs and she has painted twilit and nocturnal scenes that are mostly recognizably real but occasionally spookily

fantastic. The first and last double page spreads show us part of a slightly rundown residential area at the inner city's edge which takes in both the toys' house and the entrance to the park. So clear is her sense of place that as we look at these pictures we can follow much of the trio's route through the streets and into the park, orientating ourselves by the shapes of trees and gateposts. Once in the park, however, the adventurers' fears are pictured by Firth in Arthur Rackham-like trees with knotty faces and clutching branches.

Trish Cooke and Helen Oxenbury's *So Much* has a written text that relies heavily on the rhythms and syntax of an urban dialect of English. It is set in a simple domestic interior where 'mum and the baby' wait for family members to arrive in ones and twos for a party to celebrate Daddy's birthday, although we only discover there is to be a party at the end of the book when Daddy arrives home. This gradual gathering of the clan, however, is only the excuse for each new arrival to exclaim how much they adore the baby and want to play with him.

And we swing
and we slide
and we dance
and we jump
and we chase
all over the place,
me and Loopy
and Little Gee,
the Big Three!

Figure10 From *The Park in the Dark* by Martin Waddell and Barbara Firth.

Uncle,
Uncle Didi.
Uncle Didi came inside
with his eyebrows
raise high, high, high
and his lips scrunch up
small, small, small.
"Hello, hello," he said.
I want to kiss him,
I want to kiss the baby,
I want to kiss him
SO MUCH!"

Oxenbury alternates richly hued and lively full-page pictures of each new arrival with relatively static images in browns and creams of the family patiently waiting. The characters are finely observed and contribute to an overall feeling of homely realism. The role of the pictures here seems not unlike that of the pictures in *The Park in the Dark* and *The Little Boat*. In all three books they assert themselves as fairly clear and unambiguous representations of the events and characters referred to in the words but in each case a unique pictorial world is created that does much to influence the overall tenor of each text.

Lady Muck by William Mayne and Jonathan Heale also relies heavily upon the cadences and idioms of spoken language, but in this case Mayne has created an imaginary dialect through which the story is narrated and the animal characters communicate. Boark, a pig, goes hunting for truffles for his wife, Sowk.

Figure 11 From *So Much* by Trish Cooke and Helen Oxenbury.

Under the Beech trees he snuffled, and came upon, oh, the whifflom of the greatest pigly tasties, down under the woodland mould.

"Don't hidy there," he said. "I know you be lurking, little snack and dinner, little snap and supper." And he set to more sniffling yet, to find the nest of those best things.

The written text is on the long side for a picturebook and tells, largely through direct speech, how 'Sowky' manages to eat all the truffles found by her

Figure 12 From *Lady Muck* by William Mayne and Jonathan Heale.

husband bar one before they can sell them at market. Their ambitions to own a coach to ride in are thus thwarted. The blocks of text are broken up by Heale's pictures which come in two forms. There is a series of images, one per page, which look as if they are printed from woodblocks. These are heavily outlined in black, are mainly full page or half page rectangles and squares, rely upon a limited range of hues and – not surprisingly – possess a distinctly old-fashioned air. Facing these pictures, usually on the verso, are unframed, rather more realistic, images of the two pigs sketched lightly in pencil and watercolour against the white of the page. Neither set of pictures does more than represent scenes and events described in the written text but Heale is very adept at manipulating point of view and counterpoints close-ups of the pigs with broader perspective scenes that mark the pigs' trek to the city and the market.

Finally we return to a visual and textual world not too dissimilar to that created by Colin McNaughton. Babette Cole's *Drop Dead* is just as cartoon-like as *Have You Seen Who's Just Moved in Next Door to Us?* although her visual style is quite distinct. As storytellers neither has any interest in realism and both share a lack of respect for storytelling norms, although it is Cole who is more concerned to push back the boundaries of taste and decorum. The

Then we went to school.

Figure 13 From *Drop Dead* by Babette Cole.

content of *Drop Dead* unreels from the question asked on the first page-opening of two grandparents by their grandchildren: 'Gran and Grandad, why are you such bald old wrinklies?' The old folks' life story is what follows, tracing their development from babyhood to an imagined death and beyond. Cole takes each stage of their life and illustrates single phrases, clauses and simple sentences with images that show how time and time again the younger versions of Gran and Grandad nearly came to grief. Thus the statement, 'Then we went to school' sits below a full-page illustration of a Godzilla-like dinosaur biting a chunk out of the school roof as the two children wave goodbye to each other at the separate doors for boys and girls. Later it comes as no surprise that they lead reckless lives as film stars and get married hanging from the runners of a helicopter in flight. The pictures thus illustrate scenes, events and climactic moments in the grandparents' lives, but whereas the words remain resolutely bland ('We learned crawling, standing on one leg, running and jumping … ')

the details, as represented in the pictures, are alternately outrageous, comical and downright dangerous.

The diversity of the picturebook

There are some very clear similarities to be found amongst these texts, for example, their obviously compound or composite nature, and their relative brevity, but over and above these basic markers of the picturebook form it is the differences that I wish to draw attention to. If we consider the written texts alone we discover that they vary considerably in length and range across the most extraordinary variety of genres and registers.[6] Furthermore, there are several books that incorporate more than one form of discourse. Some books are in verse and some in prose and whereas some of the verse rhymes, much does not. A number of examples rely heavily upon the rhythms of the spoken voice, and in two of the books the written text is composed solely of unmarked dialogue (*Granpa* and *The Man*). Some of the books tell stories and some do not and with those that tell stories the kind of stories that they tell are almost as varied as the books themselves.

The pictures too are equally diverse in terms of tenor, media and style. Anthony Browne disturbs our sense of objective reality with his surrealist imagery while Patrick Benson conjures up thrilling seascapes and makes us feel the heat of the tropical sun and the freezing roar of an oceanic storm. Illustrators as varied as Colin McNaughton, Janet Ahlberg, Raymond Briggs and Babette Cole display their indebtedness to caricature while using what they have taken from this tradition to very different ends. Jonathan Heale looks back to the days of woodblock printing while Helen Oxenbury paints joyful and moving pictures of a contemporary family at play. Heale, Oxenbury, Benson, Bostock, Briggs and Burningham all use more than one style or approach to picture-making in their books – for example, monochrome as well as colour – to create contrastive effects both within the picture sequences and between pictures and words.

If we further consider how words and pictures are related to one another we find a range of different combinations. To some extent all pictures will have decorative, narrative and interpretative potential, even those that appear to stick resolutely to the task of depicting in line and colour what it is that the words say. A graceful line in a tiny monochrome vignette tucked into a corner of a page will possess a charm of its own independent of the extent to which it reflects, or offers an interpretation of, verbal meanings and even the most straightforward of representations may invite a degree or two of interpretation. In any case, 'what the words say' is rarely straightforward. It is one thing to illustrate '… she stretched out her hand/and picked up the boat … ' (event and object from *The Little Boat*), quite another to place a picture alongside the words, 'That was not a nice thing to say to Granpa'. Plain statements such as 'Then we went to school' and 'In the night something amazing happened'

(*Drop Dead* and *Gorilla*) offer far more scope to illustrators than ' ... up got Sowk from the muddy place, scratched belly with foot, rubbed her bum upon a tree to wake it up, and twirl and twitched her piggy tail till it went twang and sat up smart' (*Lady Muck*). The general rule here is, the more detail in the words, the less room there is for pictorial invention.

In addition to the differences we find in the written texts, the pictures and the shifting relationships between the two, we might also note other signs of variety. In particular we might look at features of book design such as size and shape, the positioning of images upon the page and the use made of the material fabric of the book. For example, *The Little Boat* and *The Jolly Postman* are both in landscape format, the spine running down the shorter side of the rectangle, but the former is considerably larger than the latter, and for good reason. Open up *The Little Boat* and we see how the size and the format allow for very long and narrow page-openings: perfect for allowing Benson's epic seascapes to sprawl across the pages and leak over the edge, as if the sea itself were pouring out of the book. In *The Jolly Postman*, the size and the format have a different function altogether. The landscape pages allow the postman to deliver his mail in set piece scenes involving well-known fairy-tale characters but they are also just the right size and shape for the envelopes and letters that are the *raison d'etre* of the book. Anything bigger would be too unwieldy and unreal. Anything smaller would not allow even little hands to reach in and extract the contents.

Have You Seen Who's Just Moved in Next Door to Us? is rather more conventional in shape and size, the portrait format allowing substantial portions of the street to be spread across the whole of each page-opening. Pedestrians quite properly move from left to right and lead in the end to the two foldout pages at the end where the secret of the book is revealed in a panorama four pages wide. In contrast, *Think of an Eel* and *Drop Dead* are both roughly square in format and this enables both Mike Bostock and Babette Cole to position images upon the page with greater freedom. The square page does not coerce an illustrator into designs of any particular shape so we find in both of these books a great deal of variety in the way images are disposed across the available space. In *Think of an Eel*, for example, there are long, thin, ribbon-like images that stretch from side to side of the page-opening leaving room for words above and below as well as sequences of small vignettes at the top. Bostock can also stretch landscape format images across three-quarters of a page-opening, squeezing the written text into the left-hand margin, or take each square page separately and place a vignette of a snail or a shrimp to one side above a roughly framed rectangular image in the bottom half. Cole too exploits the more open format with large scale images that bleed to the edges of the page as well as ribbon-like forms that take up the entire length of the page-opening and unframed vignettes of creatures or objects, four or five to a page.

Family resemblances

So far I have examined a selection of picturebooks, describing some of their distinctive features and emphasizing the diversity of the form. We could point up that diversity even further by considering some types of picturebook that are not represented in the list of Emil prizewinners, for example, ABCs and counting books, board books for babies and wordless picturebooks. We have ignored pop-ups and movables too – those books designed by paper engineers incorporating moving parts – although both *The Jolly Postman* and *Have You Seen Who's Just Moved in Next Door to Us?* make imaginative use of simple movable techniques. But what, in the end, does all this listing and describing achieve?

I think three important things follow from what we have done so far in this chapter, the second and third points flowing from the first. To begin with, as I argued at the outset, I consider it to be most important that we avoid presumptions in favour of any one type or kind of picturebook. If we begin by assuming that we already know what the essential characteristics of the picturebook are, then there will be less to investigate, our investigations revolving around a diminished set of characteristics. If, for example, we take the work of Quentin Blake or Anthony Browne to possess what is essential to the picturebook, then the further away from the Blake or Browne model a picturebook appears to be the less like a picturebook it will seem. By examining a range of books, and withholding judgements as to which ones are more picturebook-like than the others, we are able to construct a more generous description of the form.

Second, we reveal the heterogeneity of the form by spreading out before ourselves a collection of samples. There is no escaping the fact that picturebooks are enormously varied in terms of the forms of written text they can include, the kinds of images they can contain, the authorial intentions they can embody, the interrelationships of word and image they can support, and even the ways in which they can exploit the material fabric of the book: the paper and the card. Here is matter worth investigating. Just what is it about the picturebook that enables such teeming variety? Chapters 4 and 5 will attempt to answer this question.

Third, in 'chaining' my account by linking one book to the next through common characteristics, I wished to demonstrate the variety of relationships that exist amongst the books as well as between the pictures and words inside them. It is, of course, perfectly possible to group individual works together in categories but we do this only by selecting some features of individual works as key ones and subordinating or neglecting others.[7] *Think of an Eel*, for example, is at one and the same time a storybook and an information book. *The Jolly Postman* is a patchwork of intertextual allusions to fairy tales within which are embedded the letters, cards and junk mail that make up its core. As such it is much more than a pseudo-fairy story. And what category would *Have You Seen Who's Just Moved in Next Door to Us?* fit into most comfortably? It is neither story, nor book of verse, nor joke book, nor movable, yet it possesses some features of all these types.

A better way of understanding the nature of the picturebook is to view the form as being to some extent unbounded. This does not mean that any kind of illustrated work may count as a picturebook, but that – given the broad parameters with which we began – all manner of variations on the formula might be included. All that is required is that a new work, or a new type, should be recognizably similar to works already accepted as belonging to the form. A good example would be the wordless picturebook which really only emerged as a distinct variant in the 1970s. Despite the fact that books like *The Snowman* by Raymond Briggs, *Sunshine* by Jan Ormerod and *Clown* by Quentin Blake all fail to meet the 'interdependence of words and pictures' criterion there is enough similarity between these books and other more readily recognizable picturebooks for them to be accepted as such.

What counts, then, is the network of family resemblances that link individual examples of picturebooks together.[8] *The Man* may not look much like *All Join In* or *Drop Dead* but it has enough in common with other examples of the form for it to be included without too much strain, despite the fact that it is somewhat longer than most picturebooks. Clearly there will be cases where we might be happier placing a particular work under another heading altogether despite the fact that it possesses some picturebook-like features. This often happens when there is another category ready and waiting beyond the outer margins of the picturebook. Thus we might reasonably ask, when does a picturebook become an illustrated short story, or vice versa? And at what point does it melt into the graphic novel? None of this need be a problem, for even the most everyday concepts and categories are to some degree open-ended and possess blurred edges. At this stage we simply need to be willing to lean towards an inclusive model of the picturebook rather than an exclusive one.

In the next chapter I return to an issue raised right at the very beginning of this descriptive catalogue: the question of how words and pictures work together in picturebooks to create coherent, intelligible text. What does it mean to say, as Barbara Bader does, that the picturebook is a form that ' … hinges on the interdependence of pictures and words' (Bader 1976) and how varied are picturebooks in the way they exploit this interdependence? A number of writers and critics have attempted to classify picturebooks according to the relations that appear to exist between words and images, but as we shall see, this has proved to be a task fraught with difficulty.

Notes

1   This is not a view to which everyone would subscribe. There are many who have preferred to see picturebooks as closer to works of visual art than to literature. See, for example, Bettina Hurlimann in her book *Three Centuries of Children's Books in Europe*: 'Just as the first word-plays, the nursery rhymes, and the earliest stories, with their stilted sentences in big block

letters, help to found a future taste for literature, so picture-books prepare a future feeling for art' (Hurlimann 1967:201). See also Chiyoko Nakatani in conversation with Elaine Moss: picturebooks are 'a child's personal art gallery' (Moss 1973:136) and the writer of the introduction to Sylvia and Kenneth Marantz's *The Art of Children's Picture Books*: 'For me picture books should be perceived and valued as a form of visual art, *not* literary art' (Marantz and Marantz 1988:ix, authors' emphasis). The problem with such views is not so much that they are wrong in any *a priori* sense – picturebooks can indeed be viewed aesthetically – but that they tend to separate the artefact from its context of use. Once you cease to see picturebooks in the hands of children eager to enjoy a good read the door is opened for a reductive form of connoisseurship.

2   I shall have almost nothing to say about the picturebook as 'an item of manufacture and a commercial product'. The publishing and manufacture of picturebooks clearly have an impact upon their nature but I feel that there is more than enough matter for one book in issues of text, illustration and design.

3   The American philosopher Richard Rorty writes about the power of re-description in *Contingency, Irony and Solidarity* (Rorty 1989).

4   I carried out such a survey in 1995 for an article published in *Signal* under the title, 'The picture book: a form awaiting its history' (Lewis 1995).

5   Selma Lanes, writing about and echoing Maurice Sendak, distinguishes between three broad types of illustration in *The Art of Maurice Sendak* (Lanes 1980). In increasing order of significance these are: *graphic decoration* which adds little to the meaning of the book in which it appears, merely beautifying it; *narrative illustration* which attempts to mirror in images whatever the words say, and *interpretive illustration* which 'expand[s] a given text and add[s] a new richness of meaning to it' (Lanes 1980:47). See also Walter Lorraine's interview with Maurice Sendak in Egoff, Stubbs and Ashley 1980. See also Chapter 2 for an examination of more thoroughgoing attempts to identify different relationships between words and images in picturebooks.

6   As far as length is concerned, *Granpa* is a little over 200 words whereas *The Man* has roughly the same number of words on each one of its 64 pages.

7   Brian Alderson provides a most useful categorization of picturebooks in *Looking at Picture Books* (Alderson 1973).

8   I have borrowed the idea of family resemblances from Ludwig Wittgenstein's *Philosophical Investigations*, although here I am applying it rather differently from the way Wittgenstein uses it. He was concerned to show how concepts frequently possess 'blurred edges' and how the labels that we apply to concepts can have a range of different, though related, applications. He uses as an example the way in which the term 'game' means slightly different things when we speak of the game of snap, the Olympic games, board games and ball games. He writes:

> Consider for example the proceedings that we call 'games'. I mean board-games, card-games, ball games, Olympic games, and so on. What is common to them all? – Don't say: 'There *must* be something common, or they would not all be called "games" ' but *look and see* whether there is anything common to all. – For if you look at them you will not see something that is common to *all*, but similarities, relationships, and a whole series of them at that. To repeat: don't think, but look!
>
> (Wittgenstein 1968:31)

In this chapter, however, I am suggesting that the reason why we call different kinds of books 'picturebooks' is that they are connected through overlapping features that loosely link them together in much the same way that when we look at individual members of a family we can see that they clearly belong together, although no two members are identical. See Chapters 4 and 5 for an account of how this diversity has come about, and Chapter 8 for a discussion of how Wittgenstein's philosophy as expressed in *Philosophical Investigations* can illuminate our understanding of the picturebook.

Chapter 2

The interaction of word and image in picturebooks

A critical survey

> The big truth about picture books ... is that they are an interweaving of word and pictures. You don't have to tell the story in the words. You can come out of the words and into the pictures and you get this nice kind of antiphonal fugue effect.
>
> (Allan Ahlberg cited in Moss 1990:21)

Introduction

The picturebook began to be taken seriously as an object of academic study during the latter years of the twentieth century. The first major works in English to address the form and its nature, for example, *Ways of the Illustrator* by Joseph Schwarcz and *Words About Pictures* by Perry Nodelman were published in the 1980s (Schwarcz 1982; Nodelman 1988) and since then there has been a steady increase in the flow of articles, conference papers and book chapters dedicated to the study, criticism and analysis of the picturebook. There has been a gathering sophistication in the attempts to understand its properties but I believe we are still some way off understanding many of the picturebook's most significant features. Even though we are experienced readers of verbal text we are still learning how to read the picturebook, both in the sense of reading individual books, and in the sense of understanding how they work. In this chapter I examine some recent attempts to characterize the special ways in which pictures and words are used in picturebooks to tell stories and create imaginative fictions. Some of what follows is critical but my intention is not simply to find fault. My main aim is to establish the imperfect and provisional nature of what we know so far. I certainly have no straightforward answers to the questions that I raise but at the end of the chapter I suggest a way in which we might conceive of word–picture interactions in picturebooks that opens up possibilities for study rather than closing them down. Chapter 3 then tries to develop some of these possibilities. But to begin with, let us go back to the basic facts of reading a picturebook – what we do with our eyes and minds – and then consider some of the ways that expert readers have attempted to characterize the process.

Describing the interaction of word and image

When we read picturebooks we look at the pictures and we read the words and our eyes go back and forth between the two as we piece together the meaning of the text. In *Have You Seen Who's Just Moved in Next Door to Us?* (see page 11) the rhyme at the top of each page directs our attention to characters and events, one or two at a time, represented in the street scene below. The scene itself, however, always overflows whatever the words say about it and our eyes are tempted to wander around, roving up and down the street, inspecting the houses and their occupants, reading the captions and speech balloons, grasping (or missing) the jokes and the puns. In *So Much*, the pictures show us a family at play. The words give us the sounds and rhythms and intonations of their speech so we watch what the aunties, cousins and grans do with the baby and 'hear' their exclamations of delight and declarations of affection. In *Drop Dead*, much of the verbal text is in the form of captions to preposterous pictures so that when we read of Gran and Grandad that '[They] forget things!' we look to the picture to see what has been forgotten and smile at the old man's missing trousers and polka-dot boxer shorts.

Children reading picturebooks must also find routes through the text that connect words and images. Here six-year-old Jane reads to me from *Time to Get Out of the Bath, Shirley* by John Burningham. As she reads, she moves from the words to the pictures below the words and across the gutter to the scene on the right-hand page (words in capital letters represent book text read aloud).

J: HAVE YOU BEEN USING THIS TOWEL SHIRLEY OR WAS IT YOUR FATHER? ... (*looking at picture below*) probably her father 'cos it's got big hands
DL: Hmm
J: (*examining the picture to the right of the gutter*) She's gone on the back of the horse ... is that an owl or a bat? ... bat!
DL: Don't know ... could be
J: Oh look, there's a witch.

Time to Get Out of the Bath, Shirley, and its sister text, *Come Away From the Water, Shirley* are justly famous for their teasing quality, the way words and pictures do not seem to fully match. In the former story, Shirley is taking a bath while her mother potters around the bathroom uttering banal remarks like the one in the extract above. At each page-opening the pictures beneath the words show mother at the moment of speaking while those to the right of the gutter show Shirley to be involved in an adventure involving storybook knights and kings and queens which we may suppose is taking place in her imagination. The words act as a prompt for further investigation of the page, for on their own they simply do not tell us enough about what is going on. Jane actively scans and interrogates both pictures, searching for semantic links that will help her piece together the story.

Picturebook text is thus usually composite, an 'interweaving of words and pictures' as Allan Ahlberg puts it (see quotation at the head of the chapter). The metaphor of weaving is useful for not only does it pick out for us the sensation we have when reading a picturebook of shuttling between one medium and another, but it is also related, through sense and meaning to the term *text* which is itself etymologically and semantically close to *textile*. A text in this sense is something woven together, a cohesive patterning of inter-related strands that adds up to more than a mere accumulation of individual parts. For this interweaving to proceed, however, we need to have the images and the words displayed before us in fairly close proximity to each other. It is not much use if the two strands – the weft and the warp, so to speak – are on different pages or are so far apart that they cannot be brought together in the act of reading. If the words are on one set of pages and the pictures elsewhere in the book, as is frequently the case in longer texts and illustrated novels, then it becomes difficult for the two forms of representation to enter into the construction of the story together. We now take sophisticated combinations of word and image in books, magazines and advertising for granted but it is only relatively recently that printing technology has permitted this creative freedom. The emergence of the picturebook from earlier forms of illustrated text has been slow and hesitant and those readers interested in the development of the technology that has made the modern picturebook possible might wish to refer to Appendix 1, Developments in printing technology: bringing words and pictures together.

Musical metaphors

Despite the suggestive power of metaphors such as 'interweaving', the task of describing and analysing the interaction of text and picture in picturebooks is far from straightforward. All metaphors and analogies have their limitations and it is always a mistake to push them too far or to interpret them too literally. They may also distort what they are intended to illuminate. Take, for example, the analogy that follows the interweaving metaphor in the quotation from Allan Ahlberg's interview with Elaine Moss, 'You don't have to tell the story in the words. You can come out of the words and into the pictures and you get this nice kind of antiphonal fugue effect.' Once again we are offered an image of movement between two or more parts, this time the separate voices or lines in a piece of music. Once again the metaphor is suggestive but it will not withstand much pressure once we test it out against some real examples. There is indeed a sense in which pictures and words 'echo' or 'answer' each other in a vaguely antiphonal way and we can perhaps see it and feel it in books like *The Park in the Dark* or *The Little Boat*. But a book like *Rosie's Walk*, by Pat

Hutchins, or even *Gorilla*, is not well served by the analogy. The pictures are richer in information than the words and might be said to introduce and develop new themes rather than echo the one introduced by the words.

Perhaps it is a little unfair to push such an analogy as far as this as its purpose would seem to be to hint at a very general kind of relationship rather than account for the diversity of kinds of relationship in detail. After all, Allan Ahlberg was responding to questions in an interview rather than committing a considered view to print. Nonetheless he does suggest that there is a 'big truth' about picturebooks that his images from weaving and music can capture. In fact musical metaphors are commonplace in discussions of the picturebook and they are worth examining for what they reveal about how the picture–word relationship is sometimes conceptualized. Maurice Sendak, for example, has remarked that the true illustrator has ' ... an odd affinity with words ... almost like a composer thinking music when reading poetry' (Lorraine 1977:329). Philip Pullman, a writer with experience both of writing graphic novels for children and of studying the effects of pictures on words (see Pullman 1989, 1993), sees the interaction of word and image in the best picturebooks as being essentially a matter of *counterpoint*. The same term is used by Schwarcz in *Ways of the Illustrator* (Schwarcz 1982) and, more recently, by Maria Nikolajeva and Carole Scott in *The Dynamics of Picturebook Communication* (Nikolajeva and Scott, 2000) and *How Picturebooks Work* (Nikolajeva and Scott, forthcoming).

One of the problems with counterpoint is that different writers use the term in different ways. For Pullman, counterpoint as it has been developed in the picturebook, the comic and the graphic novel is a matter of simultaneity, the potential possessed by words and pictures in combination to 'show different things happening at the same time' (Pullman 1989:171). Nikolajeva and Scott use the term in a somewhat similar fashion, arguing that only certain books exhibit features of counterpointing and those are the ones where the words and the images provide different kinds of information that the reader must make some effort to reconcile and integrate. As an example they suggest the work of Babette Cole who often captions outrageous pictures with banal phrases, as in *Drop Dead*. The authors explain that at the outer extremity of this category lies a smaller group of books where the words and the pictures seem to be saying such different things that they appear to be contradicting each other. *Time to Get Out of the Bath, Shirley* seems to possess some elements of this kind of relationship. For Schwarcz, however, the situation is reversed: the relationship that Nikolajeva and Scott call counterpoint, Schwarcz calls *deviation* and he reserves the term counterpoint for the more specific and extreme subset where words and pictures seem opposed or contradictory (Schwarcz 1982). One outcome of this confusion is that we remain unsure whether counterpoint is an appropriate metaphor for the workings of words and pictures in all picturebooks or only in some picturebooks. And if it is the case that only some picturebooks are truly contrapuntal, then exactly which sub-category of picturebooks does the term most accurately describe?

The most important weakness of musical analogies, however, is that they risk keeping the words and the pictures apart: they might reflect each other, echo each other, weave around each other in a play of voices and images, but hardly ever do they seem to influence each other. Allan Ahlberg, for example, in the sentences that connect his two metaphors, says explicitly that 'You don't have to tell the story in the words. You can *come out of the words and into the pictures* ...' (Moss 1990, my emphasis). The following 'antiphonal effect' then suggests a kind of bouncing back and forth between the two. Ahlberg would no doubt acknowledge the mutual influence that words and pictures exert upon one another but in this interview he seems to be speaking as a creator of picturebooks rather than a reader of them. Or rather he seems to be collapsing the two roles into one, superimposing the experience of the writer ('You don't have to *tell* the story in the words') onto that of the reader ('you get this nice kind of antiphonal fugue effect').

Interanimation

The experience of reading picturebooks would suggest that as our eyes move from words to pictures and back again, far from leaving behind the meaning or effects of one medium as we enter the other, we carry with us something like semantic traces that colour or inflect what we read and what we see. Margaret Meek, in a discussion of how writers and illustrators support young readers, writes of the words of one particular book being 'pulled through the pictures' and of how 'pictures and words on a page *interanimate* each other' (Meek 1992:176,177) The liveliness of these images is appealing and suggests vividly how the two media act upon each other. Perry Nodelman's gloss on this process is as follows: '... the pictures themselves can imply narrative information only in relationship to a verbal context; if none is actually provided, we tend to find one in our memories' (Nodelman 1988:195). And again, 'Words can make pictures into rich narrative resources – but only because they communicate so differently from pictures that they change the meaning of pictures. For the same reason, also, pictures can change the narrative thrust of words' (Nodelman 1988:196). This is a most important observation for it alerts us to the fact that although pictures and words in close proximity in the picturebook influence each other, the relationship is never entirely symmetrical. What the words do to the pictures is not the same as what the pictures do to the words. Roughly speaking, the words in a picturebook tend to draw attention to the parts of the pictures that we should attend to, whereas the pictures provide the words with a specificity – colour, shape and form – that they would otherwise lack.[1]

In Anthony Browne's *Voices in the Park* for example, when we look at the picture which dominates the first page we see a rather handsome white house set in a neat lawned garden with autumn trees in the background and a white fence in the foreground. Also in the foreground, but set off to one side, a smartly dressed lady gorilla walks with her son and her dog along the pavement. The picture thus has a life of its own in that we recognize what it depicts and read some of its general significance: the clean, white neatness and smartness of the house and the purposeful air of the lady gorilla, for example. But the picture only gains the life it needs in and for Browne's story when we read the words that accompany it: 'First Voice. It was time to take Victoria, our pedigree Labrador, and Charles, our son, for a walk.' The picture is thus not primarily about the house, as we may have thought, despite its prominence, but about the characters in front of it. Moreover the words take us inside the head of one of the characters and tell us something about her personality – careful, slightly pedantic – as well as her intentions. Thus do the words breathe life into the image. They frame the image for the reader by directing attention, and offering interpretation. The central point, however, is that the image can only live and have meaning *as part of the picturebook* when informed – or 'limited', as Nodelman would say (Nodelman 1988:221) – by the words.

The reverse is also true, at least inasmuch as the words are 'animated' and given a specificity and locality that on their own they simply do not possess. Reading the words alone will tell us that here is a voice speaking, or possibly silently ruminating, on a commonplace domestic event. But the words on their own cannot tell us exactly where the event takes place, cannot convey the clear light and clean lines of the setting and nor is there any indication of gender: this could be mother or father speaking. The words clearly mean something we can understand, but on their own the words are attenuated, partial, and they only come fully to life and gain their complete meaning within the story when read alongside the accompanying picture.

There is, however, a further point to be made about what results from this interanimation. Nodelman continues, 'good picture books as a whole are a richer experience than just the simple sum of their parts' (Nodelman 1988:199). A picturebook's 'story' is never to be found in the words alone, nor in the pictures, but emerges out of their mutual interanimation. The words change the pictures and the pictures change the words and the product is something altogether different. Roland Barthes, one of Nodelman's sources here, makes a somewhat similar point when discussing what he calls *relaying* in comics and cartoons. He argues that in these mixed media forms 'language … and image are in a complementary relation; the words are then fragments of a more general syntagm, as are the images, and the message's unity occurs on a higher level: that of the story, the anecdote, the diegesis' (Barthes 1986:30). There is thus a synergy about picturebooks that ensures that if a reader wants the whole experience, then pictures and words have to be taken together.[2] And this is true even of those picturebooks where the language makes perfectly good sense on its own. Errol Le Cain's *Aladdin* works very well when the verbal text alone is read aloud, but when we see the pictures as we hear or read the

Figure 14 From *Voices in the Park* by Anthony Browne.

words, Aladdin's world is no longer the one we envisage in our heads but Le Cain's very particular world with its highly patterned surfaces and elongated figures. When we see the pictures, Le Cain's characters enter into our apprehension of the tale most determinedly.

One of the greatest advantages of looking at the word–picture relation in picturebooks in this way is that it offers a perspective on them that is more realistic than some of the looser, musical metaphors. If we are prepared to see language and image working productively upon each other then we have the beginnings of a model upon which to build an account of the picturebook that fits our experience of reading. What is lacking at the moment is a way of acknowledging and examining differences. All picturebooks may exhibit the interanimation of word and picture, but not all picturebooks do it in the same way.

Taxonomies and types

During the 1970s, 1980s and 1990s writers and illustrators of picturebooks pushed outwards at the limits of what could be said in words and pictures and how it could be said. Formal experimentation went hand in hand with attempts to address wider and more diverse audiences and more and more sophisticated kinds of subject matter. Critics and commentators have responded by looking, amongst other things, for emerging patterns and themes within the work of those who are judged to be the major practitioners. One approach has been to categorize picturebooks according to the different ways in which words and pictures are perceived to interact. I do not intend here to review every attempt that has been made at this project but I shall look briefly at three relatively recent examples to try and illustrate their strengths and weaknesses.

One of the most recent attempts to create a sophisticated taxonomy of picturebook interactions is that of Maria Nikolajeva and Carole Scott. Nikolajeva and Scott (2000, and forthcoming)[3] identify a 'broad spectrum of word–image interaction' (2000:225) reaching from *symmetry* at one end to *contradiction* at the other, symmetry being, roughly speaking, an equivalence of word and image, contradiction, a maximal dissonance. At various points along the continuum between these two poles they locate what they consider to be significant forms of interaction and these become the categories within which different kinds of picturebook are sited. The main categories are *symmetry*, *enhancement*, *counterpoint* and *contradiction*. These are explained as follows.

Words and images are considered to be in a symmetrical relationship when they come as close as possible to conveying the same information or telling the same story – roughly the equivalent of Sendak's narrative illustration. Thus if the words tell us of a boy standing in the rain in a garden, the pictures show us precisely that – a boy in a garden with the rain falling. The relationship between words and pictures becomes enhancing when the pictures expand upon the words or vice versa, the possibilities within this category ranging from minimal enhancement to significant enhancement or complementarity. In the former case (minimal enhancement) there is little difference between what the words say and what the pictures show, but in the latter case, one strand within the text will be seen to enlarge upon the other in ways which clearly affect the overall meaning. William Steig's *Sylvester and the Magic Pebble* is cited as an example of minimal enhancement, the argument being that the pictures do only a little more than echo the words and thus barely shift the text beyond the condition of word–image symmetry. On the other hand, when words and pictures enhance each other significantly something quite distinctive is held to be added to one strand of the text by the other. Beatrix Potter's *The Tale of Peter Rabbit* is, for Nikolajeva and Scott, a good example of a book where words and pictures are in such a complementary relationship. Potter's verbal text gives us the bare tale but her pictures tell us things about Peter's relationship with his family not mentioned in the words. As we have already seen, for Nikolajeva and Scott, when words and pictures counterpoint one another they offer the reader 'alternative information' so that an effort must be made to forge a connection. Contradiction, the extreme form of counterpoint, pushes the words and pictures even further apart so that they seem to be saying entirely different things.

I tried in Chapter 1 to give some idea of the sheer diversity of the picturebook. There is enormous variety within the form and categorizing the dynamic relationships between words and pictures seems to offer a means of gaining some purchase on the differences between picturebooks. A particular strength of Nikolajeva and Scott's approach lies in the fact that they not only discriminate between types of interaction but also explore the way they inter-sect with narrative features such as character, setting and point of view. In relation to these features some combinations of word and picture do seem to be relatively static and uncomplicated, the pictures appearing to do little more than shadow, or echo, the story told in the words. Others seem to demand more of the reader in terms of active synthesis and there are, indeed, those that challenge the reader with discontinuous or bizarre combinations. Nikolajeva and Scott are also careful to remind readers that the categories they describe cannot be considered to be wholly watertight, but even allowing for their sensi-tivity in this area their account gives rise to a number of conceptual and termi-nological difficulties.

Consider for example the authors' use of the term 'symmetrical'. In their view, a relationship is symmetrical when 'words and pictures tell the same story, essentially repeating infomation in different forms of communication' (Nikolajeva and Scott, 2000:225). The difficulty here is that a picture can only offer 'the same information' in the loosest possible sense and, as Nodelman demonstrates very clearly, it can only do this insofar as the words tell the reader what he or she should attend to.[4] The symmetry that many picturebooks appear to exhibit is thus illusory, an artefact of word–picture interanimation. Such relationships are often better understood in terms of the practical process of illustration, that is, the way illustrators sometimes try to match in pictures what they read in a prior written text. A further problem arises out of the fact that, although Nikolajeva and Scott purport to be exploring the dynamic inter-action of word and image, to claim a symmetrical relationship for many picturebooks is to side-step the question of interaction altogether. If the two parts of the text appear to be saying the same thing then there would appear to be no interaction to examine. The pictures and words would simply be running on parallel tracks. What would be far more useful would be an investigation into how the effect of symmetry is achieved. To what parts of a verbal text are pictures responding when the resultant impression is one of congruence or symmetry? As we saw in the case of *Gorilla*, the words and sentences that make up a narrative are not all of the same kind and some are clearly easier to set 'symmetrical' pictures alongside than others.

Similar problems arise when we consider the category of contradiction. If this is taken to mean something like 'stating the opposite' then we have the same problem as with symmetry. Nodelman's warning that ' ... pictures ... can imply narrative information only in relationship to a verbal context' (Nodelman 1988:195) alerts us to the fact that we simply cannot identify what it is that a picture 'states' in relation to the narrative outside of its animation by the words. Pictures certainly do possess an ideational function (see Appendix 2) – that is, they are perfectly capable of representing facts, events and states of affairs – but words, whether in the form of captions or fragments of narrative, will always affect how we take up and interpret those facts. In other words, the impression of contradiction is once again an artefact, a product, of the pictures and words coming together and acting upon one another rather than simply a matter of two modes offering transparently contrary meanings.

What Nikolajeva and Scott are really interested in, like most researchers in this field, are the effects of difference and incongruity, the ways in which pictures and words rub up alongside each other in ways that make us stop and think. In this respect, Denise Agosto, in her article, 'One and inseparable: interdependent storytelling in picture storybooks' follows a similar route (Agosto 1999). At the outset she distinguishes between what she terms twice-told tales – those where '... the texts and the illustrations ... tell the same stories simultaneously' – and interdependent tales, where '... the reader must consider both forms of media concurrently in order to comprehend the books' stories' (Agosto 1999:267). Twice-told tales are said to employ parallel story-telling rather than interdependent storytelling, but parallelism is simply symmetry by another name and as such must be seen as the result of interdependence rather than as a separate category altogether. However, Agosto's purpose is not to investigate the whole range, but to propose and elaborate upon a model of interdependent storytelling in those cases where there are clear differences between words and images. She begins with a diagrammatic representation of her model, dividing up the terrain into super-ordinate, inter-ordinate and subordinate categories (see Figure 15).

Agosto's two major sub-categories are therefore storytelling by augmentation and storytelling by contradiction. In the case of books that work by augmentation, '... the texts and the illustrations each amplify, extend and complete the story that the other tells'; in the case of contradiction, '... the texts and illustrations present conflicting information, such as the words describing a sunny day where the corresponding pictures show a rainstorm' (Agosto 1999:269, 275). Agosto provides some fairly clear examples of contradiction and manages to find some books where at least some features of the verbal text are illustrated in a manner that indicates something like opposition or negation. For example, in Steven Kellogg's *Pinkerton, Behave!*, a puppy in the process of being house-trained refuses to comply with its master's commands. The words tell of commands such as 'Come!' and 'Fetch!' while the pictures show Pinkerton responding by respectively jumping out of the window

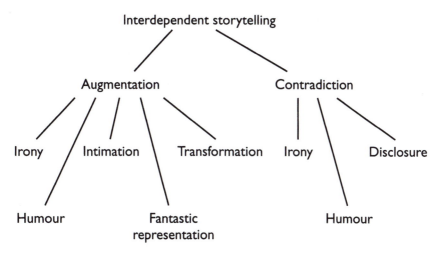

Figure 15 A theoretical model of interdependent storytelling, from Agosto 1999.

and shredding the newspaper. But the same objections could be raised here as in the paragraphs above. The putative opposition of 'Come' and the image of a dog leaping through a window is the result of an interpretative act and not the outcome of the simple co-presence of two logically incompatible statements.

A further difficulty arises out of the attempt to subdivide these two main types. Agosto provides two titles as examples of each subdivision and although she nowhere makes it explicit, it seems clear that the categories of augmentation through irony, humour, intimation etc., are intended to be categories or types of book. *Tidy Titch*, by Pat Hutchins, is thus an example of ironical augmentation and Ellen Raskin's *Nothing Ever Happens on My Block* turns out to be an example of disclosing contradiction. The problem is that, as Agosto admits, an individual book may exhibit more than one effect. Irony and humour, for example, come together more often than not: indeed, it would be very strange if they did not. In fact it would not be difficult to imagine a book exemplifying several traits at once. One of Agosto's own examples of fantastic representation – John Burningham's *Come Away from the Water, Shirley*, the sister text to the one mentioned at the beginning of the chapter – is a particularly indeterminate picturebook possessing ironical, humorous, fantastic and even contradictory features. What this suggests is that the categories as they are described are not particularly useful for characterizing individual books but are far more useful as an indication of the kinds of effects that pictures and picture sequences can have when placed alongside different kinds of verbal texts. The ironical augmentation of words by pictures, if it is anything at all, is the result of a particular kind of word–image interanimation, not a kind of book. It may well be the case that certain books exhibit very clearly a particular form of interanimation throughout, but the very fact that many books exhibit several forms, either simultaneously or sequentially, suggests that in looking at types of book, we are looking at too large a unit of analysis.

Joanne Golden alerts her readers to this fact in her chapter on the picturebook in *The Narrative Symbol in Childhood Literature*. In her own words, 'It is important to note, however, that while particular relationships between picture and text may be predominant in certain picture books, a given book may also reflect more than one type of relationship' (Golden 1990:104). Golden attempts to '... examine the nature of the picture storybook' by describing and exemplifying five different types of text–picture relationship. These are:

(i)   text and picture are symmetrical;
(ii)   text depends on picture for clarification;
(iii) illustration enhances, elaborates text;
(iv)   text carries primary narrative, illustration is selective; and
(v)   illustration carries primary narrative, text is selective.

Symmetry is again considered to be the simplest, most basic word–image relationship. Golden, like Nikolajeva and Scott, and Agosto, finds nothing to say about the interaction or interanimation of the two strands other than that the words echo, or shadow, the pictures and vice versa: 'In this type of text–picture relationship, the picture provides redundant information to the text. It serves literally to convey what the text conveys.' Once again, this is both an inaccurate description of the case and a sidestepping of the issue of interaction (although, to be fair, Golden does not claim to be examining how words and pictures interact, only how they are 'related'). Her examples are taken from *The Tale of Peter Rabbit* (remember that Nikolajeva and Scott considered this to be a good example of significant enhancement, or complementarity, not symmetry) and *Titch* by Pat Hutchins. Of *Titch* she says:

> On one page, the text reads 'Pete had a big drum' and under the text is a picture of Pete holding two drumsticks with a large drum hanging from a string around his neck. In a comparable picture on the opposite page, the text reads 'Mary had a trumpet' and a picture of Mary blowing a trumpet is depicted below the text.
>
> (Golden 1990:106)

It should be fairly clear that the pictures can only be said to convey 'literally' what the text conveys by virtue of the fact that the words are telling us what to notice and what to think of what we see. Taken away from the words in the book, the pictures might better be thought of as being symmetrical with something like 'Peter holds a drum and drumsticks', and 'Mary plays a trumpet' – that is, words from a book about 'doing things'. The pictures will not 'literally convey' anything in particular until they are brought to life by the words around them.

Golden is more helpful about clarification (type ii) and enhancement/elaboration (type iii). Pictures clarify the written text when the words alone are insufficient to carry the narrative. In Ezra Jack Keats' *The Snowy Day*, the words 'He walked with his toes pointing in, like that:' make a clear gesture towards the picture where we see exactly what kind of a walk it is. '[A]nd he made angels,' is unclear for a slightly different reason. Without the picture it is assumed we would not know that what is being referred to are 'snow angels' made by moving the arms up and down and the legs from side to side while lying in the snow. When the relationship between word and picture is one of elaboration, '... the essential narrative is conveyed in the text but the illustrations extend and elaborate the text by delineating further details' (Golden 1990:110). It is here that we begin to see that Golden's is essentially a word-centred view of the picturebook. Although she quotes with approval the picture theorist W. J. T. Mitchell on the complex word–image relationship of 'mutual translation, interpretation, illustration and embellishment' (Mitchell 1987:44) she tends to look at the words first and then the pictures to see what relationship the latter seem to have towards the former. This position becomes even clearer when we move on to the fourth kind of relationship. This is where the written text carries the primary narrative and illustration is selective, the illustrator singling out just one or two of the many scenes and events conveyed to the reader through the words.

In describing the picture–word relationship in her final category 'Illustration carries primary narrative, text is selective' she betrays a misunderstanding of how words and pictures interanimate one another and in her choice of example inadvertently reveals the limitations of her scheme. *Hey Diddle Diddle* by Randolph Caldecott does indeed appear to be a narrative told in pictures but if we were to take away the words of the traditional rhyme and (this is necessary also) forget that we ever knew them, I am not at all sure that we could make consistent narrative sense out of Caldecott's sequence of pictures. It is therefore simply untrue to say that the pictures 'carry the primary narrative'. Once again, if they appear to do so, it is only because we are guided by the words alongside or in our heads. Furthermore, to say that the text is 'selective' is to suggest that the words chronologically came after the images: the 'author' choosing which of the many features of the illustrations to mention. But this is plainly not the case for we know that Caldecott, as was his usual practice, chose a popular short text and embellished it with sequences of pictures. Golden acknowledges that this was so. If that is what happened, then would not *Hey Diddle Diddle*, along with other similar picturebooks, be better considered as an example of enhancement and elaboration, that is, of her type iii?

Once again, confusion and misunderstanding seem to take over when attempts are made to label picturebooks according to how the words and pictures seem to be related to one another, or how they interact. There is a singular lack of agreement over how categories – that is, types – of book might be described, and a pervasive lack of understanding of the nature of word–picture interanimation, particularly in relation to narrative. Individual texts are described differently by different authors (e.g. Beatrix Potter's *The Tale of Peter Rabbit*) and there is a general unwillingness to recognize that the appropriate unit of analysis is the form of word–picture interaction and not the whole book. Why should this be so?

Part of the problem, I believe, stems from the fact that picturebooks do not take kindly to being corralled into six, eight or even ten determinate categories. Part of the argument of this book is that the picturebook is a particularly flexible form of text and that picturebooks in general are extraordinarily diverse. I tried in Chapter 1 to hint at the heterogeneity of the form and suggested that one way of linking different kinds of picturebooks together is through the concept of family resemblances. Picturebook A may be like picturebook B, and B may be quite like C, but that does not mean that A and C will be much alike except in the most general terms. Furthermore, taxonomies, once established, exert a considerable magnetic attraction. If it seems that picturebooks are divisible into the complementary, the contrapuntal and the contradictory, then there is a strong temptation to make individual examples fit the available categories. If there seem to be contradictory elements to a particular book then into the bag it goes, foreclosing more detailed examination. There clearly are differences in the ways that illustrators manipulate word–picture relationships, and there clearly are books that are consistent in their treatment of those relationships, but there are also many, many books that are subtle, indeterminate and resistant to easy categorization.

Where does this discussion leave us? If neither musical analogies nor simple taxonomies will do, where might we go from here? What we need is a way of looking at picturebooks that in the broad view recognizes the interanimation that always occurs when words and pictures are intertwined as they are in picturebooks, but that also posits the flexibility of the relationship, the way it can twist and turn within the supple telling of a tale. At the risk of burdening the reader with yet another metaphor, I want to suggest that we might develop the notion of an interanimation of word and image by considering the two strands to be held together in an *ecological* relationship. Chapter 3 will expand upon and illustrate what an ecology of the picturebook might look like.

Notes

1   It should already be clear that this is a great oversimplification. Words in picturebooks can do far more than simply point to what should be attended to in the pictures, and the pictures almost always do more than dress up the words in colour and form. Nonetheless it cannot be emphasized too much that 'what the words do to the pictures is not the same as what the pictures do to the words'. For further clarification and discussion readers are advised to turn

to Nodelman's Chapter 7, 'The relationships of pictures and words', in particular, pp.193–201.

2   Lawrence Sipe adopts the term 'synergy' in his article 'How picture books work' (Sipe 1998:98) and follows *The Shorter Oxford Dictionary* definition: 'the production of two or more agents, substances, etc., of a combined effect greater then the sum of their separate effects.' This formulation, along with Nodelman's, seems to me to be more inclusive than Barthes' and thus more appropriate to the varied form of the picturebook.

3   At the time of writing neither Nikolajeva and Scott's book, *How Picturebooks Work*, nor the article based upon the book was published. The article has now been published in the winter 2000 issue of *Children's Literature in Education*. I was fortunate enough to be able to read the finished draft and the comments in this chapter are based solely upon that draft.

4   See the arguments earlier in this chapter. Also, consider Nodelman again:

> pictures can communicate much to us, and particularly much of visual significance – but only if words focus them, tell us what it is about them that might be worth paying attention to. In a sense, trying to understand the situation a picture depicts is always an act of imposing language upon it – interpreting visual information in verbal terms; it is not accidental that we speak of 'visual literacy', of the 'grammar' of pictures, of 'reading' pictures. Reading pictures for narrative meaning is a matter of applying our understanding of words.
>
> (Nodelman 1988:211)

Chapter 3

The ecology of the picturebook

N: (exclaims) She punches the king in!

DL: Hmm ... NOW THERE'S WATER EVERYWHERE!

N: 'Cos she's punched the king in

DL: Why? What do you mean?

N: She punched the king in and it probably made a splash ... she's probably still playing in the bath

DL: Yes? You mean the king falling in the water ... what that's done?

N: Yes. She's playing with her toys

DL: Ah. I see. So you don't think this is a real king then?

N: No

DL: No?

N: It's just a toy

(Nathan (N) and the author (DL) reading together
from *Time to Get Out of the Bath, Shirley* by John Burningham)

Introduction

Ecology is the branch of biology that deals with the relationships between creatures and the environments in which they live. Ecological studies within the life sciences examine ecosystems rather than individual organisms, for in the real world there is no possibility of life outside of a sustaining environment. Birds, insects, reptiles and bacteria, as well as human beings, not only exist within an environment, they are also part of the environment and as such both influence, and are influenced by, that environment. Not surprisingly, perhaps, the term has been appropriated by non-biologists and applied metaphorically in a number of different disciplines to enable the investigation of how the differing parts of a field, or factors within a process, interact and mutually influence one another. The anthropologist Gregory Bateson, in *Steps to an Ecology of Mind*, collected together essays written over 35 years, all of which explore one or another aspect of the ways in which ideas and minds shape, and are shaped by, the environments in which they emerge (Bateson 1973). The psychologist J. J. Gibson, in developing his theories of Direct Perception, posited the need for an *ecological optics* that would be truer to the facts of perception in the real world than the classical optics commonly used in psychological studies (Gibson 1986). Sociolinguists too work with essentially ecological concepts. Language and literacy is always embedded within social and cultural contexts which have a shaping influence upon discourses and utterances and which are, in turn, shaped by language and literacy events.

David Barton, in *Literacy: an Introduction to the Ecology of Written Language*, examines the development and uses of reading and writing from the point of view of their location within social settings (Barton 1994) and he makes the parallels with ecology in the life sciences very clear. He points out that there are endangered languages just as there are endangered species and that they are disappearing from the world at an alarming rate. He makes an important point about diversity too. The vitality of a language, especially a globally dominant one such as English, lies in its variety and too great an emphasis upon uniformity and conformity can have damaging effects upon both the language itself and upon its speakers.

The application of the concept of ecology to disciplines and fields of enquiry other than the life sciences is thus not without precedent, but in what ways might the concept of ecology help us in our understanding of picturebooks? The major gain is in flexibility and complexity. In claiming that picturebooks possess an internal ecology we are not claiming the exact same relationship of word and image for each and every picturebook. People and koala bears both need sustaining environments and could be said to occupy ecological niches, but human beings are so constructed that the range of environments in which they can thrive is enormous. There is scarcely a corner of the globe that they have not colonized, whereas koalas need specific trees in specific places to stay alive. Similarly, some pictures and words in picturebooks seem to be tightly bound together so that not much could be changed on either side without the narrative being dislocated or fractured in some way. In other books, the relationship is looser and freer.

Furthermore, ecosystems tend to be complex rather than simple. When we speak of organisms and their environment we are not necessarily implying a simple two-term relationship. Rather whole networks of relationships are implied. Our own bodies swarm with bacteria without which we would die and many creatures enjoy complicated symbiotic relationships with other organisms. Similarly, when we look closely at many picturebooks we find that the text has been put together from several different strands and that it is the interconnectedness of all of those strands that bring the book to life. *Have You Seen Who's Just Moved in Next Door to Us?* and *The Jolly Postman* are two very good examples of books that possess a considerable degree of complexity.

In this chapter, I use the concepts of ecology and the ecosystem in two different, but related ways. To begin with we need to see how an ecological perspective on picturebooks can refresh our understanding of how pictures and words interanimate each other. This will be the subject of the present section. In the second section I consider how an enlarged view of the ecological metaphor might help us to see how picturebooks are better understood when we consider them as texts-as-read rather than as texts-in-themselves.

The ecology of picture and word

Interanimation

If we say that pictures and words in picturebooks interact ecologically, that the book acts as a kind of miniature ecosystem, we are saying a number of things. First we are emphasizing the interdependence or interanimation of word and image. This is essentially the relationship discussed in Chapter 2. There I used the example of the first page of *Voices in the Park* to illustrate how the picture is given focus and narrative life by the opening words, and how those words gain specificity, colour and weight from the picture. The words are pulled through the pictures and the pictures are brought into focus by the words. If we translate this into ecological terms we might say that the words come to life in the context, the environment, of the pictures and vice versa.

Flexibility

But there is a second sense in which the words and pictures in a picturebook might be said to be bound up ecologically that should take us beyond simple statements about inter-relatedness. An ecology of the picturebook allows us to claim for it a degree of flexibility. Word and image, organism and environment, mutually shape each other but there is no reason to suppose that the dynamics of this relationship remain the same from page to page, let alone from book to book. We need to be careful here for in the natural world the relationship of organism to environment, and vice versa, automatically changes as the circumstances change. The temperature drops, the hedgehog hibernates. A creature's rate of reproduction grows so the food supply begins to dry up and eventually the population drops back again. In the picturebook, on the other hand, the word–image relationship is controlled by the picturebook maker or the collaborating writer and illustrator. What this means is that if the pictures change in quantity, type or function as the pages are turned these changes do not of themselves produce changes in the words for the writer is in control of those. But for a reader such changes will bring about alterations in the relationship between the two media.

By way of illustration, let us look once more at *Gorilla*. I drew attention in Chapter 1 to the way in which Browne's pictures stand as visual interpretations of the rather bare, skeletal narrative embodied in the words. The words tell us what Hannah and her father did and said; the pictures show us not only locations and appearances but also contain many embedded details that make us

Figure 16 From *Gorilla* by Anthony Browne.

pause and reflect on what seems to be happening. These seem to be the basic functions that lie at the root of the book's ecology, except that at the pivotal moment of transformation when the toy gorilla appears to come to life in Hannah's bedroom, not only is the gorilla transformed, but the text is too, and as a result the relationship between words and pictures changes. Up until the moment when Hannah throws the despised toy gorilla into a corner of her bedroom the story-in-words can just about stand alone inasmuch as it possesses both cohesion and coherence – it hangs together and it makes sense as a story. Once the toy is in the corner though, something happens to the text as well as to the gorilla. On the left-hand page, opposite the picture of a huge gorilla looming over the foot of Hannah's bed, and beneath a sequence of three square images (the only such sequence in the book), the words run as follows: 'Hannah threw the gorilla into a corner with her other toys and went back to sleep. In the night something amazing happened.' Here the text breaks off and we are not told – at least not in words – what the 'something' is that happened. Over the page, the story resumes, 'Hannah was frightened.' This is just about the only place in the book – significantly a climactic, transformational moment – where information is deliberately withheld from the reader so that the pictures must take over the narrative. They can only do this by showing what we have not been told and as this involves transformation – that is, change from one state to another – Browne needs a strip of three frames to do it. The alternative would have been to use a simple declarative sentence such as, 'The toy grew and grew'. There are other moments in the book when a somewhat similar shift of narrative weight from words to pictures occurs, but the toy gorilla's transformation is the clearest example in the book of how a story can be passed backwards and forwards between the words and the pictures.[1]

A picturebook does not always maintain the same relationship between word and image throughout. This is why it is, in the end, hard to fit picturebooks into simple, formal categories with any degree of certainty or accuracy. From the point of view of the picturebook as ecosystem, it simply means that the relationship between organism and environment, word and image, has momentarily shifted. In the case of *Gorilla*, the written text temporarily ceases to describe action and process and by way of accommoda-tion, the pictures fill the gap. As the words fall silent and give ground, the pictures are made to step up to assume narrative responsibility.

We can detect this kind of shift in relationship in many picturebooks, although the changes from page to page may not be of the accommodatory kind that we find in *Gorilla*. Sometimes we find that what we assumed was a stable relationship is far freer and more flexible than we imagined. In *Granpa*, for example, large gaps are left between the printed words and the pictures. There is no storytelling voice, no narrator as there is in *Gorilla*, and there are two separate sequences of pictures so the reader has to work hard to pull the several strands together. This task is not made any easier by the fact that the monochrome, sepia drawings on the left-hand side of each page-opening appear to represent different things on different pages. On the first page the drawing seems to be a straightforward picture of a corner of Granpa's green-house. Over the page it is perhaps best thought of as a scene from Granpa's memory stimulated by his singing of an old favourite song. Over the page again and tucked away in the corner, beneath Granpa's puzzled, 'I didn't know Teddy was another little girl' is a picture of 'Teddy' in (Granpa's?) imagination making up in front of a dressing table mirror. On the next page we are returned to the real world once more, this time possibly a corner of the garden. These shifts, from everyday life to memory to imagination and back to everyday life, and the shifts in the nature of the accompanying utterances (and thus of the word–image relationship), are not at all like the shift, discussed above, in *Gorilla*. In the first case, we have Granpa's fragment of an explanation ('There would not be room for all the seeds to grow') and the little girl's question ('Do worms go to Heaven?') hanging over a carefully arranged array of greenhouse paraphernalia, a loosely attached image that could very easily be otherwise. But over the page, the words of the song printed at the top ('One man went to mow/went to mow a meadow …') seem to be issuing from the mouths of the people depicted below. The reader is clearly being asked to link up these sets of images and words in different ways.

In Raymond Briggs' *The Man*, the variation in word–image interanimation is different again. The book begins with the kind of comic strip storytelling that was for a long time Briggs' signature style. After a single page, however, the book changes gear and Briggs slips into the dialogic manner which is sustained for most of the book. Here it seems as if the ratio of pictures to words spoken has been dramatically reversed so that the reader has far more conversation to negotiate and far fewer pictures. The speech balloons have multiplied, lost their frames and settled onto the page to form something like a playscript, and the gaps between consecutive pictures have widened as the dialogue has expanded and thickened. Three-quarters of the way through, however, there is a sudden reversion to an almost wordless block of picture strips covering three whole pages. The book then concludes in its major mode.

There is thus very often a variety of relationships to be found within

Figure 17 From *The Man* by Raymond Briggs

individual picturebooks. Within each book's ecosystem the separate parts interanimate each other while at the same time – to change the metaphor – adopting varied roles. One moment the words step forward to occupy centre stage, the next they retire to the wings or comment like a chorus on some key point of the action being played by another part of the text. In order to develop a complex and sensitive understanding of what picturebooks can do we need to retain this idea of flexibility within coherence.

Complexity

Third and finally, we need to recognize the features of complexity and diversity implicit in the concept of an ecosystem. Systems, by definition, are both multiple and organized. If picturebooks are to be considered ecologically then we might reasonably look for the organized, coherent multiplicity characteristic of such systems. It might be objected that this is unlikely given that we are only considering two modes of communication, words and pictures, but that is to assume that words are always grouped together in the same way and perform the same function, and likewise that all visual images are more or less indistinguishable. Whilst there are undoubtedly many picturebooks that are relatively plain and simple in their matching of words and images, there are also a great many that exhibit the complexity we would expect to find. The discussion of *Granpa* above makes clear that not only do relationships shift and change as we turn the pages, but also that those relationships link together a number of different strands. There are, for example, two very different kinds of picture, performing very different kinds of functions, visible at each page-opening.

Even clearer examples of complexity and diversity can be found in books such as *The Jolly Postman*, *Think of an Eel*, *The Man* and *Have You Seen Who's Just Moved in Next Door to Us?*. In Chapter 5 *The Jolly Postman* will be discussed in greater detail, but for present purposes we might simply point to the variety of types of image that the book contains. Some scenes illustrate events recorded in the rhyming text, while appended vignettes depict offstage characters or contribute extra detail to the story. The book also contains a great deal of embedded imagery such as the newspaper read by the postman in the witch's house, the various icons, postage stamps and postmarks on the envelopes and, of course, the imagery to be found in the letters and cards themselves. All of these images are relevant to the Jolly Postman's story and his round of deliveries, and they all bear some kind of relation to the written text, although that text is far from straightforward. There is the meandering rhyme that tells of the postman's meandering route but there is also much else that is not only worth looking at and reading but also highly germane to the purposes of the book. There are the addresses on the envelopes, the postmarks again, other kinds of written matter on the envelopes such as 'if undelivered ... ' instructions and again, the wonderfully inventive contents of the enclosed letters and cards.

If we refer to the complexity of such a book we are not in any way passing judgement on its difficulty. Writers and illustrators of the calibre of Allan and Janet Ahlberg are perfectly capable of ensuring that such a text is accessible to a range of ages and stages of maturity. Complexity here has everything to do with what the different kinds of pictures ask of the different kinds of words and vice versa. We might want to say that since the textual material of *The Jolly Postman* comes to us in separable sections – the rhyme, the envelopes, the letters – then this much reduces the complexity, as the words and pictures of the letters, say, form a whole unto themselves, unrelated in any substantial way to the book in which they are embedded. However, the same cannot be said for a book like *Have You Seen Who's Just Moved in Next Door to Us?*, despite the superficial similarities. In this book, as was noted in Chapter 1, the written text appears in several forms, none of which is unimportant or irrelevant: a main rhyming text, a host of speech bubbles scattered across each page-opening and the occasional shop sign. The pictures too seem to perform more than one function, and are related to the words in a variety of ways. The verses of the rhyme act a little like captions. They tell us something about the characters they refer to, but the information they provide is hardly significant and they seem to have little more to do than to point to particular characters represented in the panorama below.

> An old lady with a broom,
> At number forty rents a room.
> (Has she seen who's just moved in
> Next door to us?)

> And living down below,
> We have Michelangelo.
> (Has he seen who's just moved in
> Next door to us?)

> Move five doors along:
> Say hello to Mister Kong.
> (Has he seen who's just moved in
> Next door to us?)

On the other hand, the text contained within the speech bubbles, despite its brevity, is dense and compact with significance, but only when read in conjunction with the imagery to which it relates. The relationship here is tight and close, the words and pictures together truly transforming each other and in the process, transforming our understanding of what we see and read, sometimes to the point where the meaning resonates through two or three levels. Take, for example, the page-opening where the verses quoted above appear (see Figure 5). Scanning from the left we see first a little girl with golden hair tip-toeing away from a front door, dripping large blobs of something grey onto the pavement. From inside the house comes a voice, 'Who's been sleeping in my porridge?' The joke here hardly needs explaining. Next door, where Michelangelo is working, we have a simple case of mishearing (a theme that runs through the book like Chinese whispers). The commission for a statue of Queen Betty (Elizabeth?) has been misunderstood and the result is a Mean Yeti.

On the floor above a witch and her cat circle the room on their broomsticks, the words 'Purr' alongside the cat's broom and 'Broom!' alongside the witch's. Of course, neither word is simply a label. 'Broom' is the noise children make when they wish to conjure up in their imaginative play the sound of a powerful engine. And purring is the sound that well tuned engines make when running smoothly. Next door again is a bootmaker's. The sign over the door, 'Walker Boots', is not just a clever name for a shop selling footwear, it is also a sidelong reference to the name of the book's publishers, Walker Books.

These examples take us only as far as the gutter separating the two parts of the page-opening and, were we to continue across the right-hand page, we could identify two or three more clever manipulations of word–picture interanimation. *Have You Seen Who's Just Moved in Next Door to Us?* is an extraordinary book that repays careful study. Strictly speaking, it is not a story, for nothing happens in it that could be considered a narrative. Characters only appear once on the page showing the part of the street where they live (that is, if we ignore the final fold-out panorama where everybody turns up for a second time) so there can be no motivated action carrying over from one set of events to the next. The only characters that do appear more than once are the ones that pass on the message about the new neighbours so I suppose we could say that there is a very slight story about a message being passed on and corrupted through repeated mis-hearings, but that would be to misrepresent grossly the nature of the book. Another oddity is that thematically the book chooses to inhabit a world of immature, childish humour yet asks to be read in a layered, reflective way that brings the reader back time and time again. And again, although the book is hardly profound, it is formally complex. As such it evades easy categorization in terms of the way words and pictures interact and thus cries out to be read ecologically.

The ecology of the reading event

In the first section of the chapter I argued that the concept of ecology affords us a useful model of word–picture interaction in three different ways. First, it encourages us to see how the words and pictures in picturebooks act upon each other reciprocally, each one becoming the environment within which the other lives and thrives. Second, the notion of the ecosystem as a dynamic structure helps us to understand how the word–picture relationship might shift and change, page by page and moment by moment. Third, the recognition that ecosystems can be complex as well as flexible helps us to appreciate the heterogeneity that we can sometimes find within the picturebook. But one of the greatest advantages of looking at the word–picture relation in picturebooks in ecological terms is that it points towards the role of the reader in the interanimation of word and image. The varieties of interanimation that occur in picturebooks do so in the intercourse of books and readers and nowhere else. Barthes says that the message's unity occurs on the level of the story (Barthes

1986), but that is only another way of saying that the pictures and words work together at a semantic level, the level where meanings are apprehended. And where is this 'higher level ... of the story' if not somewhere in the reader's reading? Of course, the same could be said, and has been said, about all kinds of texts. Indeed, the idea that the reader is an active partner in the creation of meaning was a commonplace in discussions of both literature and literacy for much of the latter part of the last century. But the composite nature of the picturebook brings the issue into sharp focus. If we say with Meek that 'pictures and words on a page interanimate each other' we cannot mean that anything physical is happening. We can stare at the page for as long as we like but the pictures and words will stay quite still and determinedly leave each other alone. The only relations they share on the page are spatial ones and if any animating gets done it is because an active, meaning-seeking reader is at work.

The ecological analogy can therefore be extended to encompass the picturebook as it comes to life during what might be called the 'reading event'. The words are brought to life by the pictures and the pictures by the words, but this is only possible in the experience of reading. In this section of the chapter I explore what takes place during such reading events and discuss why they are important to the study of picturebooks. The best place to start is with an example of a reader reading.

In the conversation recorded in the extract at the head of the chapter, Nathan is reading to me from the same book that Jane was looking at closely in Chapter 2. Although Nathan and Jane were both six years old they turned out to be very different readers. Jane had no difficulties with the printed words and enjoyed reading the written text aloud whereas Nathan was still very unsure of himself and preferred me to read the words. From the beginning Jane felt she knew what the story was about (although it puzzled her greatly) but Nathan was more cautious, and when he was uncertain as to what was happening, he tended to use, in his remarks to me, modal forms such as, 'it might be ...' or 'it's probably ...'. This sensitivity towards the emergent story enabled him to make the connections recorded above. At this point in the book Shirley's mother can be seen mopping up splashes on the bathroom floor while over on the right-hand side Shirley is engaged in a mock joust with the king and has just knocked him off his mount. There is nothing in Burningham's text – either words or pictures – that makes explicit the relationship between the images on the left- and right-hand sides of the gutter (which is precisely the reason why this book, and others like it, are so useful in studying the interaction of texts and readers) but Nathan immediately recognizes that the pictures can be taken to represent two entirely different realms, the everyday-life-world on the left and the world of Shirley's imagination on the right. There is water everywhere in the real bathroom because Shirley has knocked the imaginary king off his inflatable duck into the water. 'She's playing with her toys,' says Nathan and in these few words we see the act of story-making taking place before our eyes. For Nathan, the story has suddenly become straightforward (although the text

Now there's water everywhere!

Figure 18 From *Time to Get Out of the Bath, Shirley* by John Burningham.

remains complex) and he now has a way of resolving the doubts and uncertainties expressed in his 'probably's and 'might be's. The story is now about a girl playing in her bath and giving free rein to her imagination. The author does not tell us that this is so, at least not explicitly, but Nathan knows enough about stories, books and the business of reading them to be able to make the necessary connections.[2]

Now this fragment of book-talk raises some very interesting questions about Burningham's story and about reading stories in general. We might describe to someone who had not seen the book what it was about but this would be something like an attempt at abstracting the core elements or features of the narrative, rather like offering a dictionary definition of a word. In the lived experience of reading it is a different matter entirely. We might, for example, ask when the story takes shape, for in Nathan's case it was not the same story at the beginning, or even half way through, as it was at the end. It is clear from the transcript of our conversation that Nathan held the story in suspension as we read together and he attempted to sort out what was going on. For Jane, the moment of illumination came only at the very end after she had finished. In her case, she appears to have read two stories. There is the one that took shape as she was reading about a little girl who slips down the plughole of her bath in much the same way that Alice goes down the rabbit hole, and who meets strange characters rather like Alice does. And

then there is the one that dawned on her later when she had finished and had been prompted by me (I asked her 'do you think she's really gone down the plughole?' to which she replied, very quietly, 'No, I think she's only dreaming or something.') In neither case – Nathan's or Jane's – is this a simple matter of making an interpretation of events, something that can clearly be done long after the reading of the story has taken place, as both children were concerned to establish what the events were in the first place. With some books, the story seems to take shape in our minds as we read it, moment by moment, but Jane's and Nathan's attempts to understand Burningham's tale make it plain that we construct the story out of the material provided by the text.

It is tempting to think that the construction of the story takes place in the mind of the reading reader but that would not strictly be true. The story, the living meaning of Burningham's words and pictures, is not something that takes place on the page, nor in some shadowy realm of mental events, but somewhere in the intercourse of reader and text. The text offers itself up as an object of contemplation but the attentive reader must contribute something for the story to come to life. One of the first things that very young children have to learn about reading books is that the text is in control and that not just anything will count as an appropriate response to it (see Chapter 5). You must yield to the text and withdraw from involvement in the world,3 but on the other hand you must bring to bear appropriate forms of knowledge. You must know what to do to open up the box of tricks. Consider what Nathan had to say after we had finished reading the book. I asked him which part he had enjoyed most:

DL: Which bit did you like then?
N: I like the end bit
DL: What, you mean when they were fighting, on the ducks?
N: That bit, 'cos she was still in the bath.
DL: So where do think Shirley's been all this time?
N: Playing in the bath with no water.
DL: Oh I see. So what about all this galloping around on horseback?
N: She was probably using her fingers
DL: Using her ... how would she use her fingers?
N: Like ... going like that (*making two fingers gallop like legs*)... and putting little people on her fingers
DL: Ah, I see
N: Or play men ('*Play People*')

Although it is not always easy to interpret the testimony readers provide about their experiences I think it is fairly clear from Nathan's remarks that he has something to contribute to the story which is not present in Burningham's pictures and words. We cannot exactly say that particular mental images of certain play activities were present in Nathan's mind as he read the final pages of the book, but he knows what kinds of things children do when they indulge in imaginative play, and what kinds of props they recruit to their fantasies. In other words he can fill the gaps that Burningham leaves with enough knowledge about the world and its workings for the story to begin to make sense. In addition, he also knows that sometimes it is permissible, even necessary, to allow one thing in a book to stand for another. He already understands that vital piece of book knowledge that lets us see that an imaginary king can produce a real splash – or rather, Shirley's real splash as she plays gets woven into her fantasy about storybook kings and queens and knights.

For a story to exist as an entity generated in reading there must be a successful text-to-reader direction of fit and a successful reader-to-text direction of fit. Only when these two conditions are met does the story fully come into being. As children learn to read, they must not only learn a sight vocabulary and how to segment words into their separate phonemic components, they must also learn how to make use of their knowledge of the world and of the codes and conventions of narrative employed by writers and illustrators and embedded in their texts. In ecological terms, the text – a specific combination of particular words and pictures – can only function, can only 'live' in the supporting context of a reader's engaged and active attention.

How might this analysis of the reading event help us to a better understanding of the picturebook? I think there are at least two related ways in which such a perspective can help. First, if we are prepared to accept that there can be no wholly unmediated access to the meaning of any particular picturebook then we might be less likely to assume that we already know how it works and what it means when we first approach it. We then have a safeguard against the assumption that picturebooks are all pretty much the same. Furthermore, if we are a little more cautious in our approach to them then we might be more willing not only to read them more slowly and attentively, but also to attend to the processes of meaning-making that we undergo during the act of reading. The point here is that we simply do not yet know enough about how people read composite forms of text.

Part of my unease about attempts to categorize picturebooks, especially according to word–picture interaction, arises from my suspicion that adult, expert readers of prose – academics and critics, for example – are not necessarily going to be the best readers of picturebooks. In addition, categories make us feel that we have the matter taped: labels appear to resolve mystery. But in the human sciences, to explain something is not the same as understanding it. A quasi-scientific set of categories can appear to prise open the picturebook for our inspection but it will not necessarily help us to see what is most important about it. In any case, the form is still undergoing change. A number of books published during the early 1970s radically changed the rules and prompted writers and illustrators to address a wider range of topics and themes and to experiment with formal structures. By the end of the twentieth century the picturebook landscape was very different from how it was forty years earlier and doubtless there will be further mutations in the future.

As an alternative to the technology of the matrix and the rule of the category, we might attempt something like a phenomenological approach to understanding the picturebook. This would involve patiently and carefully describing individual examples. In such a reading one would 'bracket off' judgements of quality and preconceptions about what picturebooks are 'really' like, read slowly and reflectively, attending not only to the emergent story, but also to the processes active in the ecological interchange between picture and word, reader and text. With luck, the outcome should be an account of what it is like to read particular books.

The second way in which an ecological view might help is by coercing us into taking seriously the readings that children make. There are good reasons for believing that children read picturebooks in ways that adults do not. Consider the fact that children born into the first years of the twenty-first century are likely to possess a richer and more deft understanding of visual imagery and its modes of deployment than any other generation in the history of humankind. Their world is saturated with images, moving and still, alone and in all manner of hybrid combinations with texts and sounds. This is the world in which they must function. Competence with images is now a prerequisite of competence in life. Increasingly such competence will be part of the context that young children bring to their readings of picturebooks, and however incomplete and partial those readings may be, they frequently differ in interesting ways from those made by parents, teachers, critics and academics. They sometimes see more and they often see differently. If we can find ways of gaining access to their readings we may inform our own attempts to read and understand. If we are to get better at describing picturebooks ourselves, we need to listen to what children have to say.[4]

In Chapters 6 and 8 I look again at the idea of the picturebook reading event and how it might help us understand the picturebook more fully but, for the time being, I want to return to the issue of the picturebook's heterogeneity and flexibility. In Chapter 4, therefore, we return to the question of what happens when pictures and words are placed side by side in the picturebook.

Notes

1 Not only does this sequence of words and images mark a moment of crisis, it is also the reason why the rest of the book can seem so puzzling. Browne refuses to tell us what has happened and simply shows us something happening. As a result we do not know whether the gorilla has come to life (which would mean that the events that follow 'really' occurred) or whether the transformation belongs to some other plane of experience: a dream, perhaps, or a symbol for Hannah's longing. Had Browne told us, in words, what happened, all of the mystery and much of the appeal of the book would be lost. Pictures show and words tell: a crucial distinction which many picturebook makers exploit.

2 Nathan and Jane make an interesting contrast as readers of Burningham. Nathan – the weaker reader in terms of his decoding skills – makes a more sophisticated reading of the text than Jane, who is puzzled throughout by the fact that Shirley's mum does not seem to be able to see that her daughter has slipped down the plughole.

3 The literary critic George Craig has argued that a double withdrawal is necessary when reading imaginative fictions. The reader must withdraw from the world of immediate perceptions and sensations but also from the everyday sense of self. See Craig, G. 'Reading: who is doing what to whom?' (Craig 1976).

4 The justification for pursuing this course is usually considered to be educational. It is true that a better understanding of how children read, and how they learn to read, is a prerequisite to improved approaches to teaching, but here I am arguing that children's readings, when we can access and interpret them, frequently have a backwash effect upon our understanding of how picturebooks work. They enable more sophisticated descriptions.

Chapter 4

The picturebook as process
Making it new

Introduction

If we wish to understand the picturebook we need to begin with individual examples. We need to look as clearly as possible at what picturebook makers do and what they produce and only then ask ourselves how we might set about explaining what we find. I argued in Chapters 2 and 3 against the pigeonholing of picturebooks into categories according to how the words and pictures are related or how they appear to interact. The main reason for rejecting this approach is that it does not seem to do justice to the facts. When I look at picturebooks I find in them the most extraordinary displays of creativity and formal invention. What I do not see are examples of symmetry, deviation or counterpoint. I could if I tried, but I know that in doing so I would be distorting and representing rather poorly, if not misrepresenting, how the books appear to me. Any survey of the picturebooks currently available, such as the one carried out in Chapter 1, will reveal that diversity, flexibility and adaptability are cardinal features of the form.

If you are not convinced by my limited sample, you have only to browse through the children's department of the nearest bookshop to appreciate the extraordinary variety of picturebooks.[1] At times it seems as if anything that can be rendered into two dimensions and/or printed upon, or attached to a page, will sooner or later find its way in between the covers of a picturebook. *The Jolly Postman* merely hints at the range and scope of invention found in novelty and movable books. Likewise *The Man* only gestures towards the uses to which comic and cartoon effects are put. The final years of the last century saw the introduction of the musical chip, the hologram and the flashing light-emitting diode into the picturebook (try finding these late-twentieth century technologies anywhere else in book publishing); graphic novels are further blurring the lines that divide picturebooks from other kinds of text. From the 1970s onwards, the speech and thought bubbles characteristic of the comic strip style disappeared altogether in some books giving rise to the wordless picturebook. In thirty years or so this rather peculiar formal mutation has thrived and propagated itself as illustrators have tested out its possibilities upon an increasingly visually literate population. For example, Istvan Banyai's wordless *Zoom* and *Re-Zoom* in which each successive page turn takes the reader/viewer further away from the image with which the book began is about as far away from the wordless comic strip in both method and intention as it is possible to go.

Much more could be said about the different shapes and forms that the picturebook takes upon itself, but I wish to move the argument on. I would simply suggest, in all seriousness, that the student of children's literature unfamiliar with the modern picturebook take some time to explore what is currently available and to note the exhilarating variety to be met with on the picturebook shelves of the local library or bookshop. All I wish to do here is to establish what I consider to be the most important formal properties of the picturebook and to argue for a view of the picturebook as a perpetually developing form. Barbara Bader considered the possibilities of the picturebook to be, on its own terms, limitless. In the present chapter I try to show how this is quite literally true.

The changing picturebook

The diversity of the picturebook is the outcome of its flexibility. The diversity is easy enough to demonstrate but the flexibility, the mutability, is rather more difficult to get a handle on. We might say that there are so many different kinds of picturebook because the form itself is constantly changing, but why should this be so? Were we to take the broadest view possible we would doubtless find multiple answers to this last question. To begin with, there are the changes brought about through the impact of forces external to the form itself. For example, I have already suggested, in Chapter 2, that the emergence of the picturebook as a distinct form has been very closely connected to developments in printing technology. To get words and pictures together on the same page in a manner that would permit the necessary interanimation has not been easy. As a result, the picturebook has developed in fits and starts, finally bursting into life in the second half of the twentieth century as illustrators and publishers quickly saw the potential of offset photolithography. Most histories of illustration choose the 1960s as the technological watershed, after which the picturebook was never the same again. Some changes, then, are simply due to new technologies making ever more sophisticated effects possible.

Social and cultural changes have had an impact too. Everywhere, texts are now routinely 'pictured'. Across the globe, Western culture has been pictorialized to an astonishing degree and with amazing rapidity. It is not just the high street that is now awash with photographic images, icons and other kinds of visual sign; almost all forms of reading matter from newspapers and magazines to computer screens have undergone the same change. Television channels continue to multiply and to nose their way into our private and domestic space as does the Internet and the CD-ROM. Video games often rely upon their users' ability to deduce rules and conventions, and transfer them from game to game. Advertisements are ever more ironic and oblique, exploiting consumers' increasing visual sophistication, and people now unblushingly use the term 'visual literacy' when a few decades ago the concept, never mind the term, was undreamed of. Such an enormous shift in our ways of understanding the world and ourselves will undoubtedly have had an impact upon a form of text like the picturebook that self-consciously exploits the pictorial as a way of making meaning.

There is, of course, at least one other way that innovation and change come about and that is through the experimentation of ground-breaking practitioners. From the 1960s onwards a number of particularly talented and creative picturebook makers investigated what could be done with words and pictures that could not be done with words alone. If words and pictures are different, what difference does the difference make? For example, the first adult readers of Maurice Sendak's *Where the Wild Things Are* were surprised not only by its apparently dangerous theme, but also by its formal inventiveness – the pictures that change size, page by page, and the boldly wordless rumpus at the heart of the book. That was in 1963 (first British publication, 1967). In 1970 John Burningham's *Mr Gumpy's Outing* showed what could be done by using the gutter down the centre of a page-opening to keep the words and pictures apart. By placing the words and some monochrome sketches on the left-hand side of the page-opening and wordless, full colour portraits of the animals on the other side, he made it immediately obvious that the pictures that appeared on different pages could possess different functions. In fact, you could tell more than one story in the same book by using the gutter as a kind of boundary line between different realms. The two *Shirley* books followed, along with *Where's Julius?* and *John Patrick Norman McHennessy, the Boy Who Was Always Late*. Shirley Hughes exploited the idea in *Alfie Gets in First* where part way through the story the gutter – a physical part of the book – comes to stand for a door and wall separating Alfie from his mum. A more recent development of the same idea is David Macaulay's *Black and White* where each page-opening is divided into four stories that may or may not be connected.

Also in 1970, Eric Carle punched holes in the pages of *The Very Hungry Caterpillar*, trimmed its pages to different sizes and in so doing demonstrated something else that can be done with pictures that cannot be done with written language. The truncated pages and the perforations have a purpose, whereas there would be no point at all in tampering with the material fabric of the page whereon the words are printed. Janet and Allan Ahlberg did much the same with *Peepo*, in 1981, a book where the holes in the pages add to the text rather than subtracting from it. Other picturebook makers have also realized that you can do things with pictures, and therefore with picturebooks, that you cannot do with prose or poetry. In 1992 Colin McNaughton turned *Who's That Banging on the Ceiling?* sideways so that he could take his readers floor by floor up a tower block of flats, and in 1989 Mitsumasa Anno combined, in *Anno's*

Aesop, dual narratives with a completely inverted page to tell his story of a fox who cannot read. All of these writers and illustrators of picturebooks, along with figures such as Raymond Briggs, Shirley Hughes, Philip Dupasquier, Anthony Browne and Quentin Blake have not only produced bodies of work that are visually exciting, and books that are a delight to read, but they have also all been formal innovators. They have changed the language of the picturebook and in so doing have created opportunities for others to make things in new ways.

Technological developments, social and cultural changes, artistic innovations – these all had an impact upon the shape and form of the picturebook in the last few decades of the twentieth century. However, they are all to some extent external to the picturebook itself. Even the innovations of the most talented writers and illustrators must wait upon the emergence, from time to time, of particularly creative individuals. In periods of artistic stagnation, not much will change. I now want to argue that two further factors have a shaping effect upon the picturebook and that these are factors that work from within, so to speak. The first, which I shall discuss at some length in the remainder of this chapter, arises directly out of the composite nature of the picturebook, its status as the child of two quite different parents. The second, which will be examined in the next chapter, concerns the position that the picturebook occupies as a popular kind of text for young children, its siting within the early years of childhood.

Genre incorporation

A little earlier in this chapter I claimed that the picturebook's diversity is easy enough to demonstrate but that the flexibility of the form, its mutability and capacity for change is at first sight less obvious. I could try to demonstrate this flexibility in the same way that I demonstrated diversity, by looking at a sample of books and attempting to identify changes and trace when and how they came about. The problem is that this would take us on an historical expedition for which this book is ill equipped. Diversity can be demonstrated synchronically: you simply look at the range of what is available now; change and development on the other hand can only be perceived diachronically, over time. Besides, an historical account of change is not quite what I am after. I am more concerned to reveal something of what I consider to be the open-endedness of the picturebook, its freedom from the constraints that other forms of literature must work within. To begin, let us return once more to the sample of books with which we began and examine the kinds of words and the kinds of pictures that are combined within their pages.

Those who write picturebooks, whether they are the writers only, or also the illustrators of their own work, draw upon many different kinds of discourse. In the thirteen books I have drawn from the list of Emil prizewinners there are simple narratives, spoken dialogues, non-standard English speech-forms and invented dialects, comic book exclamations and jokes, poetry (both serious and comic), pseudo-nursery rhymes for choral speaking, snippets of factual information, and a selection of different kinds of letter writing. If we were to look further afield we would soon find examples of even more language forms.[2] However, on this evidence alone I think one might reasonably come to the conclusion that, given some ingenuity, there are probably very few forms of discourse that cannot be transformed into picturebook material – always allowing for the constraints placed upon writers and illustrators by considerations of taste and suitability for children.

Much the same case may be made for the visual images that we find in the same small collection of books. Although most illustrators tend to work within a limited range of styles, and although in the present case we are looking only at the work of twelve people, we can nevertheless identify a number of different approaches to the task of illustration. There are those derived in varying degrees from the art of the cartoon and comic book; there are woodcuts; interior and exterior scenes influenced by European surrealism; closely cross-hatched images that look like coloured engravings; sketches in sepia ink; painterly images of family groups; lively line drawings of exuberant children's games; simplified images of living creatures suitable for a child's information book; and representations in water-colour of traditional English landscapes. These, of course, are simply some of the differences in style and subject matter to be found in the sample. We might also identify a wide range of illustrative uses to which these are put. There are single and double page spreads, framed plates that occupy varying amounts of page space, vignettes, icons, panoramas and so on. Once again, I think it is clear that those who provide the pictures in picturebooks have at their disposal a whole range of illustrative styles, manners and modes, many of them deriving from quite ancient traditions, none of which are *a priori* inappropriate or unusable.

We can therefore say that whatever else it is, the picturebook is *not* a genre, despite the fact that it is frequently referred to as such. Rather than confining itself to exploring the byways of any one particular type of text, verbal or pictorial, it *exploits* genres. Nor is the picturebook a format, a template that can be dropped over any suitable material, providing it with new clothes in the form of illustrations. If this were the case then all picturebooks would look more or less the same and behave in more or less the same way. What we find in the picturebook is a form that incorporates, or ingests, genres, forms of language and forms of illustration, then accommodates itself to what it has swallowed, taking on something of the character of the ingested matter, but always inflected through the interanimation of the words and pictures. The immediate result of this ability to ingest and incorporate pre-existent genres is that already existing forms are represented – that is, re-presented – and in the process re-made.

The possibilities of the picturebook are thus limitless, precisely because it makes itself out of the limitless pictorial and verbal resources that surround it.

This fundamental capacity for endless re-invention is the guarantor of the picturebook's inherent flexibility. We cannot know quite what the picturebook will look like in years to come because we do not yet know how speaking, writing and picture-making will metamorphose within the broader culture. What we do know is that resourceful artists and writers will always be ready to appropriate whatever materials are to hand in order to create new texts.

Picturing text

Over and above this basic machinery of genre incorporation there are other processes at work that help to shape the nature of the picturebook. The very presence of pictures appears to loosen generic constraints and open up the text to alternative ways of looking and thinking. Consider, as a particularly clear example, what happens to the traditional tale when it comes into contact with the picturebook. The folk- or fairy-tale is a good example of a relatively time-less genre. Its origins reach back beyond the earliest recorded stories, but during their long journey into the present fairy-tales have changed little and are structurally much the same today as they were when they were first written down. They may be re-told and variations admitted, but the essential features rarely change. Quests, trials, magical helpers, triads of tasks and brothers – these are not to be discarded. Nor are the verbal formulae that help to signify what kind of fictive world the reader is inhabiting. Care is taken to avoid degra-dation of the generic form so, although new tales can be told, they must shape themselves to the generic outlines already laid down by tradition if they are to count as additions to the genre. It is not any old tale that can count as a fairy-tale.

Now look what happens when such stories are absorbed into the picturebook. They can, of course, be simply illustrated with the key events and personages represented in the pictures, although we must remember that this is no simple process of reflection or parallelism: words and pictures are always and everywhere in the picturebook actively at work upon each other. Even the simplest picturebook versions of fairy-tales have an inflection, an accent, an angle that would be missing were the pictures not present. The fact is that once the body of a story is cut into with sequences of pictures, it becomes available for other uses. It can fall prey to the interpretative designs of the illustrator, for example. *Hansel and Gretel* as illustrated by Anthony Browne is not the same tale as an unillustrated version of the same text. Nor is it the same as, say, Val Biro's version, or Joyce Dunbar and Ian Penney's. Browne's illustrations trouble the text and they trouble the reader too. Uncertainties and doubts are introduced and the story is opened up for interpretation. We wonder about the apparent identity of the stepmother and the witch and we are drawn into pondering the significance of the small details in the pictures. Browne's pictured version of *Hansel and Gretel* re-presents the story and in the process makes it anew.

Another re-shaping of the traditional tale takes place in picturebooks. Being a relatively timeless, closed and immutable genre, the fairy-tale attracts subversion, and those most active in undermining it have been the makers of picturebooks.[3] Once again, the introduction of pictures into the telling of the tale has a disturbing effect, but this time the outcome might be the inversion of gender roles, for example, or the parodying of the conventions that govern the form. Robert Munsch tells the tale of *The Paperbag Princess* who outwits the dragon and walks away from the haughty prince while Eugene Trivivas and Helen Oxenbury invert the natural order in *The Three Little Wolves and the Big Bad Pig*. Babette Cole tells of *Princess Smartypants* who lives a rewarding life as a single 'Ms' and John Scieszka and Lane Smith relate what happened to the three little pigs from the wolf's point of view in *The True Story of the Three Little Pigs*. The same team also plays fast and loose with how to tell a tale in *The Stinky Cheese Man and Other Fairly Stupid Tales*. This is a different kind of re-shaping from Anthony Browne's mordant re-visioning of *Hansel and Gretel*, but it is driven by the same motor – the picturing of the tale loosens it and opens it up to new ways of looking.

A slightly different, though related, phenomenon can be found in some of the work of Janet and Allan Ahlberg. Books such as *Each Peach Pear Plum*, *The Jolly Postman*, *The Jolly Christmas Postman* and *The Jolly Pocket Postman* appear to have ingested and digested traditional tales so thoroughly that they have become dispersed through the body of each story leaving, in some cases, the faintest of traces. In *The Jolly Postman* and its sister texts a postmark on an envelope will sometimes be enough to evoke a complete story or rhyme. For example, the envelope containing Baby Bear's birthday card carries the post-mark 'Far Away'. There is an ellipsis here that only those already familiar with the nursery rhyme will be able to cope with. If 'far away' does not conjure up for you the phrase, 'Over the hills …' then you will not be able to identify the rhyme or appreciate the joke. Similarly, the allusion in the title of the post-man's newspaper (*Mirror Mirror*) will be lost on you if you are unfamiliar with the story of Snow White and with the British tabloid newspaper, the *Mirror*. In these books the reader is confronted not with a pictured version of an individual tale, but with a network of visual and verbal allusions and cross-references that draw upon a host of different tales. The sleight of hand that the Ahlbergs perfected was to dissolve the boundaries between individual stories and rhymes and posit a fictive world that was continuous across all stories. There is thus a deliberate manipulation of narrative levels in these books, something that is still only rarely found in prose fictions.

The picturebook is therefore just as much a process as it is a form of text. We might refer to this process as 'picturing', a term I have already used somewhat casually once or twice in the discussion so far. The term is a rather awkward one, but it is useful, not only as a label for the loosening and liberating effect that pictures have upon words, but also to distinguish the processes at work in picturebooks from those in illustrated books. The distinction between these two kinds of text – picturebook and illustrated book – is far from straightforward as it is always in the end impossible to ignore the influence of pictures on words, even when illustrations are few and far between. But there is certainly a difference between the illustration of a pre-existent text, such as *Treasure Island*, say, and the creation of a picturebook where words and images are envisaged as roughly equal textual partners.

Double orientation

One of the reasons why pictorialization – the promiscuous mixing together of words and images – is able to shake loose generic bonds and derail expectations, is that it enables the picturebook to look in two directions at once and sometimes permits picturebook makers to play off one perspective or view against the other. I think that this inherent double orientation is probably what Schwarcz, Golden, Agosto and Nikolajeva and Scott are trying to grapple with when they attempt to distinguish between symmetry, enhancement, counterpoint, deviation, augmentation, contradiction and so on (see Chapter 2). But I believe that they mistakenly identify as characteristic of particular picturebooks something immanent in all picturebooks. They mistake potentiality for a circumscribed actuality. Nodelman gets close to this potentiality when he writes of the words and pictures in picturebooks always bearing an ironical relationship to one another (Nodelman 1988:221). The term 'irony' however, seems to be far too literary and too powerfully suggestive of satire and sarcasm to effectively sum up what happens when words meet pictures on the page.[4]

As examples of double orientation, the ability to look in two directions at once, let us examine some word–image combinations from four books, two from our sample – *Gorilla* and *Drop Dead* – and two from *The Dancing Class* by Helen Oxenbury and *Way Home* by Libby Hathorn and Gregory Rogers. The page layout pattern in *Gorilla* is one that Anthony Browne has used many times. It consists of a page-opening with all the written text on the left-hand side, usually alongside or beneath a small, square framed image, and a large wordless plate on the right-hand side. The smaller pictures in *Gorilla* often depict linking scenes – Hannah, the gorilla or Hannah's father moving from one place to another – and in one scene Hannah and her companion are shown returning home from their night's excursion. The words convey the situation thus: ' "Time for home?" asked the gorilla. Hannah nodded a bit sleepily. They danced on the lawn. Hannah had never been so happy.' The last two sentences are reflected in the large plate to the right, but ' "Time for home?" ' is represented in the smaller picture by an image of Hannah riding on the gorilla's shoulders. Nowhere in the text is there any mention of how Hannah gets home and we only learn of her mode of travel through the picture. There is thus an

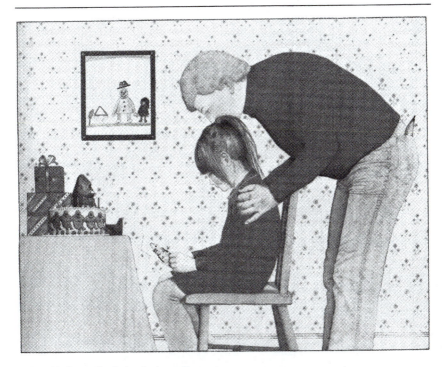

Figure 19 From *Gorilla* by Anthony Browne.

ellipsis in the text which the picture fills. Here the double orientation is simply a sharing out of information between the two modes so that each one says something that the other does not. Nikolajeva and Scott, as well as Golden, would no doubt consider this to be an example of enhancement whereas for Agosto it would be a type of augmentation.

At the very end of *Gorilla*, however, there is a very different kind of double orientation. The last double page spread shows, in the smaller picture, Hannah dashing downstairs and in the larger, Hannah in profile seated on a dining chair in front of a small pile of presents on the table while her father stoops over her from behind with his hands on her shoulders. The words accompanying these images are as follows: 'Hannah rushed downstairs to tell her father what had happened. "Happy birthday, love," he said. "Do you want to go to the zoo?" Hannah looked at him.' The key words here are the last ones, 'Hannah looked at him', for in the picture we can see quite clearly that she is not looking at him at all but down at a picture she is holding of a gorilla, presumably a birthday card. This dissonance between what the words say and what the pictures show might be considered to be insignificant, especially if we have a desire for the story to end in a traditionally happy way, but it becomes important when we realize that a theme running through the images in the book has been that of looking and being looked at: of making, and failing to make, eye

As we grew older we played different games.

At six years old.

At ten years old.

At sixteen years old.

Figure 20 From *Drop Dead* by Babette Cole.

contact. Hannah and her father never manage to look each other in the eye, even at the end of the story, whereas much of the central portion of the book shows Hannah and the gorilla either facing each other or gazing at each other with affection. In the light of this pictorial theme, the lack of congruence between the final words and the final image, casts a slight shadow over the book's ending.[5]

In *Drop Dead*, the mood is altogether lighter. Babette Cole combines her spare text with wilfully playful and silly images and she uses the picturebook's capacity for double orientation to create a number of jokes. For example, when Gran and Grandad reach the pre-teen stage in their life story we are told that they played different games, 'At six years old. At ten years old. At sixteen years old.' The words thus tell us absolutely nothing about the nature of the games, that role having been left for the pictures. What we see are two children bowling along on scooters, then on bicycles and then on motor bikes. So far the

play between the words and pictures is closely akin to the first example from *Gorilla* described above, the pictures filling the gaps left by the words. But there is rather more going on here, for in each little scene we are shown the six-, ten- and sixteen-year-olds being pursued by a lion, first roaring after the children's scooters, then puffing after their bicycles, then smilingly mounted on a motor bike much like the ones the youngsters are riding. This extra twist gives the page something of what might be called the *Rosie's Walk* effect: apparently ignorant participants are pursued by a beast not mentioned in the text.

Helen Oxenbury is keenly observant of the ways in which babies, toddlers and the adults that surround them behave. *So Much* is a good example of her ability to portray families wittily but accurately, and with affection. In *The Dancing Class*, a small, foursquare book for pre-schoolers, she tells the slight, but amusing story of a little girl's disastrous attempts to learn how to dance. The first page-opening shows her flinging herself around the sitting room watched by her mum alongside the words, 'Mum said I should go to dancing classes.' They buy tights – big ones, into which mum says she will soon grow – and ballet shoes, under the watchful eyes of a shop assistant who looks as if she has been on her feet too long, and then it's off to the dancing class. The little girl, looking warily and nervously about, gets changed alongside all the other boys and girls and mum says, ' "We'll just make your hair tidy like the others." ' Over the page we see a troupe of little girls practising at the barre and skipping in a circle around the teacher who looks on appraisingly. ' "Heads up, tummies in, knees straight and point your toes," ' she says.

It is at this point that Oxenbury displays most clearly her ability to exploit the double orientation of the form to send the reader different kinds of messages. The teacher's words simply tell us what the children are asked to do and hint at the kind of voice that such characters habitually use: we can almost sense the tone, brisk and jolly but determined and directive. The pictures, however, show that the newcomer, with her loosely tied shoes and baggy tights, is not yet able to comply. She leaps and skips about throwing her arms out while her companions make rather more dainty and restrained movements. Furthermore, the teacher's appraising look is directed solely at her new pupil. She neither frowns nor smiles but rests her chin on her right hand, the elbow supported by her left, as if she were thinking 'I wonder if we can do anything with this one!'. The effect is finely judged and very droll – at least for the adult reader, the one accompanying the child to whom the book is being read – for it is unlikely that young children would fully understand the dance teacher's expression, gesture and posture, even if they had seen adults behaving in this way, for they are never themselves in such a position. *The Dancing Class* is thus one of many fine picturebooks that possess a dual address, one message being for the child reader and one for the adult who shares the experience. The effect is brought about partly through playing off rather bland words against quite detailed and keenly observed images, but also partly through manipulation of the image itself.

Finally, a more serious and disturbing use of the picturebook's capacity to look in two directions at once can be found in *Way Home*. In this book the pictures aspire to a kind of realism that seems to be derived from film or video (another visual mode that the picturebook will happily draw upon). The images are raw and dark and possess a documentary immediacy. Shane's story, his finding of a kitten and his tortuous journey home through a benighted city, is narrated in a street-wise, jazzy register. Although there are plenty of clues and hints along the way, few first-time readers are prepared for the discovery at the end of the story that Shane is actually homeless and his 'home' is a shack made of rough planks and cardboard hidden away amongst the refuse and garbage of an empty lot. The final image of the book is of the dimly lit interior of Shane's dwelling, and the final words, printed below the picture, are, 'Here we are. We're home!' The dissonance of word and image here rests almost entirely upon our common understanding of the meaning and connotations of

Figure 21 From *Way Home* by Libby Hathorn and Gregory Rogers.

the single word 'home' and what it means to 'go home'. Throughout the book, we see a child on his way home and little do we suspect what the pictures are about to reveal to us.

Of course, there are very many picturebooks that are far less self-conscious about their double orientation. Many books, perhaps most, conform to something like Sendak's narrative illustration – words and pictures apparently welded together in an apparently symmetrical relationship – but in the picturebook there will always be some degree of double accenting. Picturebooks always open at least two windows upon the text so that we might see it in more than one light. As a result, they tend to feel more open and permeable than more determinate forms. You can start by simply looking at the pictures and ignoring the words, or enter the book part way through to enjoy a particularly appealing picture. Best of all, you can take it as a composite whole and appreciate its openness, three-dimensionality and sheer novelty.

Finally, I want to bring the discussion so far up to date. I argued in Chapter 3 that an ecological perspective on picturebooks tells us that the words are never just words, they are always words-as-influenced-by-pictures. Similarly, the pictures are never just pictures, they are pictures-as-influenced-by-words. Thus the words on their own are always partial, incomplete, unfinished, awaiting the flesh of the pictures. Similarly the pictures are perpetually pregnant with potential narrative meaning, indeterminate, unfinished, awaiting the closure provided by the words. But the words and the pictures come from outside the picturebook; there is no picturebook house style or fixed approach, no set of genre conventions, no preferred forms of text. The picturebook is thus emphatically not itself a genre. It is an omnivorous creature, ingesting, absorbing, co-opting pre-existent genres – other ways of speaking, writing, picturing – in order to make its texts, and as these genres change and mutate within society, so does the picturebook. It constantly renews itself by adapting to whatever languages and images are available to it and this gives the form an open-ended quality. We can never be sure exactly what the picturebook will do next as it is forever becoming and never completed. It turns its face to the unfinished future rather than to the preservation of the forms of the past.[6]

But not only does the ingestion of already existing forms confer a high degree of open-endedness and freedom upon the picturebook, it also provides picturebook makers with opportunities to take the separate parts, the pictures and words, off down different paths. There is no rulebook that says you have to try to mirror in the pictures what the words say; besides, this kind of symmetry is always more apparent than real. The potential for what I have called double orientation – the looking in more than one direction at the same time – is always present in picturebooks. It can be suppressed, as it is when words and pictures appear to parallel each other, but close looking reveals more often than not that somewhere in a picturebook, what its maker wants to say can be found somewhere in between what the words tell and the pictures show. In the next chapter I explore what it means for the picturebook that its makers are not only dealing with a form of text that is uniquely flexible and malleable, but are also creating imaginative fictions for an audience for whom the world itself is in a perpetual state of becoming.

Notes

1   See Note 4, Chapter 1, p. 29.

2   For example, the Emil list contains no dialogues with the reader as in *How Do I Put it On?* by Shigeo Watanabe and Yasuo Ohtomo; no lists of labels as in *The Baby's Catalogue* by Janet and Allan Ahlberg; no sports commentary as in *Goal!* by Colin McNaughton; no instructional text as in *How Dogs Really Work* by Alan Snow; no fairy- or folk-tales; no counting rhymes; no nonsense rhymes; no parodies; no alphabet texts; no Bible stories.

3   At first sight this may seem puzzling for there would appear to be nothing inherently subversive about the process of placing pictures alongside stories; but we should first of all appeal to the facts once more and consider the very large number of picturebooks that parody, or otherwise subvert, the fairy-tale genre. We then need to ask why this should be so and, furthermore, why picturebooks in particular should be so active in this process. These questions are taken up in more detail in Chapters 5 and 6.

4   Nodelman completes his chapter on 'The relationships of pictures and words' as follows:

> Because they communicate different kinds of information, and because they work together by limiting each other's meanings, words and pictures necessarily have a combative relationship; their complementarity is a matter of opposites completing each other by virtue of their differences. As a result, the relationships between pictures and texts in picture books tend to be ironic: each speaks about matters on which the other is silent.
>
> (Nodelman 1988:221)

5   For a fuller discussion of this theme, see Chapter 7. This final scene is, in fact, even more complex in structure than I have indicated here, for Browne employs colour to bring father and daughter together at the same time as retaining the distance between them by refusing them the intimacy of eye contact. There is indeed a resolution here, but it is not a straightforward one.

6   I have borrowed here from the Russian critic and theorist Mikhail Bakhtin a claim that he makes for the novel. The writings of Bakhtin and his circle – in particular, *The Dialogic Imagination, Problems of Dostoevsky's Poetics, Speech Genres and other Late Essays* and Volosinov's 'Discourse in life and discourse in art' – have influenced much of the present chapter along with parts of Chapters 3 and 5 (Bakhtin 1981; Bakhtin 1984; Bakhtin 1986; Volosinov 1976).

Chapter 5

Picturebooks at play

These are my shoes. Do I put them on like this?
(From *How Do I Put it On?* by Shigeo Watanabe and Yasuo Ohtomo)

Introduction

In the last chapter I argued that the composite nature of the picturebook predisposes it towards openness and flexibility. Unlike the relatively fixed and stable genres of fiction, it constantly evolves through its assimilation of the images, discourses and text types generated outside it. However, the existence of a predisposition towards freedom does not necessarily mean that in each and every case that freedom must be exercised. Picturebook makers could, if they wished, choose to mirror as closely as possible those genres and text types that have proved to be durable and popular, suppressing the form's potential for double orientation. Some writers and illustrators of picturebooks follow precisely this route, but the fact that many others do not, that the garden of the picturebook is a riot of strange hybrids and glorious mutations, still requires some explanation. A formal account of the picturebook is not enough and we must do more by way of exploring the cultural context within which the picturebook flourishes in order to arrive at a fuller understanding of its nature.

In the next two chapters, therefore, I approach the subject of the picturebook's freedom and flexibility from an entirely different direction. In this chapter I consider the special relationship that exists between picturebooks, the child reader and the concept of play. The implied reader of many picturebooks is one for whom reading and the world of fiction are only gradually taking shape, and this open-endedness in the learner, this state of perpetual becoming, is matched by an open-endedness and freedom from constraint in the picturebook. Picturebook makers respond to the child's need for play with playfulness in word and image. In the latter part of the chapter I go on to identify a number of picturebooks that exhibit playfulness and freedom from constraint in a particularly bold and striking way. Then, in Chapter 6, I consider the picturebook's predilection for play under a different description and discuss in detail the way in which the most playful books have been characterized in recent years.

Children, learning and play

I make the assumption throughout this chapter that a special relationship exists between picturebooks and young, emergent readers. In doing so I am aware that I will be making some readers uneasy. Writers of children's books often deny that they write for a specific audience or a particular age range and there is an understandable reluctance on the part of many readers – teachers, critics, scholars – to view picturebooks as being the province of the youngest children only. There are good reasons for such doubts. Many picturebooks seem to be just as keen to appeal to adults as to children. We need look no further than *The Jolly Postman* for an example of a picturebook that addresses readers possessed of different levels of competence and maturity. Some picturebooks are designed to appeal primarily to older children and adolescents rather than the youngest readers and there are some now in print that do not seem to be addressed to young people at all. Raymond Briggs, for example, is particularly skilful at turning his adaptations of comic strip art to ends other than telling stories to children. *When the Wind Blows*, *The Tin-Pot Foreign General and the Old Iron Woman*, and *Ethel & Ernest* are fine picturebooks but they are not for the youngest. Despite these reservations I think there is ample reason for believing that the vast majority of picturebooks are produced with a young and inexperienced readership in mind.

If this is the case then we might posit an interesting, and perhaps unusual, relationship between writer/illustrator and reader. Unlike writers for more mature and accomplished readers, writers and illustrators of picturebooks address an audience for whom what counts as reading and what can legitimately go into a book are concepts that are still being learned. For young children, books are, as we shall see, highly unusual objects. We are not born knowing what to do with them, and studies of parents and pre-school children sharing picturebooks reveal very clearly that children learn what books are for and what reading is as they gradually get used to handling and talking about them with their parents and care-givers.

Catherine Snow and Anat Ninio in a chapter from Teale and Sulzby (1986) entitled 'The contracts of literacy: what children learn from learning to read books' summarize much of the most interesting work that has been done in this field. Based upon numerous observational studies of pre-school children and adults interacting with picturebooks, the writers identify seven inter-related contracts, or negotiated understandings, about how to deal with, talk about and make sense of books. These are as follows.

(i) Books are for reading, not for manipulating. Self-evident though this is for practised readers, it is far from obvious for beginners for whom things in the world are for chewing, throwing and banging on the floor. Children must learn that books belong to the category, 'objects of contemplation' and not 'things of action' (Werner and Kaplan, cited by Snow and Ninio 1986).

(ii) In book reading, the book is in control, the reader is led. When reading, readers must submit to the agenda set by the book. In early picturebook sharing sessions, joint attention must be established so that parent and child are looking at the same picture, and it is the picture that must become the focus of interaction and discussion. 'The picture is the topic' as Snow and Ninio put it (Snow and Ninio 1986:124).

(iii) Pictures are not things, but representatives of things. Much puzzled scratching of pages and grasping at images goes on in the earliest book interactions as children sort out the difference between objects and illustrations of objects.

(iv) Pictures are for naming. In other words, the proper response when seeing a picture in a book is to say something appropriate to it. Later, this behaviour will be necessary in the presence of the printed word if children are to continue their lessons in reading. Just as artists can draw toy cars, writers can 'draw speech', and you need to be able to say what it is they have drawn (a word) when you look at it.

(v) Pictures, though static, can represent events. Pictured objects are named, but pictured events elicit accounts of 'what happened'. Thus actions (e.g. digging, climbing, running) and happenings (e.g. falls, collisions) sow the seeds of narrative. With the support of an adult they also help children come to 'see the point'. Children do not automatically understand why pictures are sequenced in the way that they are. As we saw in Chapter 2, picture sequences do not of themselves suggest particular narratives and the ability to invest represented objects and events with narrative meaning must be learned.

(vi) Book events occur outside real time. You can stop reading (or looking at the pictures) then return later and take up from where you left off: the characters and events remain unchanged (see vii).

(vii) Books constitute an autonomous fictional world. Book events, book characters and book time are all separate from real events, real characters and real time. They stay still while you contemplate them. Children often make life-to-text and text-to-life remarks such as 'I've got one of those' when listening to stories and looking at pictures in picturebooks to establish connections between the book world and the real world, but nonetheless the two realms must come to be seen as distinct.

Snow and Ninio's article makes fascinating reading but it makes the acquisition of the contracts (or rules of book-behaviour, if you prefer) sound a terribly serious affair. What is missing is any recognition of the role of play in acquiring and securing these understandings. Learning to read and learning to find your way around books is not just a matter of learning the rules. Young children, either with or without adults present, almost always play with what they are learning. In the case of language they make up jokes and silly rhymes and invert the rules that they have most recently acquired in topsy-turvy fashion.[2] All of these play activities have them roaring with laughter for in discovering the proper relation between a label and the thing to which it applies you have also learned what is improper, and the improper is almost always funny. Mikhail Bakhtin, whose work on language and the novel I have relied upon a great deal in this book, writes that laughter destroys what he calls 'Epic distance', the aloof, untouchable objectivity of certain kinds of language and text.

> As it draws an object to itself and makes it familiar, laughter delivers the object into the fearless hands of investigative experiment – both scientific and artistic – and into the hands of free experimental fantasy. Familiarization of the world through laughter … is an extremely important and indispensable step in making possible free, scientifically knowable and artistically realistic creativity …
> (Bakhtin 1981:23)[3]

When children are able to play with language and with text we can be sure that they are in no danger of mistaking nonsense for sense, have understood the rules and are in possession of a competence that they can apply creatively in their own use of language.

Young children are permanently on the borderline between ignorance and understanding and this very inexperience appears to liberate picturebook makers from pre-existent notions of what a book should look like and what it should contain, and offers them the freedom to create new kinds of text. This, then, is one way in which we might draw together the picturebook, reading and the concept of play. If the form within which you are working is particularly flexible and adaptable, and if your primary audience does not have too many preconceptions as to what might be found in a book – excepting only that it should offer the possibility of meaning and delight – then all manner of things become possible. Such a claim might seem to fly in the face of the view that texts must conform to genre conventions of some kind if they are to possess any kind of meaning at all, but we should remember that, as I argued in the last chapter, picturebooks shape themselves to the genres and images out of which they are constructed. The picturebook is therefore not wholly free to make itself up from scratch. It must use whatever building blocks are already available but, for the reasons given above, it is able to use them in free and innovative ways. On the other hand, we should not assume that the only genres and text types available to the picturebook maker are those most readily recognizable from prose fiction. Any form of language, spoken or written, is capable of being appropriated and put to use. In order to be meaningful, picturebooks – however unconventional – must simply be linked to discourses and text types that offer access to comprehensible forms of life.

For example, consider how picturebooks often draw upon and are structured around children's games. In books like *Peepo* by Janet and Allan Ahlberg, *Would You Rather ...* by John Burningham, *Mrs Armitage on Wheels* by Quentin Blake and *How Do I Put it On?* by Shigeo Watanabe and Yasuo Ohtomo, forms of life – that is, modes of action and ways of being – that are entirely familiar to children (though often long forgotten by adults) are mimicked by the text structures. In *Peepo*, the game of covering one's eyes and then peeping out is mapped onto a text that both literally and metaphorically offers glimpses into the life of a young family. *Would You Rather ...* reflects the daring games with which children tease each other, addressing the reader directly with questions and challenges such as, 'Would you rather ... jump in the nettles for £5/swallow a dead frog for £20/or stay all night in a creepy house for £50'. *Mrs Armitage on Wheels* works somewhat like *Mr Gumpy's Outing* in that a gradual accumulation of detail eventually leads to catastrophe. Just as children build towers out of dominoes and wooden blocks, piling them ever higher until they collapse, the eccentric Mrs Armitage keeps adding 'improvements' to her bicycle until it too, being top heavy and unwieldy, also collapses. The little bear in *How Do I Put it On?* plays at putting his clothes on wrongly, asking the reader 'Do I put [my shoes] on like this?' as he hangs them on his ears. The book thus transposes into textual form an example of the kind of silly nonsense game common in many families. In all four of these children's books, as in many more, children's predisposition towards play meets head on the picturebook maker's freedom to play.

How Do I Put it On? is a good example of how sensitive picturebook artists can appeal to the child's love of topsy-turvy rule-breaking. At first sight it does not appear to be a particularly radical kind of text and it would certainly not tax the comprehension of the youngest pre-schooler familiar with the difficulties of dressing oneself. It presents, on the left-hand side of alternate page-openings, an item of clothing accompanied by the words, 'This is my shirt [cap, shoes, etc.]' To the right is the bear with the item used incorrectly ('Do I put it on like this?') Over the page, the left-hand side is simply printed with the word, 'No!' (this is the point where even the youngest emergent reader can anticipate what is coming and join in) while the right-hand side depicts the bear wearing the item of clothing correctly above a sentence following the pattern, 'I put my shirt [cap] over [on] my head'. The reason that this is comprehensible to young children is that it transposes an activity with which they are very familiar into a text for contemplation. Nevertheless, it is clearly a text that involves the breaking of a number of rules. If we take as something like a story-telling norm the tale told in the third person past tense which gradually unfolds a sequence of events involving a number of characters, then *How Do I Put it On?* appears to be highly unconventional: a character in the world represented on the page addresses the reader directly and the sequence of events that follows does not go anywhere in terms of plot. Furthermore, as a substitute for narration, forms of language familiar from speech are used that treat the pictures as if they were the context of a conversational exchange ('*These* are my shoes ... Do I put them on like *this?*'). The behaviour depicted in the book is itself a rule-breaking form of activity. To judge from the changing expressions on his face the bear knows perfectly well that what he is doing is incorrect and is well aware of the proper way to get dressed. The whole book is a joke that the young reader is invited to share, but it is likely to appear funniest to the child who has just mastered the difficult art of dressing.

The breaking of rules and the flouting of conventions do not necessarily imply obscurity or complexity, but they do suggest a strong connection with forms of play. So far I have claimed that writers and illustrators feel licensed to play with the form of the picturebook by the very inexperience of their readers. In addition, I have suggested that picturebook makers recognize this need for play in children and frequently respond with forms of text that are game-like and playful. Play is what children do, not because they are in a state of innocence, but because they are perpetually learning, perpetually becoming, and the best picturebook makers are their allies in this.

The playful picturebook

In this second part of the chapter I offer a more detailed account of some picturebooks that I consider to be particularly playful and discuss the different ways in which they adopt game-like disguises, break rules and subvert conventions. Two or three of the titles from the original sample display at least some of the characteristics that I am interested in – let us say, *Gorilla*, *Granpa*, *Have You Seen Who's Just Moved in Next Door to Us?* and *The Jolly Postman*. All four of these books bend, stretch or break the rules and conventions of storytelling. *Gorilla* leaves us wondering whether the toy really did come to life; *Granpa* does not even bother to tell a story but offers readers a sequence of fragments to piece together as best they can; *Have You Seen Who's Just Moved in Next Door to Us?* replaces narrative movement with a collage of cartoon imagery, puns and jokes and *The Jolly Postman* invites us to enact in play the opening and reading of letters. Browne, Burningham, the Ahlbergs and McNaughton seem to be able to do things with books composed of pictures and words that would be very unusual if attempted in prose alone. They seem willing, even keen, to play around with the possibilities of the form, exploring just what effects are possible when pictures are made to rub up against groups of words. Such books are thus playful, not in the sense that they are necessarily fun or funny – although of course they often are – but in the sense that they do not take settled forms of proceeding, such as genre conventions and the usual strategies for structuring narrative, as wholly binding. Let us now look at some of the ways in which the impulse to play has spread throughout the whole of the picturebook form.

The Jolly Postman or Other People's Letters is an excellent place to begin for it seems to exhibit playfulness in a number of different ways. To begin with it possesses that game-like quality that I identified in books such as *How Do I Put it On?* and *Peepo.* Lying behind the text of *The Jolly Postman* is a common or garden 'let's pretend' activity. The Ahlbergs themselves have explained that the origins of the book lie in their own daughter's wanting to have letters of her own to open and read, and the brilliance of the invention lies in having such an activity embedded within a book. A young child can thus listen to, look at and enjoy the story of the postman's meanderings and also play at opening and receiving (other people's) mail. It might be objected that the contents of many of the envelopes are beyond the understanding of young children – the advertising flyer from Hobgoblin Supplies Ltd, for example, or the solicitor's letter to B. B. Wolf Esq. c/o Grandma's Cottage – but this would be to miss the point. On their own, away from the guidance of an adult, children can use *The Jolly Postman* to play at reading as they usually do when given the opportunity. They enact as much of the process as they have seen and can manage, learning the rules of reading through taking them to be the rules of a game.

In order to make this desire for play realizable, the Ahlbergs have had to take some liberties with the fabric of the book. They have incorporated a little paper engineering into it by making some of the pages double up as envelopes, and in so doing they have placed their work within a tradition that goes back to the beginning of the nineteenth century. Books which are as much games and toys as they are texts to read were as popular in the 1800s as they are today. Movables of all shapes and sizes – dissolving pictures, panoramas, pop-ups, flap and slot books – were first devised around two hundred years ago and have never completely gone out of fashion. They are particularly interesting as they demonstrate clearly the way in which the inclusion of pictures – picturing – always seems to make text more malleable and prone to hybridization and mutation. Amongst other things, pictures can be made to fold and bend, to stand up and simulate a world of three dimensions, to be shaped and truncated in various ways: all things that it would be pointless doing to pages printed with words. The end result of such fabrication is a group of picturebooks that blur the dividing line between games and toys on the one hand and 'proper' books on the other. *The Jolly Postman* just about qualifies as such a book-toy although the brilliantly inventive combinations of words and pictures make it clear that this is far more a text to be read and enjoyed rather than a toy to be manipulated, as is the case with some of the more elaborate movables.

There is one more way in which we might claim a playful nature for *The Jolly Postman* and that is at the level of story. As I observed in the last chapter, a good deal of the Ahlbergs' work seems to be set in a storyland where characters from disparate tales meet and interact, precipitating the events that make up the newly created narrative. Thus although Cinderella will go on forever suffering the slights and indignities visited upon her by her sisters every time the story is made anew by a listening or reading child, in *The Jolly Postman* we can peep behind the scenes and see just a little of what happens in the 'happy

So Cinders read her little book,
The Postman drank champagne
Then wobbled off
    On his round again
            (and again and again – Oops!)

Figure 22 From *The Jolly Postman* by Janet and Allan Ahlberg.

ever after'. We discover that the prince has a liking for Hawaiian shirts and champagne and that Cinders does not seem to be able to relinquish her apron, symbol of the domestic servitude she has recently left behind, despite her elevation. The letter she reads comes from Peter Piper of the Peter Piper Press and accompanies a 'newly published', illustrated version of her own dramatic tale. By playing with the otherwise fixed and immutable shapes of stories such as Cinderella, the Ahlbergs create fictive space where new stories can come into being.

A different kind of playing with stories can be found in *On the Way Home* by Jill Murphy. This tells the story of Claire who, having fallen from a swing in a playground and grazed her knee, makes her slow way home telling fabulous, tall tales to her friends about how the accident occurred. The cause of Claire's injury is withheld from the reader at the outset – all we know is that she has hurt herself – so that we only discover the real reason for her injury at the very end of the book when she dissolves in tears on her doorstep in front of her mother. All we know about Claire at the beginning is that she has a hurt knee and is making her narratively devious way home. In this respect the story pivots around the establishment of an enigma and the delaying of its resolution.

As the pages are turned the reader is allowed to eavesdrop on one prepos-terous tale after another. Abigail is told how the bad knee was caused when Claire struggled to escape the clutches of a big bad wolf; Paul hears of the flying saucer that picked Claire up and then dropped her; Amarjit is told that it was a fight with a crocodile that caused the damage. Later in the book other friends hear of witches, giants, ghosts, gorillas and so on – in fact, all of the stock char-acters and figures from children's tales. Claire's stories are, from the beginning, clearly incompatible and thus, as with other cumulative tales, lead absolutely nowhere. They do not advance an overall plot, do not thicken or enrich an overall story, do not even advance our understanding of Claire as a character for we know what she is like after two or three pages. Rather in the manner of *Tristram Shandy*, they actively inhibit rather than promote development.

Claire is an untrustworthy narrator and the differing accounts of her acci-dent clearly belong to the tall-tale tradition, what Susan Stewart in her book *On Longing* refers to as the 'festive display of accumulation over balance' (Stewart 1984). However, although Claire's tales can clearly be seen as fabulations, she is not a particularly fabulous narrator. She may possess Scheherazade's ability to keep them coming but she herself is portrayed as a perfectly ordinary, suburban schoolgirl. Thus for many readers her tales are not so much fabulations as fabrications – that is, untruths or lies and therefore monstrous not just in a narrative sense but in an ethical sense too. When Nathan read *On the Way Home* he was fascinated by Claire's stories, whereas Jane was concerned about her lies.

In order to produce these effects Jill Murphy plays around with a number of narrative devices such as the embedding of minor stories within the major story and the withholding of important information from the reader, and in so doing plays with the reader's expectations. We don't expect stories to follow this strangely repetitive pattern and are surprised and delighted and/or horri-fied at Claire's bare-faced cheek. Another book that leads the reader on into unexpected territory is Chris Van Allsburg's *The Mysteries of Harris Burdick*. Once again the question of whether what we read is fact or fiction is central, but this time it is the readers of the book rather than the book's characters who might have reason to doubt what they are told. There is an introduction, written by Van Allsburg himself, wherein it is explained that the pictures we are about to see were intended to illustrate a number of different stories. They were left behind at the offices of a children's book publisher along with a few fragments of text – a title and a caption for each illustration – by a mysterious figure named Harris Burdick. Burdick had promised to come back the next day with the stories to which the pictures were an accompaniment, but he never returned. According to the introduction, these pictures, along with their titles and captions were now being published in book form for the first time.

On the pages that follow, large, monochrome drawings are placed to the right of each double page spread over against the titles and captions on the left. Opposite a picture of a darkened bedroom where tiny globes of light are drifting in through the open window to hover over a sleeping boy is the title, 'Archie Smith, Boy Wonder', and the caption, 'A tiny voice asked, "Is he the one?" ' Later in the book another picture shows a harp sitting in the foreground on a rock beside a stream. In the background, back-lit against a clump of bushes, a boy and his dog peer at the instrument through the branches of the overhanging trees. Here the title is, 'The Harp'; the caption, 'So it's true he thought, it's really true.' Several pages further on a nun, watched by two impassive male clerics, sits on a plain hard-backed chair hovering in the air twenty feet above the floor in the nave of an otherwise empty cathedral. The title: 'The Seven Chairs'; the caption, 'The fifth one ended up in France'. As with *On the Way Home*, there is no sense in the book of a developing narrative, each page-opening being complete unto itself, but unlike Jill Murphy who piles on the detail so that by the end of the book we are glutted with stories, Van Allsburg teases us with their absence. The invitation in the book – not exactly explicit, but hardly implicit either – is for readers to create their own. In this extraordinary book we are presented with an elaborate fiction as if it were fact and then left to do our own storying on the basis of the fragments that Van Allsburg has created for us. All stories leave gaps for readers to fill but Van Allsburg seems to have asked himself whether he could create a picturebook where almost all the responsibility for the generation of the narrative rests with the reader.

Finally, let us look at one of Anthony Browne's early works, *Bear Hunt*. In this book Browne equips his hero, a small, white bear, with a magic pencil which enables him to draw his way out of a series of traps created by a pair of hunters who are trying to catch him. He strolls, rather insouciantly, along a path through the jungle as one of the hunters approaches with a net, but before the net can fall, the bear draws a rope stretched between two pegs in the ground and trips the figure up. Later he is about to be lassoed so he starts to draw a curved horn. The hunter then finds himself attached by his rope to a rhinoceros. Later still, the bear is caught in a bamboo cage. He draws himself a saw and cuts his way out. At every moment of crisis he appears to be able to slip out of the fictional world that Browne has created for him and into the realm more properly occupied by his author/illustrator, for it is the latter who actually creates the images that embody the fiction. We do not normally expect characters in stories to tamper with their surroundings in this way, or otherwise to alter the fiction of which they are a part. To emphasize this slippage between realms, whenever his bear is in the act of drawing, Browne strips away the colourful, surreal jungle that acts as backdrop to most of the scenes and places the character against a blank, white surface. He thus appears to float in the ether, somewhere alongside his own creator.

I began this chapter with the claim that the makers of picturebooks enjoy a very special and rather peculiar relationship with their primary audience of young readers. With each new book they create they are making afresh the experience of reading for a generation of readers who do not yet know what reading is nor what books are and can do. This is one of the reasons why the picturebook is so flexible and so diverse in form. However, a number of the books described above, and in particular, *The Mysteries of Harris Burdick*, are clearly not intended for the youngest, least experienced readers. They break rules and undermine expectations but it can hardly be said that they do it in the spirit of the playful pre-school child. If they are playful texts, then it is a playfulness that needs rather more explanation than I have been able to provide here. There is the playfulness that seems simply a delight in the picturebook's possibilities, its capacity for endless variation, and there is the playfulness that smacks of a conspiracy between the picturebook maker and the child, but there are other explanations on offer too. In the next chapter I take a close look at an approach to rule-breaking and subversion in the picturebook which sets the form within the context of the wider contemporary culture.

Notes

1   The idea of writing being 'drawn speech' comes from Vygotsky, L. 'The pre-history of written language' in Vygotsky (1978).

2   Kornei Chukovsky discusses children's need for topsy-turvy nonsense in *From Two to Five*. Deprived of nonsense written and published for them, as children were during Stalin's rule in Russia, they will simply make up their own. (Chukovsky 1963.)

3   Bakhtin is writing about the effects of comedy and laughter in certain kinds of novelistic writing but the point seems equally applicable to children and their texts.

Chapter 6

Postmodernism and the picturebook

WARNING: This book appears to contain a number of stories that do not necessarily occur at the same time. Then again, it may contain only one story. In any event, careful inspection of both words and pictures is recommended.

(From *Black and White* by David Macaulay)

Introduction

Although young readers of picturebooks might be said to be relatively unsophisticated and unworldly, the same could hardly be said of their writers and illustrators. Those who write, illustrate, design and publish picturebooks live and have their being in the complex contemporary world that we all share; it has been suggested that the makers of picturebooks like *The Jolly Postman, On the Way Home, The Mysteries of Harris Burdick* and *Bear Hunt* are doing no more than responding to the tenor of the times and either consciously or unconsciously importing the approaches, techniques and sensibilities of postmodernism into their work.[1] This shift from playfulness to postmodernism is important for a number of reasons. It not only introduces a technical vocabulary into the discussion but explicitly connects picturebooks with larger social and cultural developments. However, despite the fact that the influence of postmodernism on the picturebook is a phenomenon that has been observed and commented upon a number of times in recent years, I believe it remains poorly understood. The terms postmodern and postmodernism have been appearing with some frequency in academic works devoted to children's books but such works rarely offer much by way of illumination for the reader unfamiliar with the relevant literature. In what follows, therefore, I describe some of postmodernity's defining features and provide some examples of how these features have influenced writing for adults before returning us to the children's picturebook with an account of the ways in which some picturebooks might be considered to qualify as postmodern.

Postmodernity and postmodernism

David Lyon, in his book *Postmodernity*, makes a most helpful, and relatively straightforward, distinction between postmodernity on the one hand and postmodernism and the postmodernist artefact on the other. 'As a rough analytic device,' he writes, 'it is worth distinguishing between postmoder*nism*, when the accent is on the cultural, and postmoder*nity*, when the emphasis is on the social' (Lyon 1994:6). Thus, postmodernity refers to the condition that Western society finds itself in subsequent to the undermining of many of the ideals of the Enlightenment – in particular, the eighteenth-century belief in progress and reason that suffered such damaging shocks in the twentieth century. Postmodernity is thus the outcome of 'the exhaustion of modernity' (Lyon 1994:6), that is, the epoch ushered in by the eighteenth century and the Enlightenment. Postmodernism, on the other hand, refers to the cultural and intellectual phenomena that have grown out of the rubble and that have blossomed since the 1960s in the form of buildings, paintings, works of literature and other cultural forms and artefacts. Postmodernism (or post-modernism), particularly for artists and cultural critics, is thus a reaction to or transcendence of modernism in the arts, or both.

Despite the fact that the terms postmodern, postmodernism and postmodernity are freely used in a bewildering range of contexts, most writers on the subject tend to agree that there are a small number of core features that characterize both the works of postmodernism – the books, the architecture, the theories – and the experience of living in a postmodern world (that is, postmodernity). Before turning to look at how postmodernity has influenced the world of literature we need briefly to consider these key features.[2]

The key features of postmodernity

Indeterminacy

In the postmodern world we are a lot less sure about the nature of objective reality, our own selves and the products of our hands and minds than they used to be. The more we know about the world the less stable and certain it seems. Instead of our knowledge and understanding growing steadily in a cumulative way, science and philosophy, along with many other disciplines, seem to be telling us that we will never be able to be sure of anything, once and for all, ever again. Early in the century Werner Heisenberg's uncertainty principle articulated the dilemma most elegantly for science, and in recent years astrophysicists and cosmologists have come to see the universe as a deeply unsettling place. The philosophy of science turned its back on Enlightenment views of progress and reason with Kuhn's formulation of the *paradigm shift*, the idea that scientific explanations only work within an accepted framework of concepts and understandings and that the frameworks themselves – the paradigms – are subject to periodic upheavals and revisions (Kuhn 1996). The human universe too has become a far less stable place. The more we know about other societies and cultures, the more we become attuned to difference and the less confident we become in our judgements of what constitutes normal human behaviour. Literature has responded to such developments by placing an increased emphasis upon undecideable outcomes and irresolvable dilemmas. In place of the obscurities of the modernist text – the difficulties of Joyce, Eliot and Pound – we now have the indeterminacies of the postmodern text. As we shall see, it is not uncommon for readers of the postmodern to be left not knowing which way to turn.

Fragmentation

Postmodernism suspects totalization, attempts to unify and synthesize being considered the imposition of an ideological, and thus spurious, order. According to Ihab Hassan, postmoderns prefer the 'openness of brokenness, unjustified margins' (Hassan 1986, 505) to the tendentious unity brought about by the various forms of artistic closure. The metaphor of 'unjustified margins' is a useful one for it suggests graphically the refusal to tidy up loose ends. Rather than attempt to pull everything into shape at the last minute, and thus create an illusion of order where none in fact exists, the postmodern artist or writer is likely to let the ends remain loose and visible: indeed they may well be moved to the foreground to emphasize the fact that wholeness and completeness are not honestly achievable. Collage, with its juxtaposition of disparate elements, is thus a favourite postmodern method.

Decanonization

Perhaps the most widely disseminated tenet of postmodernism is that the governing narratives of our culture – *les grands recits* – have broken down (Lyotard 1984). We are less likely now to trust blindly in authority than were the citizens of previous ages. Fewer and fewer people believe wholeheartedly the overarching stories we tell ourselves about ultimate values, truth, progress and reason because the authorities that underwrote such stories – the church, rationality, science – are no longer viable. Jean-Francois Lyotard, in his seminal work *The Postmodern Condition*, defined postmodernism, loosely, as, ' … incredulity towards metanarratives'. The very fact that it is possible to speak of the most fundamental beliefs as 'stories' suggests the extent to which the unquestioning acceptance of them as revealed truths has atrophied. Moreover, there is no court of higher appeal to which we can turn to help us choose between one story and another. For example, religion still survives in the West as a real presence in the lives of some people but for increasing numbers, it has become simply one of the many ways we have gone about explaining our existence to ourselves. With the grand narratives in ruins at our feet all we have left are *les petits recits*, stories that do not aspire to global significance, but operate at the level of discrete language games. Such stories work insofar as we can invest in them and turn them to our ends but there is little left now in which the postmodernist can put absolute trust.

A further effect of decanonization is the ironing out of differences in value between cultural artefacts and images. The more our lives are invaded by relativism, the harder it becomes to feel confident about absolute standards in art and life and the boundaries separating pop- and high culture become blurred. Our television screens convey into our homes live performances of, for example, Mozart's *Don Giovanni*, but during the intermission we can catch up on the latest episode of another kind of opera at the push of a remote-control button. Similarly, modern printing technologies can place high-culture images such as the *Mona Lisa* on the same plane as portraits of film stars.

Irony

Indeterminacy, fragmentation and decanonization inevitably lead to irony. Whether we like it or not, modern life and culture is massively 'double-coded', images and ideas coming to us ready equipped with an ironic spin that tells us not only what we are looking at but also how to look at it. High Street and television advertisements are today so much more 'knowing' than they were and the consumer at whom they are aimed is expected to understand the allusions and get the jokes in the act of reading the text. Again, the more that relativism invades our lives the harder it becomes not to speak and think in quotation marks, and the more we become aware of ourselves saying what we say and doing what we do. Thus in the postmodern world it is almost impossible to act, to create, to think unselfconsciously in the expectation that others will automatically understand us.

Hybridization

The dissolving of boundaries, the fragmentation of wholes, the flattening out of differences between high and low are all held to be characteristic of our postmodern condition, and they have all contributed to the rise of bizarre hybrid genres and artefacts. Skyscrapers capped with motifs borrowed from Chippendale furniture are now possible, the non-fiction novel emerges from the blending of journalism and imaginative literature and on television docu-soaps import the conventions and expectations of cheap, serial melodrama into the real lives of hospital or airport staff. Nothing is sacred any more for the canons have faded that told us of the great and the good and that kept high culture and low in separate compartments. The boundaries have dissolved, inviting a promiscuous mixing of forms. In such a climate parody and pastiche flourish too as the cultural forms of the past become accessible and available to all.

Performance and participation

The more that authorities dissolve and the more authors and artists abrogate responsibility for leading readers and viewers towards sense and meaning, then the more readers have to write the text they read. Much art is now conceived in terms of performance and participation, the role of the onlooker or participant in the process being deemed as important as any product. In such a climate the craft element in art, the idea that the artist possesses superior manipulative and creative abilities, has withered away and much art in recent years has taken the shape of installations, ready-mades and immaterial concepts.

Postmodernism in literature

How, then, have these trends within the larger culture affected the writing of fiction? The main influence has been upon the structures and conventions that have traditionally been shared between writer and reader. We expect a well-constructed, well-told story to have – to put it crudely – a beginning, a middle and an end. We expect to find more or less convincing characters interacting in an imaginary world according to the dictates of a plot which the author usually takes the trouble to resolve in some more or less satisfying way. Stories seem to follow rules and although the rules might differ for different kinds of stories – fairy-tales, school stories, thrillers, romances, etc. – we do not usually expect the rules to be broken or abandoned. We expect something like a decorum, a sense of fittingness, to prevail within the fictions that we read and we very soon notice when incongruities intrude.

For example, we would not normally expect an author to step out onto the stage of his on-going fiction to inform the reader about exactly what it is he is up to, but such interruptions are commonplace in postmodern writing. Take for example the following passage from the novel *How Far Can You Go?* by David Lodge (Lodge 1980). Lodge would not consider himself to be a postmodern writer, but his academic interest in the subject has prompted him time and again to employ postmodern devices within his otherwise realistic novels. Here, a group of old friends who have not met for some time raise the subject of the accidental death of the daughter of some other, absent friends.

> "Yes," said Edward, shaking his head, and looking at his toecaps, "that was too bad."
>   Adrian and Dorothy had not followed this and had to have it explained to them, as you will, gentle reader. Two years after Nicole was born, Dennis and Angela's next youngest child, Anne, was knocked down by a van outside their house and died in hospital a few hours later. I have avoided a direct presentation of this incident because frankly I find it too painful to contemplate. Of course, Dennis and Angela and Anne are fictional

characters, they cannot bleed or weep, but they stand here for all the real people to whom such disasters happen with no apparent reason or justice. One does not kill off characters lightly, I assure you, even ones like Anne, evoked solely for that purpose.

"Of course, they blame themselves for the accident, one always does," said Miriam ...

(Lodge 1980:125)

This kind of intrusion of the author's voice into the fictional conversation of the characters is rather different from the traditional author strategy of appealing to the 'gentle reader', despite the fact that Lodge makes such an appeal at the beginning of the passage. What we experience here is a deliberate interruption of the drama that throws the fictional nature of that drama into high relief. We are suddenly aware that the story is precisely that, a story.

Consider a further, related example. In a short story by the Latin American author Julio Cortázar entitled 'Continuity of Parks', a man is described as reading a novel in a high-backed, green velvet armchair in his study. The novel he is reading tells of a desperate but resolute murderer who follows an avenue of trees that leads to a house; he climbs the stairs and locates the study, ' ... and then, the knife in hand, the light from the great windows, the high back of an armchair covered in green velvet, the head of the man in the chair reading a novel.' Thus is someone murdered by a character in the story that he is reading (Cortázar 1968).

What is it that these two examples have in common? In one the author steps out from behind the curtain to address his audience, his readers, and in the other an 'unreal', fictional character is made to commit a 'real' murder. In both examples, figures involved in the creation of a fiction or belonging to the fiction refuse to stay in their assigned places and, like Anthony Browne's little bear in *Bear Hunt*, cross boundaries to take upon themselves roles they would not normally occupy. The effect is to disturb the expectations of the reader and once again to push into the foreground the fictional nature of the story.

A rather different example of a device that can unsettle expectations can be found in 'The King of Jazz', a short story collected in Donald Barthelme's *Great Days*. Two trombonists are playing in the same group and one is managing to produce wonderful new sounds that have never been heard before.

'What's that sound coming in from the side there?'
'Which side?'
'The left.'
'You mean that sound that sounds like the cutting edge of life? That sounds like polar bears crossing the Arctic ice pans? That sounds like a herd of musk ox in full flight? That sounds like male walruses diving to the bottom of the sea? That sounds like fumaroles smoking on the slopes of Mt. Katmai? That sounds like the wild turkey walking through the deep

soft forest? That sounds like beavers chewing trees in an Appalachian marsh? That sounds like an oyster fungus growing on an aspen trunk? That sounds like a mule deer wandering a montane of the Sierra Nevada? That sounds like prairie dogs kissing? That sounds like witch grass tumbling or a river meandering? That sounds like manatees munching seaweed at Cape Sable? That sounds like coatimundis moving in packs across the face of Arkansas? That sounds like –'

'Good God, it's Hokie! ...'

(Barthelme 1979:59–60)

Here the ludicrously extravagant imagery and continuous piling up of comparisons cuts across our expectation of how metaphors and similes should be constructed and how they function within a story. The story itself stalls and comes to a stop while the writer belabours the reader with an excessive amount of detail. Metaphors and similes usually function to bring a story to life, to help a reader to experience the realism of the tale, but here the lack of proportion brings us up short and undermines imaginative involvement in the story.

Postmodernism and metafiction

Postmodern fictions are usually unsettling, sometimes very funny and occasionally completely bewildering, but what is the justification for considering them to be specifically postmodern? How do these fictions display postmodernity? The most obvious connection between these three examples and the list of characteristics discussed above lies in their authors' unwillingness to permit the reader to enjoy an uninterrupted illusion of a secondary world. Amongst other things they are concerned to remind the reader that literary fiction is not a window onto, or a mirror of, the real world but a fabrication that temporarily deludes us into believing that 'real' people are engaged in 'real' events. Furthermore, such stories often imply that the everyday-life-world itself will not withstand too much scrutiny, and that our own lives, with all their randomness and chaos, are only endowed with sense and meaning through our persistent liking for and belief in stories.

Some postmodern fictions offer the reader alternative endings, resisting traditional forms of narrative closure and embracing indeterminacy as a narrative principle. Others loop back to the beginning in a continuous circle, suggesting that unity – the consistency of beginning, middle and end – is in the end simply an illusion. Yet others are reduced to mere fragments and scraps, leaving readers to piece together whatever story they can. All of them, however, have one thing in common, they are all inherently metafictive; that is, they comment upon, or direct attention to, the nature of fiction in the process of creating it. Postmodern fiction is not interested in the traditional satisfactions and consolations of story, but it is interested in the nature of fiction and the processes of storytelling, and it employs metafictive devices to undermine the unreflective and naïve reading of stories. Postmodern fiction does not accept traditional modes on their own terms and always wants to say something to the reader about the nature of the fictive experience in the midst of that experience.[3]

However, postmodern fiction and metafiction are not, strictly speaking, the same thing and it is most important to distinguish between them. Postmodernism in fiction, as in its other cultural manifestations, is very much an historical phenomenon. The extracts quoted above by way of illustration were all written after 1960. In fact, the most uncompromisingly postmodern novels and stories were written in the 1960s and 1970s although precursors can be found in such figures as Vladimir Nabokov and Jorge Luis Borges. Metafiction, on the other hand, is very much an a-historical notion. It is much more like an approach or set of devices, for undermining expectations or for exposing the fictional nature of fictions. As such it has tended to appear from time to time throughout history. Lawrence Sterne's *Tristram Shandy*, with its black page to mark a death and space for readers to add their own descriptions is essentially metafictive, as are passages in Rabelais' *Gargantua and Pantagruel* and *The Thousand and One Nights*. One can see why metafictive devices are essential to the postmodernist enterprise, with its sustained attack on all manifestations of authoritative order and unity, but we should not make the mistake of assuming that the two concepts are identical.

The postmodern picturebook

The claim that certain picturebooks may be considered to be postmodern rests largely upon some very compelling parallels between the picturebooks in question and the kinds of prose fiction for adults discussed above. We need to bear in mind the distinction between the postmodern and the metafictive, but to begin with we need to examine the ways in which picturebooks and postmodern novels can sometimes appear to be playing similar games. However, as picturebooks possess some features that prose fictions do not, rather than attempt to squeeze my examples into a typology derived from novels and short stories, I have grouped them into five rather loose categories of my own devising into which both prose and picturebooks can fit.

Boundary breaking

Boundary breaking occurs when characters within a story are allowed by their author to wander beyond the narrative level to which they properly belong. I have already discussed this effect in *Bear Hunt* by Anthony Browne and also in the adult novel *How Far Can You Go?* (Lodge 1980) and the short story 'Continuity of Parks' (Julio Cortázar) so I shall not linger on it here but will simply add to these two titles some further examples.

In *The Story of a Little Mouse Trapped in a Book* by Monique Felix a mouse appears to be confined within the page upon which she is represented. She pushes at the sides in her attempts to get free, then nibbles around the edges to cut out a square of paper from the page, folds the square into an aeroplane and flies down to safety 'out' of the book and into the 'real world' depicted beyond the ragged edges that are left. *Simon's Book* (Henrik Drescher), *Benjamin's Book* (Alan Baker), and *The Book Mice* (Tony Knowles) all rely upon similar effects. Benjamin, for example, is a rather clumsy hamster who gets into scrapes through such tricks as walking across the page upon which he is represented leaving a trail of muddy paw prints behind him. In attempting to wipe the page clean he only makes matters worse. John Burningham's *Where's Julius?* manages the curious feat of having one character trespass upon the inner fantasies of another.

Excess

Excess usually involves the kind of disregard for literary norms that we saw exemplified in the extract from 'The King of Jazz' but it may take the form of any kind of gigantism that upsets our expectations. Interestingly, picturebooks often have an 'over the top' quality. They frequently involve a stretching and testing of norms – linguistic, literary, social, conceptual and ethical as well as narrative. Such books push at the outer limits of what constitutes the normal and the acceptable and seem to pose the question, 'how far is it possible to go?'

Jill Murphy's *On The Way Home* is a good example of a book that exploits a specifically narrative and ethical excess. Are Claire's stories 'tales' or 'lies'? Whatever they are, they are deliberately heaped up in that 'festive display of accumulation over balance' that prevents us from forming a conventionally satisfying narrative as we read. The unthinkable or the unmentionable appears with startling regularity in picturebooks. Alarming, disturbing or exciting possibilities are put to the test in *Would You Rather ...* by John Burningham. In this book narrative is abandoned altogether and the reader is invited to chose between extraordinary, exciting or disgusting possibilities. Many of the options on display are grotesquely humorous in the manner familiar from children's comics and cartoon strips while others put social norms to the test. Indeed, the book can cause embarrassment in children as they recognize the enormity of some of Burningham's suggestions.

Angry Arthur by Hiawyn Oram and Satoshi Kitamura takes a different form of excess as its theme: the extravagant results of a temper tantrum. Once again there is an accumulation that goes well beyond the bounds of realism, but in this instance there is a clear metaphorical purpose to the depicted events. The eponymous anti-hero is so angry at being prevented from watching late night TV that his rage brings on typhoons and earthquakes. In the real world the actual results of bad temper are rather more localized but the images of chaos in the book serve as the perfect objective correlate for the sense of boundless outrage experienced by angry infants. The dissolution of one's personality in blind rage is well portrayed in the loss of a universe.

Indeterminacy

Indeterminacy is the opposite of excess. In the latter case readers are offered an accumulation of one sort or another way beyond the norm for realistic stories; in the former, they are left with very little information. The contrast between these two extremes reminds us of the fact that a sense of the real in stories depends upon what Susan Stewart calls 'an economy of significance' that is governed by generic conventions (Stewart 1984): writers (or in the case of picturebooks, writers and illustrators) must neither say too much nor too little or they risk losing the reader.

All stories are built upon gaps – writers and picturebook makers cannot describe, explain or show everything – but some picturebooks expose those gaps for us and thus reveal the comic absurdity of the situation we are left in when textual props are missing. For example, *How Tom Beat Captain Najork and His Hired Sportsmen* by Russell Hoban and Quentin Blake has at its heart a series of three testing games that are simultaneously present and absent. Womble, Muck and Sneedball are named and (partially) illustrated but we are never allowed to learn their precise nature. Blake's illustrations hint at their complexity, and Hoban offers one or two clues about scoring and procedures, but the three games remain a pungent lack throughout the story.

Time to Get Out of the Bath, Shirley also relies upon an absence, but here it takes the form of a withholding of information about how two sequences of images are related. The pictures and words on the left-hand pages clearly relate to the images on the right but we are left to make up our own minds about the precise nature of the relationship. In *Come Away From the Water, Shirley*, the companion piece to *Time to Get Out of the Bath* ... Shirley visits the beach with her parents but then appears to be fighting pirates and finding treasure at the same time as her mother, reclining in a deck chair, is exhorting her to behave herself.

Another book that leaves relationships and outcomes obscure is *Black and White* by David Macaulay. The four stories told in the four quarters of each page-opening are depicted in four separate styles, one of them entirely word-less, another packed with the kinds of visual puns that some picturebook illustrators delight in. There are hints and suggestions embedded in the pictures that the four stories might be connected but Macaulay makes no efforts to explain how, or indeed if, this is so. In fact, he prints a warning label on the title page: 'This book appears to contain a number of stories that do not necessarily occur at the same time. Then again, it may contain only one story. In any event, careful inspection of both words and pictures is recommended.'

Parody

Parody is inherently metafictive as it involves a refusal to accept as natural and given that which is culturally determined and conventional. As a literary device it is usually associated with satire and ridicule and may thus seem an unlikely trait to find in children's picturebooks, but in fact picturebook makers often lean towards this particular mode. The aim of parody in the picturebook, however, is not to ridicule any particular author or style but to poke fun at the conventions, manners and affectations of a particular genre. *The Worm Book* by Janet and Allan Ahlberg is an excellent example of how a relatively rigid form – the child's 'information book' – can be undone by placing straight-faced captions beneath silly pictures: 'All good worms have a beginning, a middle and an end ... Worms with two beginnings, a middle and no end are apt to injure themselves ... Worms with two ends, a middle and no beginning get bored.'

A more sophisticated parody of a non-fiction, information text can be found in *How Dogs Really Work* by Alan Snow. This book comes complete with table of contents, index, cut-away pictures with keys, labels with arrows, inset diagrams and so on. The target of the parody is clearly the glamorous books that have proliferated in recent years showing the insides of everything from skyscrapers to ocean liners. Snow's book, however, shows caricature dogs opened up to reveal pulleys, levers and valves and the text purports to explain how doggy behaviour can be explained in terms of the rudimentary, Heath Robinson-like machinery shown in the pictures. Thus, in the section headed, 'Legs and Getting About' we read:

> Legs are organs of support and locomotion in animals (and humans). In dogs, the legs are fixed at the four corners of the main body, (see diagram 1). Nearly all dogs have four legs, even the short funny ones that sometimes look like they may not, (see diagram 2). Legs are powered by energy generated from the food the dog eats.

As befits this kind of manual everything is shown in the greatest possible detail, and there are lots of handy hints for the prospective dog owner ('Make sure you are running your dog on the right fuel. If you are not it may affect the dog's performance.').

It is worth noting that both of these books – and there are many more like them – rely upon forms of non-fiction. As we have seen already in Chapter 4, it is not the only genre that is parodied in picturebooks but it is certainly a popular one. In the case of fiction, the most frequently parodied form is the fairy-tale or folk-tale and I suspect that, as with the information book, such tales are easy prey for parodists because they tend to conform to fairly fixed and immutable conventions and are well known and widely dispersed within the culture. Less inflexible and less popular genres are less easy to subvert. Tony Ross, for example, has rewritten many folk- and fairy-tales from a parodic point of view, and – as I have already observed in Chapter 4 – Babette Cole turns gender roles upside down in *Princess Smartypants*. Eugene Trivivas and Helen Oxenbury turn the folk-tale tables in *The Three Little Wolves and the Big Bad Pig* while the same story is given a twist by John Scieszka and Lane Smith in *The True Story of the Three Little Pigs*.

Performance

Many picturebooks are constructed to be deliberately interactive and partici- patory. Picturebooks with tabs to pull, flaps to lift, wheels to rotate, pages to unfold, holes to peep through and, most recently, buttons to push and sounds to listen to, are now quite commonplace. Notable examples include: the popular *Spot* books; the elaborately engineered works by Jan Pienkowski such as *Haunted House* and *Robot*; the books of Eric Carle and Ron Maris with their cut and shaped pages; much of the work of the Ahlbergs, in particular *Peepo*, *The Jolly Postman*, *Yum Yum* and *Playmates*. More recent examples include: *Making Faces* by Nick Butterworth – a book where the reader is encouraged to pull faces in a built-in mirror – *Tom's Pirate Ship* by Philippe Dupasquier, where each double page spread consists of two nearly identical pictures which the reader must scrutinize to find what is missing from one of them; *Say Cheese* by David Pelham, a pop-up which is shaped in three dimensions like a wedge from a circular block of cheese and *Where, Oh Where, is Kipper's Bear?* by Mick Inkpen which contains a tiny torch that lights up at the end of the book.

Books such as these are not particularly concerned with undermining, or resisting the creation of, a secondary fictive world through manipulation of the text. Instead they foreground the nature of the book as an object, an artefact to be handled and manipulated as well as read. They are thus metafictive to the extent that they tempt readers to withdraw attention from the story (which, it must be said, is often pretty slender) in order to look at, play with and admire the paper engineering. One of the characteristics of a well-told tale is that as we read it our awareness of the book in which it is written tends to fade away, but when the material fabric of the book has been doctored in such a way as to draw attention to itself, it is less easy to withdraw into that fictive, secondary world.

Pop-ups and movables tend to produce a degree of unease amongst chil- dren's book critics and scholars for they often do not seem to offer much in the way of a reading experience at all. For this reason they are sometimes consid- ered to be more like toys than books, objects to play with rather than to read. There is some justice in this view, but it is far too simplistic for it tidies up too neatly something that, if we are honest, rather resists pigeonholing. We might better understand the movable if we view it as a hybrid, a merging of two, otherwise incompatible artefacts: the toy and the picturebook. Under this description, movables are both books that can be played with and toys that can be read.

Picturebooks: postmodern or playful?

Boundary breaking, excess, indeterminacy, parody and performance are all strategies or devices that authors and illustrators can use to push what can be done with the picturebook to its limits, but they are also frequently used by writers of fiction for adults to unsettle readerly expectations. The view that some picturebooks can be considered to be postmodern arises out of this parallel between the picturebooks in question and certain kinds of novels and stories for adults. It seems to me, however, that the parallel is more to do with the structural and formal features of the books than with the cultural sensibilities of the authors and illustrators. The bear in *Bear Hunt* and Julius in *Where's Julius?* slip the bounds of their narratives not to make a point about the instability of the postmodern world but to recruit the reader to a textual game.

The point might become clearer if we return to the distinction between postmodernity and postmodernism. If we wish to say that John Burningham, David Macaulay and John Scieszka are making, or have made, postmodern picturebooks then we must be prepared to consider whether their books reflect the instability, indeterminacy and fragmentation evident within the wider culture, or whether they are an explicit and self-conscious rejection of the tenets and practices of modernism in the arts. Neither argument, I believe, can be made in a wholly satisfying way. The picturebooks in question rarely unhook themselves totally from mainstream literary norms and none possesses the apocalyptic, endgame quality – that feeling of pirouetting gaily on the edge of an abyss – that is found in much postmodern art.[4]

On the other hand, writers and illustrators working in the last three or four decades have obviously been exposed to exactly the same postmodernizing influences as everyone else. Like the rest of us they daily soak up the increasingly ironic messages and images in advertising and the media; observe the effects upon the visual arts of the artist's abdication of responsibility and authority, and experience the flattening out of high- and popular-cultural differences. It would therefore be reasonable to suppose that such influences might find their way into their books. Illustrators in particular tend to be magpie-like in their approach to the world of imagery, taking whatever they wish from the visual world around them, transmuting and making use of it whenever they can. Indeed, if we accept the arguments in Chapter 4, we should expect writers and illustrators to import into the picturebook whatever is to hand. For this reason, if for no other, we might expect some picturebooks to possess postmodern features.

I believe that this leaves us with two possible versions of the postmodern picturebook: a weak view and a strong view. In my opinion the strong view – that is, that postmodern picturebooks are postmodern in exactly the same ways that adult novels and stories are – is not wholly sustainable. There is simply too little continuity between the books and the wider culture to which they are supposed to belong. The weak view – that is, that picturebooks will inevitably be influenced by some of the numerous manifestations of postmodern culture – is altogether more believable.

Another way of looking at the matter is to shift attention from the problems of how we might locate picturebooks within a particular historically located culture to the formal and structural parallels that clearly do exist between the books that we are concerned with and the literature of the postmodern age. In other words, it might be more realistic to make a case for the metafictive in picturebooks rather than the postmodern. As I observed above, metafictive devices did not just appear in the 1960s when the first recognizably postmodernist writings were published. Writers have occasionally played games with their texts and with their readers at many periods throughout history. Textual rule-breaking in this sense – the a-historical sense – returns us to the arguments I put forward in the last chapter. The question of why many picturebook makers feel free to abandon settled modes of storytelling may best be answered by taking a good close look at the nature of the form within which they are working and the audience to whom that work is addressed.

Notes

1   My own first attempt to write about this subject was published in *Signal* as 'The constructedness of texts: picture books and the metafictive' (also collected in Egoff, Stubbs Ashley and Sutton 1996). Other relevant texts include:

> Moss, G. (1992) ' "My Teddy Bear Can Fly": postmodernizing the picture book'; Styles, M. (1996) 'Inside the tunnel: a radical kind of reading – picture books, pupils and postmodernism'.

2   The list that follows here has been adapted from Hassan, I. (1986) 'Pluralism in Postmodern Perspective'.

3   According to Patricia Waugh in her book *Metafiction: the Theory and Practice of Self-conscious Fiction* (Waugh 1984) strategies characteristic of the metafictive postmodernist include:

> The over-obtrusive, visibly inventing narrator: the storyteller who steps out from behind the curtain to address the reader directly (see John Barth's 1969 *Lost in the Funhouse* and Robert Coover's 1969 *Pricksongs and Descants*).
>
> Ostentatious typographic experiment: enlarging, distorting, inverting or otherwise manipulating the print on the page to foreground the objectivity of the book (see Federman's 1971 *Double or Nothing*, and the work of Alasdair Gray, Christine Brooke-Rose, Donald Barthelme and Ronald Sukenick).
>
> Explicit dramatization of the reader: addressing the reader as if he or she were a character in the tale (see Italo Calvino's 1981 *If on a Winter's Night a Traveller*).
>
> Chinese-box structures: embedded stories, one inside the other that can regress through many levels (see John Barth's 1969 'Menelaiad' from *Lost in the Funhouse*).
>
> Incantatory and absurd lists: over-extended or bizarre lists like the one from 'The King of Jazz' (see page 92).

Over-systematized or arbitrarily organized structural devices (see Walter Abish's 1974 *Alphabetical Africa*).

Total breakdown of temporal and spatial organization of narrative: the rejection of authorial control so that readers decide the order in which chapters should be read (see the works of B. S. Johnson).

Infinite regress: plot sequences structured so that they circle endlessly like a Moebius strip or permanently defer closure (see William Burroughs' 1985 *Exterminator!* and John Barth's 'Life-story' (Barth 1969)).

Self-reflexive images that deliberately call attention to themselves (see many of the works of Vladimir Nabokov).

Critical discussions of the story within the story (see John Barth's 1982 *Sabbatical* and David Lodge's 1980 *How Far Can You Go?*)

Continuous undermining of specific fictional conventions such as the slippage between narrative levels already discussed (see Muriel Spark and John Fowles).

Use of popular genres such as science fiction, pornography and the western to draw attention to narrative conventions (see examples of *romance* (John Barth's 1982 *Sabbatical*, Margaret Drabble's 1969 *The Waterfall*); *science fiction* (Kurt Vonnegut Jr's 1959 *The Sirens of Titan* and 1979 *Slaughterhouse Five*, Donald Barthelme's 1976 'Paraguay'); motifs from *pornography* (Gore Vidal's 1969 *Myra Breckinridge*, Robert Coover's 1969 'The Babysitter'); the language of *comic books* (Clarence Major's 1975 *Emergency Exit*); the *family saga* (John Irving's 1978 *The World According to Garp*, Vladimir Nabokov's 1969 *Ada*) and the *western* (Richard Brautigan's 1976 *The Hawkline Monster: a Gothic Western*).

Explicit parody of both literary and non-literary texts (see Gilbert Sorrentino's 1980 *Mulligan Stew*, Alan Burns' 1969 *Babel* and Thomas Pynchon's 1975 *Gravity's Rainbow*).

4   The exception is perhaps *The Stinky Cheese Man and Other Fairly Stupid Tales* by John Scieszka illustrated by Lane Smith. In its flouting of just about every narrative and bibliographic convention it betrays a high degree of self-consciousness (Scieszka and Smith must surely have done their research) and a disturbing willingness to look loss of coherence directly in the face.

Chapter 7

A word about pictures

N: That looks like a fan.
DL: What is it do you think?
N: A towel

(Nathan (N) and the author (DL) reading together
from Time to Get Out of the Bath, Shirley by John Burningham)

Introduction

It may seem strange in a book about picturebooks to leave the chapter on
visual images to near the end, but there are good reasons for placing it here
rather than at the beginning. Throughout I have tried to keep in view
picturebooks as whole entities rather than separate them into their constit-
uent parts. Indeed, I began by claiming that picturebooks are quasi-literary
objects, more closely related to books than to paintings, prints and drawings.
This is so because the words and pictures that make up a picturebook are
bound within covers, are arranged sequentially, together comprise a text that
is frequently, though not always, narrative in kind, and which is intended to be
read. Had I foregrounded the picturebook's pictures by discussing them in the
first chapter, I would have risked making them seem too much like discrete
entities that have an existence apart from the overall text within which they
are embedded.

   A number of previous studies of picturebooks have given the pictures pride
of place but there was a time when it was necessary to defend the idea that the
pictures in picturebooks made an important contribution to the meaning of
the text. Joseph Schwarcz, for example, summarizes in his Introduction to
Ways of the Illustrator some of the history of how pictures and illustrations in
children's books were dealt with in the past. He shows how limited were the
responses of critics and reviewers who saw picturebook images as merely
tasteful or drab, beautiful or undistinguished. At best, picturebook pictures
were said to 'harmonize' with the written text. Schwarcz saw his own book as

contributing to the movement away from this condescending approach to the visual image toward 'the examination of the illustrator's work as a means of symbolic communication' (Schwarcz 1982:4). He therefore began with the following questions: 'In what ways does the illustration, an aesthetic configuration created for children, express its contents and meanings? How do its elements combine and its structures operate so as to carry the messages to which we are asked to relate?' (Schwarcz 1982:4). He did go on to ask, 'How does the illustration relate to the verbal text?' but it was the pictures that had to be dealt with first.

It is no longer necessary to defend the right of pictures to be considered in this way. Non-specialists, as well as critics and scholars, are now much more at ease with both the idea and the practice of 'reading pictures'. In this chapter, therefore, I have not attempted a review of all that is currently known about pictures and how they work but have restricted myself to a discussion of five key features of the visual image and have linked these to examples of children attempting to make sense of picturebook illustrations. I then briefly examine one of the most recent attempts to develop a grammar of the visual image.

Some key features of the visual image

Line

In the extract set at the head of this chapter, Nathan and I are at the beginning of Burningham's book and are looking at the first page-opening after the title page. On the right is the first picture of Shirley in her bath. Her mum reaches out towards her daughter holding a towel in her left hand. The towel is white with sketchy blue stripes, or possibly fold lines, running along its length. The towel hangs downwards from where it is held at one end and Nathan, quite rightly, points out that it looks like a fan. He is in no danger of really mistaking the towel for a fan as the context clearly calls for a towel, but he does have a point. Burningham's sketch-like, non-naturalistic style stiffens the towel somewhat so that it looks more rigid than it should – it does indeed look like a fan.[1] If we look at the image carefully we can see that it is the towel's black outline and the blue marks fanning out downwards that give the impression of stiffness. In other words, we see the shape as a rather fan-like towel because of Burningham's handling of line.

In this case it is the quality of line that is important. Contour lines not only outline characters and objects but can be made to animate them. Quentin Blake's drawing in *All Join In* explodes with movement and energy, his characters leaping from sofas, chasing mice and hurtling down snowy mountainsides. None of this violent and helter-skelter movement is created through conventional signs of motion, the dashes and streaks familiar from comics. It is the outcome of vigorous drawing and broken outlines allied to a sure grasp of gesture and an understanding of how to suggest action (see below). In contrast to Blake's swirling, jagged and jittery lines, Jonathan Heale's drawing in his foursquare prints for *Lady Muck* – each one framed in solid black – is bold and strong, creating thick, black outlines and shadows which impart a sense of stasis and timelessness. Not much happens, at least physically, in these images, but in the vignettes and scenes which face them, usually on the left-hand side of each page-opening, the paler, more delicate outlining allows for a greater degree of realism and a touch more animation.

Line can be used for purposes beyond separating figure from ground and suggesting animation. The lines, dashes and scorings of hatching and cross-hatching can be used to darken individual colours to suggest shadows and textures, and to model features. In *The Little Boat* Patrick Benson uses this device for a multitude of purposes. He shows us shadows cast by umbrellas on a sunny beach, the smooth roundness of children's legs, the rise and swell of waves at sea, the shimmering of the sea's surface in a flat calm and the glistening scales on the flanks of a giant fish. Anthony Browne uses hatching and cross-hatching too, but rather more sparingly and frequently in contrast with other effects. In *Gorilla*, as Hannah is swung through the trees away from her home and off to the zoo, the blue sky is darkened with cross-hatching in its upper two-thirds causing the moon and stars to shine out brightly. In the lower third the cross-hatching gives way to horizontal hatching strokes which allow for a lighter sky just above the roof tops. A frightened ginger cat leaps into the air from the top of a wall and beneath it the hatching changes direction appearing to propel the cat into the air. In *Voices in the Park*, the 'third voice' sequence begins with Charles peering out of a window in his home, the interior walls of which are densely hatched and cross-hatched, the directions of the hatching serving to clarify the succession of receding empty rooms and doorways. The plate on the facing page shows Charles in back view looking out across the green lawns of the park, most of which are an undifferentiated green except for the foreground where the vertical hatching darkens the tone and suggests the individual blades of grass. The cross-hatched shadow of Charles' mother leans in from the left and falls – both literally and metaphorically – across Charles' back (see Figure 4).

Colour

Colour is perhaps the next most basic feature of picturebook pictures. This is not to suggest that picturebooks are always, or have to be, coloured. A number of successful books have relied upon monochrome drawing only, but the vast majority of picturebooks are now printed in colour. Line and colour together can be used to produce simple shapes that in the hands of an illustrator such as Dick Bruna can be transformed into the forms of everyday objects that infants can recognize and name. Modulation of colour and further variation of line produce more complex forms that can be placed in relation to one another, perhaps in an illusory space extending backwards from the picture plane. Thus, cartoon characters can walk down suburban streets, stuffed toys can play in the park and old-fashioned postmen can cycle down country lanes. Line and colour, then, are the two basic elements out of which the more complex features of pictures are built. In the next extract we see clearly how important colour can be in creating the world that the reader sees.

Nathan and I are looking at the fourth page-opening of *Time to Get Out of the Bath, Shirley*. The picture to the right shows some knights in armour galloping through a forest towards the figure of a girl, Shirley, who is hanging from a branch suspended above a waterfall. In keeping with Burningham's non-naturalistic approach, the colour scheme is rather odd, the forest floor being a purplish blue and the background – the space between and beyond the trees – a deep red. The reader is thus placed in a position not unlike that in the first extract. The picture is realistic up to a point but it possesses features that do not seem to fit.

DL: ... so what's going on over here?
N: (*snorts with laughter*)... in the water ... but there's no splashes (*looking at the horses apparently galloping on the surface of some blue water*) there's two bunny rabbits
DL: that's right ... is that water, do you think?
N: No ... probably the blue path
DL: Hmm ... could be couldn't it?
N: They ... they've gone into the ... mm devils ... in the red thing
DL: Into the devils? What do you mean?
N: Yea ... mm hell
DL: Oh I see
N: 'Cos it's red (*the background to the riders*)

Nathan's mistakes are fairly obvious: he initially sees the horizontal blue band upon which the riders seem to be galloping as water, and then compounds the mistake by taking the red background to be a sign that Shirley, and the knights, are now in hell. Bizarre though these interpretations are, they are directly linked to colour cues. Unlike in the first extract, where the context is clear enough for Nathan not to genuinely mistake the towel for a fan, here the events in the picture sequence have become so strange that he is much more at risk of misunderstanding what is going on.

Colour thus plays an important role in building up the basic image but of course it possesses other functions too. The vibrant red of the baby's dungarees in *So Much* keeps him very much at the focus of our attention. He is easy to find even when he is surrounded by the much larger adults and is especially prominent in the pictures which depict, in tones of brown, grey and black, the other family members waiting for the next arrival. In fact, this muted palette acts as a clear signifier of the boredom depicted so clearly in these images. Colour can also connect or separate significant characters and objects, both within single pictures and across whole sequences. At the beginning of *Gorilla*, for example,

Figure 23 From *Where is Monkey?* by Dieter Schubert.

the red of Hannah's jumper is contrasted with the blues associated with her father, signalling their lack of contact. By the end of the book the two characters are brought closer together, not only through the father's hands on Hannah's shoulders, but also through the matching reds of their clothing.[2]

Action and movement

Since most picturebooks tell stories of one kind or another they must deal with commonplace features of narrative such as motion, action and the passing of

Figure 24 From *Where is Monkey?* by Dieter Schubert.

time. Characters move through landscapes and interact with others, tasks are performed and events depicted, quests are followed and challenges met, and what the words tell of these things the pictures are frequently required to show. As a result, picturebook illustrators tend to be particularly adept at calling forth motion out of stillness and duration from instantaneity. For example, imagery that arrests motion immediately prior to its completion can suggest the rapid or violent movement of objects, people and animals. In *All Join In* Quentin Blake's characters chase after a mouse, toss pots and pans about as they clear out a kitchen and are thrown off a sledge at the bottom of a particularly steep slope and in each case we are shown the moment just before events reach a climax. Similar moments can be found in *The Park in the Dark* where Barbara Firth chooses to depict the three friends on a swing at the high point of an upward arc, moments before the descent (see Figure 10), and in *Drop Dead* where there are many pre-climactic images of jumping, flying and falling.

Less convulsive movement is often portrayed through what can appear at first glance to be simply a frozen gesture. Barbara Firth's toys walk, twist and turn convincingly but more has gone into their animation than simple stopped motion. In fact, frozen gestures of the sort sometimes found in unposed snapshots can look distinctly awkward and not at all animated. Firth's skill enables her to use the dynamics of her designs to animate the still figures and she recruits our knowledge of facial expression to help us interpret posture. Sometimes, however, it can be difficult to interpret the stilled gesture appropriately if an illustrator is unable to clarify the true nature of a movement.

Consider, for example, the following two extracts from a conversation with Jane about the wordless picturebook, *Where is Monkey?* by Dieter Schubert. *Where is Monkey?* is the tale of a stuffed toy, the monkey of the

Figure 25 From *All Join In* by Quentin Blake.

title, who is dropped by his young owner on a trip to a wood or park. The toy is found by a pack of rats who play with it and mistreat it for a while before it is passed on to various other groups of forest creatures. At one point it is carried off by a magpie who pulls out one of its glass eyes. In the second extract with Jane, she begins to tell her version of the story. The first plate shows the little boy reaching out with his left hand towards his toy monkey which is tucked up in bed in a box beneath a chair (see Figure 23). The figures and objects in the background make it clear that mother and son are about to go out for a cycle ride but Jane is momentarily unsure whether the reaching gesture is one of 'putting' or 'getting' as there is no unambiguous vector associated with the movement.

J: (*quietly commenting on the first picture only*) Well first of all the little boy puts the monkey ... no he puts the monkey in a chair ... under the chair in a box and then after that he gets him out ...

Such misinterpretations are easy to make at the beginning of a book, particularly one such as this where there are no words and no preceding sequence of
pictures to contextualize the actions. But later in the story, when the magpie
has appropriated the monkey, Jane has a similar problem, for a similar reason.

J: ... and it catches the monkey and it goes back to its nest ...(*laughs*)
        teeth!
DL: Hmm
J: ... and glasses and eyes ...
DL: Yes
J: glass eyes
DL: I think they must be glass eyes mustn't they?
J: And he puts a pin in his eye 'cos he takes one of his eyes out
DL: Hmm
J: ... 'cos it's shiny

The picture is intended to show the magpie trying to detach one of the toy's glass eyes but the arrangement of elements within the image is confusing, for although the bird seems to be leaning backwards and thus pulling, a clear vector formed by the bird's beak and the thread attaching the glass bead to the toy's head runs diagonally downwards from left to right, suggesting a pushing movement (see Figure 24). Jane therefore initially perceives the taut thread to be a pin being pushed into the toy's fabric ('he puts a pin in his eye …') and then swiftly corrects herself without disturbing the flow of her narration ('… he takes one of his eyes out').

Diagonals within pictures can create strong directional thrusts as the tendency to read from left to right interacts with our sense of gravity moving things downwards. Thus the diagonal from bottom left to top right always appears to ascend while the diagonal from top left to bottom right appears to descend. This opposition is clearly illustrated in a page-opening from *All Join In* where some typically Blakean children are caught in the act of sliding (see Figure 25). On the right a group of four on a sledge are depicted hurtling left to right down a snowy mountainside. On the left another group are taking turns to slide, right to left, down an elephant's trunk, but so powerful is the force of the vector that leads upwards from left to right that at least one of the children could easily be seen as shinning up the trunk rather than slipping down it.

Rudolph Arnheim points out in his book *Art and Visual Perception* that sometimes the postures in which artists freeze their subjects to gain the most animated effect are not even found in the real world (Arnheim 1974). Galloping animals such as horses, for example, are still often shown with both fore and hind legs outstretched – as is the lion chasing the children in *Drop Dead* (see Figure 20) – although the serial photographs of Eadweard Muybridge revealed long ago that quadrupeds only adopt such a posture when leaping and never when running. The distortion comes about because 'Action pictures portray motion precisely to the degree displayed by the figure' (Arnheim 1974:424). Thus the depiction of rapid movement requires the full extension of the limbs even when such extension is 'unreal'. Slower, more sedate movement would require much less stretching and distortion.

Size and location

If we return for a moment to the misfortunes of Dieter Schubert's lost monkey we can examine how two more features of the visual image – the size and location of separate elements – affect our understanding. Having satisfied its craving for the bright shiny glass eye, the magpie drops the monkey and it falls past some bumblebees into a lake or stream below. Jane, and another reader, Martin, on reaching this point in the picture sequence, both make the same error – they both see the bees as catching the monkey.

Figure 26 From *Where is Monkey?* by Dieter Schubert.

M: he drops it into the sea ... he drops it from there
DL: Hmm
M: The bees grab it and drop it in the sea.

J: And ... and then it falls and some bees try and catch it but they can't because it's too heavy and it goes into the water and goes down to the bottom ...

The reasons why both children read the picture in this way are partly to do with the fact that the whole story has been structured around the serial abduction and mistreatment of the monkey so it makes sense to anticipate a further, similar episode. But their reading is also prompted by the way the elements of the picture are organized. The tiny bees are placed close to the picture plane making them much larger than is necessary and granting them a significance that they do not possess within the story. Moreover, one of the bees overlaps the figure of the monkey as it falls behind suggesting that the monkey is being borne on its back. A closer look at this image, however, reveals that the bees appear to be fleeing the falling object rather than trying to catch it. Size and location are therefore key factors in determining what we see, but it is not the absolute size that is important. Large objects in the background are not only diminished in size but also in significance, and small elements can be given prominence either by moving them closer to the picture plane or by bringing them closer than another larger, but more distant, object.

For example, in *The Little Boat* the tiny scrap of expanded polystyrene, no bigger than a child's hand, is brought forward towards the viewer and placed at eye level in the picture where it is becalmed in the middle of the ocean. This automatically makes it seem larger but on turning the page we find it brought even closer still as a giant fish rears up out of the depths and seizes it between its jaws. The fish, pressed up against the picture plane seems truly monstrous, but given the absolute size of the little boat, the fish can be no more than, say, one or two feet long. Another creature brought vividly to life, though only partly through its size and position, is the chimpanzee behind the bars of its cage in *Gorilla*. The poignancy of this image is brought about through the interanimation of many design features: the contrast in style with the relatively flat and non-realistic images around it; the severing of the creature's face into bands by the strips of white page which are also the cage bars; and the chimpanzee's level stare that meets our gaze and implicates us in its plight. But it is the fact that this is a life-size portrait, crammed up close to the reader's own face, and foreshortened so that the muzzle seems to push out through the bars that makes us pause. These features are discussed in greater detail in Appendix 2.

There are a number of further ways that an object's or person's location within the picture might influence meaning. High and low, right and left are all locations that can have significance. William Moebius suggests that figures positioned up high may be interpreted as in ecstatic or dream-like states, or may be possessed of high social status or a positive self image. In contrast, a low position might suggest low status or low spirits. Important figures are usually centred but can, in another picture, be both literally and metaphorically marginalized. The left-hand side of a picture, Moebius claims, is a position of relative security while figures on the right are likely to be ' ... moving into a situation of risk or adventure' (Moebius 1986:140). Nodelman, following Arnheim, suggests that we are likely to identify with figures on the left, especially if they have their backs to us so that they appear to be seeing what we are seeing.

However, much clearly depends on the overall design of a particular book. High and low, left and right, can be readily identifiable locations within clearly framed or differentiated images. On pages where the pictures are mere vignettes or are only partially framed so that the words push in from the side, however, or where pictures are irregularly sequenced down or across the page in asymmetrical arrangements as they are in some parts of *The Man*, *All Join In* and *Drop Dead*, then high and low, left and right have no significant value. When we speak of such positions we make the assumption that the objects or figures concerned are located within a scene. Thus, Barbara Firth's three toys are positioned to the far right in front of a panorama of the park at the moment when terror strikes them and drives them home. Similarly, Anthony Browne's Hannah slumped on the ground, low down in front of the television set, is clearly miserable whereas Charles and Smudge excitedly at play in *Voices in the Park* are high up in trees, on slides and climbing frames. In fact, when we examine a range of different types of picturebook, and types of picturebook imagery, then we find that such positional codes are in fact used sparingly. Again, see Appendix 2 for a more detailed discussion of these locations.

Rather more commonplace is the convention that places figures in motion facing left to right. Sometimes this is taken to be a feature unique to the picturebook but Arnheim makes it clear that pictorial representations have been read from left to right ever since the advent of 'sequential thought ... recorded in linear writing'. (Arnheim 1974:33) This deeply ingrained habit creates a powerful vector, causing us to perceive movement from left to right across a picture as freer, easier and more natural than movement in the opposite direction. Thus Rosie the hen from *Rosie's Walk* plods steadfastly around the farmyard across each of the page-openings from left to right, dragging our eyes with her and inviting us to turn the page to see what happens next. Max from *Where the Wild Things Are* sails from left to right into the land of the Wild Things, only reversing the direction when he deems it time to return home. Further examples can readily be found in most narrative picturebooks. Thus Browne's dogs, Albert and Victoria, pursue each other around the park in the direction of the next page turn and the Jolly Postman's 'round' is in one direction only. Almost no one walks leftwards down the street in *Have You Seen Who's Just Moved in Next Door to Us?* and *The Little Boat* sails west to judge from the contrast between its point of departure and its point of arrival (from British seaside resort to Caribbean beach), but does it by sailing east, that is, to the right. So strong and all-pervasive is this bibliographic habit that its inversion almost always has a significance for the characters in the story. Anyone attempting to move from right to left can usually be seen to be deliberately interfering with the general movement of characters in the story, to be blocked in some way, to be returning from adventures or to possess a sinister purpose. A good example comes at the end of *The Park in the Dark* when the three toys, having had fun playing on the swings in the locked park, are frightened by a late commuter train rushing across the scene from the right-hand edge. The three friends turn tail and run towards the left-hand edge, back in the direction of home.

Symbolism

Each of the extracts taken from readings and discussions with children have so far in this chapter turned upon mis-readings of the illustrators' intentions. We could therefore be forgiven for believing that young children quite frequently make such mistakes and that learning to 'read pictures' is for them an arduous and slow process. In fact, the very opposite is true. Children are sometimes puzzled by what they see in pictures (see Maureen Crago on 'Incompletely Shown Objects in Picture Books' (Crago 1979)) but mistakes such as the ones we have been examining here are actually quite rare and in every case have been caused by visual ambiguity or – sad to say – inept illustration. What is remarkable is not the fact that they make mistakes (in one sense they are not making mistakes at all) but rather the speed with which they recognize and interpret what happens in the pictures they look at. Nathan simply sees the fan-like stiffness of the towel just as Jane sees the magpie pushing a pin into the monkey's eye and Martin sees the monkey on the bee's back. There are, however, some features of visual images that are not so instantly recognizable.

Take, for example, the different ways in which Jane and Martin come to an understanding of the identity of the old man who finds and rescues the dilapidated toy in *Where is Monkey?* Immediately after the episode with the magpie and the bees, the toy is hooked out of the stream into which he fell by an elderly fisherman and taken home to be repaired. The next extract is Jane's response to this sequence of pictures.

J: … it goes into the water and it goes down to the bottom where a big fish finds it *(turns page)* and the man is fishing and he catches some fish and it also catches the monkey.

DL: That's right

J: And luckily it's a toy-mender

How does she know that the old man is a 'toy-mender'? There is no written text to tells her that this is so. She does it by rapidly identifying the key features of the final plate of the page-opening (the man inserts a key into the lock of a cottage-like building which has rows of dolls and toys in the window and a sign above the door), recognizing the general significance of the sign (a red cross) and fine-tuning this understanding with the aid of supplementary information (the bits and pieces of dismembered doll stuck to the wall around the cross). This act of interpretation she carries out swiftly, and equally swiftly translates it into the phrase 'toy-mender'. She is probably unaware of these acts of judgement and interpretation but in narrating her story she reveals how her reading rests upon an implicit understanding of how elements within pictures are arranged and how pictures can exploit the symbols of a common culture.

Now contrast Jane's response to that of Martin.

M: Found the Monkey

DL: Hmm … Hmm

M: *(quietly)* Takin' it back to his place *(turns page)* takin' it in his house … stitchin' it up

DL: Hmm

M: Then he's in a bowl of water … an' dryin' it

DL: Why do you think he's doing all that?

M: Don't know

At this point in our conversation, if Martin was aware of the symbolic significance of the red cross he was not letting on. Later, however, when the book was finished and we were discussing it, he revealed with some prompting that he did understand.

DL: ... when he gets caught by the man with the fishing rod ...
M: he gets repaired
DL: he takes him home
M: Look teddy ... ambulance ... toys
DL: Ah, right
M: He's an ambulance
DL: I wondered you see why the man repaired him ... do you know what that is?
M: It's an ambulance cross

The red cross symbol is almost universally recognized and understood so it would be strange if children, at least in the western world, were unaware of its significance. Nodelman is correct, however, to maintain that 'All symbols are inherently arcane' (Nodelman 1988:107) inasmuch as the meanings of symbols such as the red cross are hidden from those who do not possess the knowledge necessary to unlock their secrets. If you are born into a culture that neither uses nor recognizes the red cross – let us say, an Islamic society where the red crescent symbolizes medical assistance – then no amount of looking at the symbol alone will force it to reveal its significance (though I imagine you could work it out within the story from the surrounding textual information). On the other hand, authors and illustrators may well employ symbols that are not derived from the everyday-life-world of a specific culture and that only resonate within a particular book or within that author's or illustrator's oeuvre.

Take, for example, the following group of children discussing with their teacher some of the puzzling features of Libby Hathorn's and Gregory Rogers' picturebook story about the homeless child, *Way Home*.[3] They pause to examine the *trompe l'oeuil* end papers which are designed to look like crumpled paper. At first, before they have read the story, they are concerned only with the surface features of the image. (Individual letters indicate different speakers. VB is the teacher.)

T: and this is supposed to be creased-up paper
P: it looks like tin foil

Later, having read and shared the book and having been primed to look for meanings beyond the superficial, they are prepared to suggest ways in which the endpapers may relate symbolically to the theme of the story.

A: that's the newspaper he's lying on
VB: yes it seems all scrunched up doesn't it?
P: and crumpled

VB: what is it?
A&P: paper
T: when I first saw it I thought it meant he'd have a lot to climb over
C: I thought it meant his life was a bit crumpled

(Burdon 1996)

The key here is the expectation on the part of the children that images in a book of this kind may possess meanings over and above what is represented, allied to a willingness to use their understanding of the story to generate a plausible interpretation. An image of crumpled paper is what it is, but in the context of the picturebook *Way Home*, it carries a clear symbolic charge. Clearly there can be no appeal to a standard meaning as in the case of the red cross, but the interpretative processes at work are essentially the same.

Manipulation of line, colour, action conventions, object size and location, and symbolism are only a few of the ways in which pictures can be made to possess meaning. Illustrators also concern themselves with the way images are framed; how the preponderance of certain shapes can influence the reader's understanding; how facial expression and gesture can be translated from real life to the printed page and so on. Readers of the present book who are interested in researching the subject further could turn to Jane Doonan's detailed and accessible book, *Looking at Pictures in Picturebooks* or the first six chapters of Perry Nodelman's *Words About Pictures*. A slightly different approach is taken in D. A. Dondis' *A Primer of Visual Literacy*, but this book too is helpful (Doonan 1993; Nodelman 1988; Dondis 1973).

A grammar of visual design

So far we have examined how some of the discrete features of an illustration – the lines, colours and symbols – might contribute to the meaning and effectiveness of the whole, but we have not as yet considered what kind of contribution might be made by any *structural organization* a picture may possess. In the Introduction to *Words About Pictures* Perry Nodelman hints at such pictorial structures when he writes, '[semiotics] suggests the possibility of a system underlying visual communication that is something like a grammar – something like the system of relationships and contexts that makes verbal communication possible' (Nodelman 1988:ix). The idea of such a grammar of the image is not new. Indeed, artists themselves have sometimes sought for such an underlying structure. Many painters in the early years of the twentieth century, in particular those drawn towards abstraction, sought analogies from verbal language to support their efforts at uncovering a universal visual language. However, it is semioticians who have been the most persistent seekers after the grail of a visual grammar.

Roland Barthes' attempts in the 1960s to analyse the image syntactically foundered on his inability to identify both the discontinuous elements, the

Figure 27 From *Gorilla* by Anthony Browne.

separate units, within the continuous field of the image that might be taken to
correspond to the words, phrases and clauses of verbal language. Without such
a 'vocabulary' it would seem that there could be no grammar. For these and
similar reasons, there has been much scepticism over the possibility that pictorial representations will submit to anything like a grammatical analysis. Nevertheless, a further attempt has recently been made to outline a grammar that
can be applied to the full range of visual images – paintings, cartoons, photographs, advertising layouts, diagrams, maps and so on – and a full account has
been published under the title, *Reading Images: the Grammar of Visual Design*,
by Gunther Kress and Theo van Leeuwen (Kress and van Leeuwen 1996). I
provide in this final section of Chapter 7 a short introduction to this grammar,
explaining some of the technical terms involved and supplying some simple
examples, drawn from picturebooks, of the grammar in action. I have provided
a fuller account, adapted to the picturebook image, in Appendix 2 as at the
time of writing little work has been done to apply the grammar to the kinds of
pictures that appear in picturebooks.[4] We will begin with one or two examples
and then examine the underlying principles of the grammar, concluding with a
further example of how the grammar might apply to picturebook images.

In *Gorilla*, Hannah and her friend spend some of their evening in the

Figure 28 From *So Much* by Trish Cooke and Helen Oxenbury.

cinema. Sitting in the darkness they watch a 'Supergorilla' streaking across the screen from left to right. For Kress and van Leeuwen this image would be typical of what they call an *action process*. In other words it is – rather obviously – an image of something happening. Somebody – an *actor* – is doing something. Picturebooks are full of action processes for they are primarily concerned to represent, in words and sequences of pictures, doings and happenings, most often in the form of narrative. We can tell that this is an action process rather than, say, a *conceptual process* like a diagram in a textbook because the image involves a *vector*, a strong directional thrust. In this case the body of Supergorilla himself forms the vector, pushing from left to right. He is therefore not only a *participant* in the action process (the character or object who is 'doing something'), his torso and arms also direct our attention to what or where the action is directed. In this case, the action (flying, or streaking through the sky) is not directed at anything or anyone, so it is therefore a *non-transactional* action process. This fragment of an image structure, if put into words, might be represented as 'Supergorilla (actor) streaks (action process) through the sky'.

In *So Much*, on the other hand, the image of Aunt Bibba arriving at the house is organized in such a way that her left arm points towards the baby as she stoops down towards him (see Figure 28). This arm forms a vector, or directional thrust, linking Aunt to baby in a *transactional* process, unlike Supergorilla whose action is non-transactional. Aunt Bibba, who is the main actor within the image, reaches out to the baby who is *the goal*. Transcoded into words we might say that 'Aunt Bibba (actor) greets (action process) the baby (goal)'. Sometimes, of course, a picture will represent an *interaction* rather than an action, the process being bi-directional and the participants taking the roles of actor and goal either simultaneously or sequentially. Thus in Briggs' *The Man*, the boy and the Man threaten each other at the same time with, respectively, a mobile phone and a match, the aerial of the phone and the shaft of the match forming vectors that link Man to boy and boy to Man (see Figure 17). Similarly, Uncle Didi from *So Much* makes to kiss his little nephew as the baby points with a delicate index finger. Here the baby's finger and his uncle's pouting lips form two tiny but distinct vectors linking the two figures together (see Figure 11).

The terms *action process, conceptual process, vector, participant, transactional, non-transactional, actor and goal* have all been borrowed from the systemic functional grammar developed by M. A. K. Halliday and his associates[5] and they tell us immediately that this is not like the traditional grammars taught in school. In this grammar, structure – whether of verbal language or visual imagery – is conceived in terms of meaning and function. In other words, the authors are not interested in dissecting the image into its separate features (line, colour, shape, etc.) and analysing them apart from each other, but are looking at the way the structure of an image contributes to what that image says to us. The participants in an image – the people and things that have roles to play – are organized upon the page, and are related to one another, in various ways. The principles of this organization, and the ways in which it contributes to how we understand the image, are what the grammar seeks to reveal.

The grammar is systemic because it involves the artist and/or illustrator (or writer when applied to verbal language) in making selections from different areas, or systems, of possibility. Thus, when language users speak, write, draw or paint they make choices – more or less unconsciously depending upon the circumstances and context – from the available resources in order to realize in sound, writing or pictures whatever it is they want to 'say'. Languages are therefore *systemic* in that they are composed of interlocking systems that require users to choose between options that the language makes available to them in order to realize their meanings. For example, if I want to tell my daughter to tidy her room I have to make vocabulary choices so I might refer to her by her first name, her full name or by her private, family pet name. I can also choose from a number of sentence forms: the imperative ('Go and tidy your room'); the interrogative ('Have you tidied your room yet?') or the declarative ('I'd like you to tidy your room'). Similarly, if I take a group photograph of my friends I might ask them to look straight into the camera lens or look away; to smile or not; to stand formally erect or to relax. Each choice made will affect the final meaning of the utterance or image. In the case of Supergorilla, Browne had the option of making the image transactional or non-transactional (the superhero could have been about to catch a falling victim); it could have been uni-directional or bi-directional (another figure could have attacked Supergorilla head on making both figures actors and goals). Of particular importance here is that the choices are about alternative structures rather than individual features such as line, colour, texture, etc. Structure is taken to be directly concerned with the construction of meaning and is not merely a formal skeleton holding the various parts together.

The functional aspect of the grammar is thus rooted in its concern with meaning. Kress and van Leeuwen maintain that, even today, most grammars tend to be formal, examining the separate parts of a language in isolation from its semantic aspects. In contrast, systemic functional grammar focuses upon the relationship between structure and meaning and is concerned with the uses to which images are put. The authors approach the task of analysis and description in this way because they begin from the assumption that visual imagery, like verbal language, is a form of *social semiotic*.[6] In other words, the signs from which images are composed have developed socially, in the interactions of image makers and their reader or viewers. What makes visual images intelligible is that makers and users alike share common understandings about how the world – real and imaginary, outer and inner – can be represented, and about how images can be and are used. The pictures in picturebooks, for example, possess certain functions that mark them out as being different from the pictures in art galleries, car maintenance manuals or photograph albums. Our images are part of the fabric of our shared culture and are put to use for various ends. Moreover, since visual languages, just as much as verbal ones, are concerned with encoding and communicating meaning, the developed system exists as a 'semantic pool' from which those inducted into the culture may draw.

Let us examine one more example of the grammar in action. Consider the picture in *Granpa* where the old man skips along his garden path watched by his granddaughter. We could give a formal account of the image of Granpa emphasizing the fact that the figure of the old man is the most salient feature of the picture. He bears the most visual weight on account of his location, shape and

Figure 29 From *Granpa* by John Burningham.

size, but this would not tell us a great deal about how the organization of the image structures the meaning. If, however, we transpose the analysis into the terms of functional grammar we might say that Granpa is here a major participant who is an actor involved in a non-transactional action process: that is, he is doing something, but not doing it to, or aiming it at, anyone else. His depicted action has no goal and is thus analogous to the category of 'intransitive verb' in verbal language. In words we might say, 'Granpa is skipping'.

If we now look at the whole picture rather than just the image of Granpa we can identify a further participant, the granddaughter. Once again, in formal terms we could say that although she is a relatively small figure she gains weight and salience through her overlapping of the house in the background where the regular oval of her head stands out against the rectilinear shapes behind. Also, positioned as she is to the far left of the picture she balances the larger figure of her Granpa just right of centre. In terms of the semantic relations within the picture, however, and employing the terms of functional grammar again, we might say that here there are two major participants, one a *reactor* (the girl) who through the eyeline of her gaze creates a vector that involves her in a *transactional* process (watching) directed towards a *phenomenon* (Granpa skipping). Transcoded into verbal language, we might say, 'the girl is watching Granpa skipping'.

Analyses of picturebooks which focus upon how the images work have been influential in the study of the picturebook since at least the 1980s and one can see perfectly well why this should be so. It seems fairly obvious that the more one knows about how pictures come to possess meaning seemingly cannot fail to be of value in our researches into how the picturebook works. Kress and van Leeuwen's grammar, for example, helps us to understand more clearly how the pictures in a book like *Gorilla* contribute to the story. Once we begin to notice reaction processes in pictures we soon realize that although the printed text tells us what Hannah, her father and the gorilla did, either by themselves or to and with one another, the pictures show more looking and watching than doing. There are scenes of action (Hannah's father works at his desk and walks to work, Hannah walks upstairs and rushes down again the following morning, and the gorilla swings through the trees and climbs the wall of the zoo) but many of these processes, such as the small scenes of walking to and from home, contribute little semantically to the unfolding story and function almost like the grammatical words in a sentence, a kind of connective tissue linking the parts of the story together.

In contrast, the scenes involving reaction processes seem highly significant. In its pictorial aspect, *Gorilla* is very much a book concerned with looking and being looked at. In the opening pages Hannah is shown reading a book, looking at television and watching her unresponsive father. He in turn reads the newspaper and ignores his daughter. All these images confirm the girl's isolation and alienation from her surroundings. To make matters worse, as I have already observed, Hannah's father never makes eye contact with his daughter, and this is true even at the end of the book when he stands behind Hannah to look at her birthday card, and despite the fact that the printed text says that she looked at him. In none of these scenes is there any 'bi-directionality' to the reaction processes. In contrast, once the toy gorilla has apparently come to life (watched, of course, by the horrified doll), Hannah and the gorilla do little else but gaze into each others' eyes, the vectors of their eyelines following the same path. They then look at the gorillas in the zoo, though here their looking is merely implied as they are positioned with their backs to the reader, and later we see them several more times face to face although again, in only one of these latter scenes are Hannah and the gorilla actually depicted with an eyeline connecting them. They have eyes closed as they kiss goodnight and are swivelled through ninety degrees so that Hannah has her back to the reader as they dance. This selective use of uni-directionality and bi-directionality in reaction processes makes a powerful contribution to the meaning of the story. The real father cannot be reached and the close social bond established and maintained through the primary sense of sight is transferred to a substitute father in the shape of the gorilla.

In cases such as this an increased sensitivity to pictorial structures seems to be extremely helpful. One might have spotted the 'looking and watching' theme without knowing about reaction processes but the systematic and organized nature of the grammar provides us with a way to focus our looking. Even so, when we come to analyse picturebooks we can only make use of our increased understanding of visual structures if we combine it with other kinds of knowledge. Our understanding of reaction processes in *Gorilla* would have been of limited use if we had not already known a good deal about Browne's story. Analyses of the pictures in picturebooks always need to be fed into an understanding of the book as a whole, and if our fine dissections of structure do not help us to understand more about the story to which they are contributing then they are of limited use to us.

Grammar, however, is not the end of the road. In the next chapter I make some provisional suggestions about how pictures in picturebooks might be re-described in such a way that we are able to see how much more is involved in understanding them than the ability to analyse them aesthetically, semiotically and grammatically.

Notes

1   Burningham's style in this book, and elsewhere, presents the unwary reader with many opportunities for misunderstanding. In several of the extracts that follow it is the children's mis-readings that are illuminating.

2   This is a complex concluding image. As I have already remarked in Chapter 4, Hannah does not look at her father despite what the text says. On the other hand, the red of their clothing undeniably draws them much closer together than they were at the beginning of the book.

3   I am grateful to Vanessa Burdon for allowing me to reproduce some of her unpublished work involving children discussing picturebooks.

4   Two attempts to adapt Kress and van Leeuwen's grammar to children's picturebooks are:

   Unsworth, L. 'Exploring multi-modal meaning in literature for children' in, Unsworth, L. (forthcoming), and Williams, G. (1998) 'Children entering literate worlds'. See also, Williams, G. (1996) 'Reading and literacy'.

5   See, for example, Halliday, M. A. K. (1985) *An Introduction to Functional Grammar*.

6   See Halliday, M. A. K. (1978) *Language as Social Semiotic: the Social Interpretation of Language and Meaning*.

Chapter 8

How do picturebooks come to possess meaning?

Language is a labyrinth of paths. You approach from one side and know your way about; you approach the same place from another side and no longer know your way about.

(Wittgenstein 1968: Remark 203)

Introduction

In the last chapter I reviewed some of the ways in which we could be said to read pictures. This involved looking at how the structure of images influences their meaning as well as how their individual features contribute to what we make of them. But there is much more involved in understanding the meaning of picturebook illustrations than this. In order to understand what that 'more' might involve, we need to be able to see the question of how pictures in picturebooks come to have meaning in a new way, and that will involve us in shifting our ground to get beyond where we now stand to gain a new perspective, a new way of looking at the subject. One of the ways we can re-orient ourselves in relation to a topic is to re-describe it, to enfold it in a different vocabulary so that the labels we attach to it are slightly alien, making it, to some extent, unfamiliar.

I propose to tackle the question of how picturebook pictures mean – and by extension, how picturebooks themselves mean – from the point of view of one the twentieth century's most influential philosophers, Ludwig Wittgenstein, a figure much concerned with the question of how things come to possess meaning. Philosophy may seem rather remote from the writing, illustrating and reading of picturebooks and it may seem to be a little late in the day to be introducing a new theoretical perspective on the topic, but there is much in Wittgenstein's later writings that may help us to see picturebooks in the fresh light that we need. I also hope to show that much of what Wittgenstein has to say about pictures, language and meaning sits very comfortably alongside the kinds of things that I have been arguing throughout.

Natural history, language games and forms of life

I do not propose to go very deeply into the complexities of Wittgenstein's thought, but a little background will be necessary before we can begin to make use of his insights. His first philosophical writings, published in 1921, were concerned to establish, once and for all, exactly how language maps on to the world of facts and what conditions must exist for language to be able to represent the world of facts accurately.[1] Later, in the years between 1929 and 1951, he came to reject the views expressed in this work and began to revise his approach to philosophy, basing his thinking upon a close examination of the ways in which we use concepts in our everyday lives and how we express them in language. His most famous work from these years is *Philosophical Investigations*, which he left unfinished and which was published posthumously. A great deal of further, fugitive writing was collected by his students and friends, and published in a number of separate volumes.

In these later writings Wittgenstein attempted to rid philosophy of what he saw as the metaphysical dead-ends into which it had got itself. Puzzling questions such as how the mind and mental events relate to the body and the brain; how words and ideas are connected to things, and how we can possibly know anything about what others are thinking and feeling, were slowly unravelled through a patient examination of the 'deep grammar' of language. For this reason Wittgenstein is often considered to be a 'philosopher of ordinary language', although this is only partly true. He was concerned with languages rather than language, and was interested in ritual and ceremony, art and music, arithmetic and algebra as well as the speech and writing of everyday life. It would be more accurate to say of Wittgenstein that, in the words of one of his interpreters, H. L. Finch, his later philosophy was based 'on the kinds of common agreements that make cultural life possible' (Finch 1995:34).

Such common agreements or conventions were, for Wittgenstein, not simply convenient and arbitrary agreements amongst social groups, but were as 'deeply woven into the structure of human life as anything could be' (Finch 1995:34). Such a formulation brings his way of thinking quite closely into line with the preoccupations of, say, anthropologists, socio-linguists or social semioticians. However, Wittgenstein never allied himself to any school or system, either within philosophy or elsewhere and, in fact, was mistrustful of movements and schools for he saw them as placing restrictions upon thought which should – for a philosopher at least – be as untrammelled as possible. For this reason his writing, as well as his thought and teaching, tended to be aphoristic and discontinuous. *Philosophical Investigations*, for example, is largely composed of short paragraphs which he called Remarks. Sometimes these are linked together in short chains, but at other times they jump suddenly from one subject to another.

Because of his belief that the things we do and say, and the ways that we understand the world, are inextricably bound up with our natures as biological, social and cultural human animals, he came to see that languages, and the things that we mean by them, arise out of our natural history and out of particular forms of life. By the phrase 'forms of life' he meant the many modes of being and doing through which we live our lives. Following Wittgenstein, we can imagine a military form of life, a primary school teaching form of life, a book publishing form of life, a book illustrating form of life, a tennis playing form of life and so on. Embedded within such forms of life are the languages – or *language games* as Wittgenstein came to call them – which are expressive and constitutive of them.

There are potentially an infinite number of forms of life, and therefore of language games, and new ones are coming into being all the time (think of all the practices and forms of language that surround the personal computer revolution and use of the internet). It is this multiplicity of ways of using language that Wittgenstein argued is responsible for trapping us into hopeless metaphysical quandaries. He compared language to a labyrinth that could easily confuse us into believing in fantasies and illusions (see Remark 203 quoted at the head of the chapter). Consider as an example of such confusions Wittgenstein's discussion of family resemblances that I alluded to in Note 8, Chapter 1. In his Remarks on the nature of the concept of a game, he maintains that although we can limit the use, and thus the meaning, of such concepts for this or that purpose, there is no reason why we may not consider the concept of 'game' *in general* to be unbounded, or to possess 'blurred edges'. What links different games together is not some singular essence but a network of family resemblances. Part of Remark 66 in Philosophical Investigations goes like this:

> Consider for example the proceedings that we call 'games'. I mean board-games, card-games, ball games, Olympic games, and so on. What is common to them all? – Don't say: 'There *must* be something common, or they would not all be called "games" ' – but *look and see* whether there is anything common to all. – For if you look at them you will not see something that is common to *all*, but similarities, relationships, and a whole series of them at that. To repeat: don't think, but look!
>
> (Wittgenstein 1968:31)

In these few words we have an excellent example of Wittgenstein's method. He says we should not be fooled by the fact that we use exactly the same word for all these different activities. The word does not label a single common characteristic. When we look at words in this way we get ourselves into endless difficulties trying to find that one, elusive defining feature applicable in all cases. If, on the other hand, we look carefully at how we use the term in normal everyday life, we will see that we use it differently at different times; and we use it differently because we play different language games when we speak of the Olympic games and the game of snap. Moreover, these different language games arise out of quite distinct forms of life (cultural practices). Far better, then, to recognize that what makes all games 'games' is a network of overlapping features and resemblances that loosely link individual examples together.

Meaning in different ways

Many fascinating things follow from this way of looking at concepts and language in use, but here we are concerned solely with how it might help us to look at picturebooks in a new way. First we need to recognize that exactly the same argument about forms of life and language games can be applied to the concept of meaning itself. We can imagine the term 'meaning' meaning different things in different contexts as we play different language games with it. When people say, 'What I really meant was …', or when they look up the meaning of a word in a dictionary, or when they reflect on the 'meaning of life' they are not only doing different things but also pursuing different, though related, ends. So when I pose the question, 'how do picturebooks come to have meaning?' we must not necessarily expect to find a single answer. Scattered throughout Wittgenstein's writings are references to four different ways in which human beings make sense of the world. Although he never gathered them together anywhere or codified them in any way, he returns time and again to four distinctive dimensions, or aspects, of meaning. These are: meaning as physiognomy, or what he sometimes called 'face'; meaning as use; meaning as custom, and meaning as rule-following. In what follows I explain each of these dimensions and try to show how they might open up different perspectives on the picturebook.[2]

Meaning as 'face' or physiognomy

At various points throughout *Philosophical Investigations*, Wittgenstein maintains that we often recognize what something 'means' in the way that we recognize a face. We do not have to think about it, we simply recognize it when we see it. We simply 'read off' its meaning in the act of recognition. He famously distinguished between seeing something and recognizing it for what it is on the one hand, and 'seeing as', or seeing something under a particular aspect, on the other. If, for example, I look at a random group of shapes that I have doodled on my notepad I might say, 'if I try hard, I can see this as a horse, but if I look at it another way I can see it as a tree'. We are all familiar with the kind of drawing that is deliberately designed to create ambiguity so that at one moment a particular arrangement of lines appears to represent an old woman's face and then moments later we seem to see a young woman in a full skirt and feathered hat. In *Philosophical Investigations* Wittgenstein used the well-known alternating image of the 'duck–rabbit' to distinguish between this kind of 'aspect seeing' and the circumstances of normal perception. Although it is perfectly reasonable to speak of the drawing as looking now like a duck, and now like a rabbit, it makes no sense at all to speak of the arrangement of shapes and volumes in front of me as looking like a keyboard. Nor does it make any sense to say, when I look to one side of my keyboard, that I see an assemblage of black plastic and shiny metal as a reading lamp. When I look at these things I simply see a keyboard and a lamp. Their meaning, their sense, is immediately apparent to me and there have to be very special circumstances for me to want to say that I am seeing them as something.

If we apply this way of thinking to the perception of visual images, we can see that unless there are special circumstances of ambiguity or obscurity, the pictures in picturebooks deliver up their meaning directly. When I turn the pages of, say, *Lady Muck*, I see pictures of pigs and parts of pigs in various positions and from various angles. If I am asked, 'What do you see?' I might say, 'I see a pig rubbing its rump against a tree', or alternatively, 'I see a picture of a pig rubbing its rump …'. What I am unlikely to say is, 'I see an arrangement of lines and colours as a picture of a pig'. This of course just sounds foolish, but more is at stake here than proper or improper uses of language. The sentences do not just dress up the experience in more or less appropriate words and phrases, they give us important clues about how we understand or misunderstand the world around us. Wittgenstein always recommended looking closely at how we use artefacts, images or words in normal circumstances to try and untangle the confusions that language can lead us into. In this case we have a useful corrective against some of the misunderstandings into which semiotics might lead us.

Semiotics has taught us to think of words and pictures in terms of *signification*, that is, in terms of signifiers and the meanings, or signifieds, that attach to them; but ways of analysing and investigating pictures like the ones outlined in the previous chapter naturally tend to focus upon the signifiers: the shapes, volumes, lines, colours, structures, participants and vectors that can be identified within the images. These are the perfectly proper subject matter of semiotic analysis, but attention to such features should not lead us into believing that when we look at a picturebook we are somehow seeing lines, shapes and colours to which we apply meaning. Meaning does not have to be read into the signifiers on the page, we simply read off the meaning of what we see from the image before us. In *Lady Muck* we see pigs, in *Think of an Eel*, eels, in *So Much*, humans at play.

We see this perfectly clearly in the way children look at and talk about picturebook pictures. 'It catches the monkey and it goes back to its nest …' says Jane; 'He drops it into the sea,' says Martin, and 'She's punched the king in!' exclaims Nathan. Only when there are problems or ambiguities – that is, special circumstances – do the children resort to looking closely at the individual features of the picture and attending to the image's material nature. Nathan notices the rigid lines on Shirley's towel and remarks, 'That looks like a fan', a perfect example of seeing an aspect: 'seeing as' rather than simply seeing.

What this suggests is that if we wish to understand more about how picturebooks are put together and how words and images interanimate one another we are going to have to pay far more attention to the ways in which readers perceive them, and to do this we must pay attention to what they say about what they see. Much more is needed than the systematic analysis that semiotics provides. I have already tried to suggest the importance and useful-ness of listening closely to what children tell us as they read, but consider two further examples.

Here is Nathan right at the beginning of *Where is Monkey?*

N: Well there he's playing with ... there he's making a cage for the monkey.
DL: Hmm
N: There she's taking the little boy to the wood with the monkey and there they're feeding the ducks ... and he thinks it's a worm.

He comments on each of the pictures in turn telling me not only what he sees but also how he interprets what he sees. This in turn helps me to see the book differently. As an adult I begin for the first time to notice the ambiguity at the beginning of the book that I discussed in Chapter 7. I see that for Nathan the boy and his mother are going to a wood and not a park and, most inter-esting of all, I realize how, in the final frame, Nathan's looking is different from mine. As the ducks crane their necks to peck at Monkey's dangling tail his owner reaches upwards to keep his precious toy out of the reach of the hungry birds ('he [a duck] thinks it's a worm ...'). Nathan is about the same age as the boy in the story and he looks at the picture as a fellow toy-owner. Furthermore, he allows the pantomime of snapping beak and protective gesture to take him inside the duck's head ('he thinks ...'). In contrast, I see the beginnings of a story about a fond parent taking her son out for the afternoon. I 'see' the hungry duck, of course, and yet I do not see it. At least I do not see it as Nathan sees it. Adult and child, we look differently and therefore see different things.

Here again is Jane using what she sees in Jill Murphy's *On the Way Home*. Having read some of the story together I try to prompt her into thinking about where all Claire's stories come from. I'm intrigued by the fact that each story makes use of a stock character from children's popular culture – fairy tales, science fiction and the like – but Jane has noticed something that I have missed.

DL: Where do you think she gets her stories from? I mean, she makes up a lot of stories doesn't she?
J: 'Cos the swing sort of did drop her didn't it? ... because she fell off ... and in all the stories it's dropping isn't it?
DL: Oh I see. She gets dropped every time doesn't she?

Jane is not interested in my agenda; indeed why should she be? She is far more alert than I am to the way in which each tall tale involves a fancy-dress version of the original experience of falling off a swing and hitting the ground with a bump. Once again, Jane's looking teaches me to see the book differently.

Meaning as use

Much of the early part of *Philosophical Investigations* is given over to the argument that in order to discover how it is that words possess meaning for us in speech and writing we should attend to how we use them. More than once Wittgenstein likened language to a tool-box.

> Think of the tools in a tool-box: there is a hammer, pliers, a saw, a screwdriver, a rule, a glue-pot, glue, nails and screws. – The functions of words are as diverse as the functions of these objects ... what confuses us is the uniform appearance of words when we hear them spoken or meet them in script or print. For their *application* is not presented to us so clearly.
>
> (Wittgenstein 1968:6)

Halliday's functional grammar referred to in the previous chapter is based upon similar principles. Words and groups of words possess meaning for us – that is, meaning in use – by virtue of the functions they perform. Words are not simply labels, they get things done within the language and within the world as people speak and write.

In Wittgensteinian terms, of course, much will also depend upon the language game you happen to be playing. For example, the single word 'plate' might possess a whole range of different functions according to where and when and how it is used. In a classroom, a non-English speaker might be taught the word as part of the process of learning the correct labels for everyday objects, whereas in a busy restaurant kitchen a harassed chef might bellow the word at one of his underlings when a dish is ready to be served. The function, the use to which the word is put, gives us the meaning.

If we now turn our attention to the visual codes of pictures we can see that the same considerations apply. The meaningfulness of a picture for any particular viewer will not depend solely upon his or her ability to read off its representational sense – whether it shows a pig, an eel or a human being – but will also depend upon the function, the use to which the picture is put. In the case of the pictures in picturebooks, this is first and foremost a matter of contributing to a sequence which in most cases, though not all, serves to engender a narrative. Apart from the first and last images in a picturebook the pictures are always preceded and succeeded by other pictures and the whole is held together in reading through ecological processes of anticipation and retrospection, along with the interanimation of word and image.

The peculiar function of picturebook pictures is strikingly revealed when we set them alongside other kinds of pictures serving other ends. We mount family photographs in albums and use them as a record and as an aid to memory, to remind ourselves of high points in our lives and to live these over again in imagination. We visit art galleries and summon up particular kinds of knowledge and sensitivity to enjoy specifically aesthetic sensations. We scan catalogues and holiday brochures – with a critical eye, if we have any sense – using the artfully composed photographs to help us in our judgements of what and whether to purchase. Sometimes picturebook pictures are used for ends other than the ones for which they were created. Print shops often remove illustrations from books and frame them, turning them into free-standing art objects, and every year a prestigious gallery in London mounts an exhibition of the work of children's illustrators where original drawings and paintings by figures such as Edward Ardizzone, E. H. Shepard and Quentin Blake may be bought and savoured, not just aesthetically, but as investments.

If we are to understand picturebook pictures, therefore, we must recognize and understand their particular function. This much is uncontroversial and hardly new, but less often acknowledged are the 'language games' that are played with and around picturebooks and what these reveal about the forms of life into which they might fit. Thus the same picture, or set of pictures, might be viewed and understood quite differently by different groups of people or at different times. For example, a 'big book' version of *The Park in the Dark* might be used in early years' classrooms during literacy lessons (Martin Waddell and Barbara Firth's popular *Can't You Sleep Little Bear* is often used in British class-rooms for this purpose). Typically a whole class would read the book together under the direction of a teacher during Shared Reading times. The emphasis might be placed upon understanding and enjoying the story, but equally the teacher might direct the children's attention to some feature of the language, its vocabulary, grammar or textual formation. In these circumstances Barbara Firth's pictures would tend to be somewhat marginalized as the focus of the ten or fifteen minutes would be largely upon learning about some feature of language use. At best the pictures might be taken as props or prompts in the service of a language-learning task.

Later on the same day, however, the same book might be shared as bedtime reading by one of the children in the class with a parent or sibling. In these circumstances parent and child, through negotiation and joint agreement, might reverse priorities and focus almost exclusively upon the pictures. Questions such as 'What are the toys doing now?' might be asked and discussed and parallels between the toys' behaviour and feelings and those of the child considered. The visceral thrill of rushing through the air on the swings in the park might be recovered through talk and play as child and parent examine the picture depicting the toys in the playground.

Elsewhere the same picture might be the subject of a student assignment in the semiotics of the visual image, and the page-opening in question, along with others from the same book scrutinized for features that will submit to the kinds of analysis discussed in the last chapter. Where child and parent enter into an imaginative recreation of the toys' nocturnal adventure, the semiotician is more likely to focus upon vectors, actors and processes. It might be objected that these three different contexts and uses of the visual image are not entirely mutually exclusive; after all, the adult student can still enjoy the imaginative experience and in learning to read at school, the child cannot completely ignore the pictures that accompany the words. Nonetheless, the ways in which readers and viewers use the illustrations substantially affects how they understand them and what it is they are doing. There is, for example, no shortage of anecdotal evidence that children often consider reading for pleasure at home and learning to read at school as two entirely different activities.

Meaning as custom

There is a strong temptation for citizens of the technologically developed west to view the making of meaning through ritual and custom as something peculiar to pre-modern societies. Where tribal dances and ritual forms of greeting still exist we are more likely to find them as part of a tourist package, tailored to entertain visitors to exotic lands, than as part of a living society. We certainly would not expect such forms of behaviour to have a role in twenty-first century culture, yet Wittgenstein is adamant that ritual and custom are fundamental to all human culture and experience.

For all our apparent freedom from the constraining customs and ceremonies of the past, we still order our lives according to routines and patterns that exercise a high degree of influence upon our behaviour. We still greet people in characteristic ways; we manage meetings and behave within them in a highly ritualistic fashion; there are customs in pubs (buying rounds) and on the football field (the congratulatory huddle when goals are scored); and in Britain there are times when it is acceptable to talk to strangers (when asked for directions) and times when it is not (on buses and trains, although there are signs that this venerable custom is changing). Some forms of life are more clearly structured around routines and rituals than others, and some areas of our lives are relatively free of rigid constraint, but there are few moments in the day when we are not subject to at least some form of behavioural regularity (how many people cannot turn out the light at night without reading at least one page of a book or magazine?)

Not all ritualistic forms of life are associated with typical uses of language – Wittgenstein's language games – but they do all involve characteristic uses of the body. For Wittgenstein ritual is first and foremost a kind of body language. We make use of a whole lexicon of facial expressions, gestures and postures when we enter into even commonplace forms of ritualistic behaviour. It is never enough to learn the appropriate forms of words or the correct ways of speaking, whenever these are necessary; you have to learn what to do with your physical self, how to hold yourself, when to nod, when to smile, when to come close and when to withdraw. Think of the religious and military forms of life (two institutions suffused with ceremony and ritual) and then think of the extent to which 'body language' enters into them: the kneeling, standing, sitting, bowing of heads, prostration, closing of eyes in the former, and the saluting, marching, presenting of arms, emphasis upon carriage and bearing, turning of heads, etc., in the latter. But it would be a mistake to imagine that in acting in these situation-specific ways, and in the rather less rigidly constrained forms of everyday life, we were simply 'acting out' roles or following rules. Rituals, customs and routines are structured at the deepest level by these patterns of behaviour in much the same way that utterances, either in speech or writing, are governed by generic patterns.[3]

If we consider the ways in which the pictures in picturebooks, and indeed picturebooks themselves, are involved in ritualistic ways of behaving, it is not difficult to find contexts and circumstances where young children are introduced to particular ways of handling, using and understanding the images with which they are presented. In fact, some of the research referred to earlier in Chapter 5 treats directly of the ways in which pre-school children are inducted into how to talk about the pictures in picturebooks. In an article in the *Journal of Child Language* entitled, 'Turn the page please: situation specific language learning', Catherine Snow and Beverly Goldfield discuss recordings of a mother and child looking at and talking about the illustrations in Richard Scarry's *Storybook Dictionary*. The same pictures were returned to over and over again, each time eliciting the same language from both parent and child. Snow and Goldfield begin with an acknowledgement of the vital role that routine plays in such interactions and then 'trace the child's acquisition of the linguistic means for talking about a given picture' (Snow and Goldfield 1983:551). They then try to identify what it is about the routine of repeatedly discussing a picture that enables a child to do it for herself.

They propose that what the child learns is a strategy that can be used elsewhere with other pictures and books and at times when the adult is not present, but they display a curious ambivalence about the processes involved in the way in which they write about them. Several times they refer to a 'mechanism of acquisition' but elsewhere write of an 'acquisition strategy'. The use of these two terms, 'mechanism', and 'strategy', suggests a vacillating between what are, in fact, two incompatible views of human behaviour. If what is acquired is a mechanism then it does not make sense to speak of a child's actions – his or her learning to talk about pictures in a specific way – as something that he or she does. To ask 'what is the mechanism?' is to ask how the machinery works. Mechanisms are something over which we have no control; they are things that happen to us, or within us, rather than activities in which we actively and consciously engage. On the other hand, the term 'strategy' suggests something far too self-conscious; a way of proceeding that has been decided beforehand according to consciously understood rules. In the authors' terms children learn to 'identify a situation, remember what is said in it, say [it] … the next time the situation recurs' (Snow and Goldfield 1983:567), but this is to confuse rule-governed behaviour with rule-following behaviour. Our actions are rule-governed when they exhibit regularities such as when our morning routines carry us from the bathroom to the breakfast table to the bus stop in the same way every working day. We are rule following when we see what we have to do to achieve certain ends and consciously take up and attempt to follow those rules. When pre-school children pick up picturebooks, look at them and talk about them in certain ways, it is highly unlikely that they are self-consciously following rules or acting strategically.

Why do Snow and Goldfield slip into this confusion? Part of the reason I believe is that they work with a reductive and attenuated notion of a routine, the repeated situation in which the learning takes place. Indeed they deliberately exclude from consideration everything other than what they consider to be the key factor of looking at the picture. 'The situation is defined by the act of looking at a particular page in a particular book; other factors such as time of day, location of the activity, and previous or subsequent activities, are irrelevant to the situation' (Snow and Goldfield 1983:553). Wittgenstein's notion of routine and custom grounded in bodily action seems to me to be closer to the truth of what actually happens. When children learn from their parents and care-givers how to handle, look at, read and interpret the pictures in picturebooks they do so in routinized social contexts that involve practices – ways of sitting, looking, sharing, page-turning, pointing and so on – in which are embedded the processes of conversational turn-taking and information exchange (the picturebook language game). They do not simply trade disembodied words and ideas. The process is neither mechanistic, nor is it super-rationalistic. It is structured through more or less settled dispositions to behave in certain ways that guide and focus the child reader's attention, understanding and ability to interpret and question.

This kind of process can be seen even more clearly in the way that classroom practices in literacy teaching are changing in British schools. The National Literacy Strategy introduced in 1998 not only established comprehensive teaching objectives in reading and writing, but, more radically, prescribed particular teaching methods. Shared and Guided Reading require that classes and groups of children behave in particular ways. Interactional routines are specified and times for speaking to the teacher and times for remaining silent are strictly managed. In effect this amounts to an attempt to determine once and for all the routines and customs of the literacy classroom and a crucial part of the process involves managing the children's behaviour, not simply what they read, to whom and when.

Meaning as rule-following

This is probably the least helpful aspect of meaning as far as our understanding of pictures in picturebooks is concerned. Wittgenstein's preoccupation with rule-following was in large part determined by his desire to demystify, or de-metaphysicalize our understanding of language and of the world. In brief, his view was that rules were fundamentally a matter of convention and cultural practice, and that this was the case whether the rules in question were those governing a game (let us say, chess) or a mathematical procedure (say, the rules for generating a number sequence). For Wittgenstein, there are no mysterious essences lying beyond the sets of rules that we follow. Rules do not give us access to something that pre-existed their formulation; they are not windows upon a secret realm of meaning. The meaning arises directly out of the following of the rules.

The meaningfulness of rule-following for children is nicely captured in an essay entitled, 'The role of play in development' from *Mind in Society* by the Russian psychologist Lev Vygotsky (Vygotsky 1978). He shows clearly how children's earliest games involving imaginative play rely heavily upon rule-following. He argues that forms of imaginative play such as pretending a cardboard box is a car, or a cushion wrapped in a blanket is a baby, first arise when children begin to experience desires that cannot immediately be satisfied. They would like to be grown-ups, to drive cars and to nurse babies, so they re-create such experiences in imagination using appropriate objects as props. In the course of the game the objects lose their determining force and cease to behave like boxes and cushions. They take on new meanings within the game (cushion = baby, box = car) and this is brought about by the children's actions which are in turn governed by what they see the grown-ups doing. In other words, in order to enjoy the game you have to play 'according to the rules' (that is, doing what the adults do). Following the rules delivers up the meaning, the desired new experience.

That there is rule-following involved in the reading of picturebooks the work of Snow and Ninio demonstrates quite clearly. You have to learn what to do with the pictures and the book if you are to get anything out of them. There are ways of behaving, rules to follow if you are to animate and interanimate the words and the images. But this kind of rule-following is in need of heavy qualification. To begin with, as I tried to show in Chapter 5, learning how to follow the rules is more often than not accompanied by a fair amount of rule breaking. Once you have mastered the rules you are then at liberty to test them by inverting them and trying them out in different contexts. In the process of learning, the proper use of the rules goes hand in hand with their improper use.

More importantly, however, we should recall that Snow and Ninio refer to contracts and not rules. The term 'contracts' suggests something negotiated, the result of repeated processes of interaction and exchange between adult and infant. Moreover, we know that the learning involved tends to take place in heavily routinized situations. Ritual and custom play a very important part in children's early book experiences and we have already seen how rule-governed behaviour can easily come to seem like rule-following behaviour. Children do not learn to read and understand picturebooks as they might, at a later date, learn to play a new board game: by reading the rules and attempting to apply them. The processes involved are much more akin to being inducted into a cultural practice. For Wittgenstein, the following of rules and the following of rituals and routines both grow from the same root stock: the deep conventionality of human behaviour. We do things in the way that we do because we have a natural history, a way of living and being that leads us into particular forms of life with their attendant language games.

Where does this leave us? In attempting to escape a one-dimensional language, be it art-critical or semiotic, it is tempting to look for a path that will lead us to the 'correct' way to think about picturebooks, to search for a language that will enable a proper way of looking, a proper response and a proper form of analysis. But the first very general lesson we can learn from Wittgenstein is that we gain meaning from picturebooks in a number of different ways. This in turn suggests that from the point of view of academic study there might be a number of different routes into appreciating and understanding the subject. We can apply the methods of semiotic analysis to picturebook images or look for the ways in which pictures and words interanimate one another. We can try to understand the picturebook as an object of aesthetic contemplation or as an imaginative experience for a child. We can understand it as embedded in its contexts of use, both constrained and enabled by routines and rituals. All of these possibilities are open to us by virtue of the fact that picturebooks can be and are seen under a number of different aspects: they deliver up their meanings to us in a number of ways. But I am not at all persuaded that all perspectives are equally useful, and this is because from Wittgenstein we learn a further lesson. This is that as human beings we are able to understand each other's meanings because at bottom we are like each other, we share a natural history. In one of his more gnomic Remarks, Wittgenstein said that 'If a lion could talk, we could not understand him' (Wittgenstein 1968:223). In other words, the 'form of life' a lion takes is so far removed from our own that even if a lion had language and even if we could understand that language, we could not understand *him*. Human meanings and human understandings are rooted in our distinctive forms of life – in our natural history – and in the end that is why I believe that however we go about our reflections and analyses, we will always weaken our understanding of picturebooks if we remove them from the natural and normal contexts of their use.

The purpose of this book has been to explore the nature of a relatively new and not particularly well-understood form of text. I have tried to avoid too many preconceptions and attempted to follow Wittgenstein's advice to look closely and only then to think about what you find (' ... don't think, but look!') Of course, processes of reflection are never so straightforward and are probably much more like an interanimation of what you see with what you know. I began with a small corpus of books which I take to be reasonably representative of the form as a whole, and have drawn – rather eclectically – upon ways of thinking about them that I hope go some way towards explaining why they are how they are. I have no doubt that there is much missing from my account, but I hope that an image of something like the contemporary children's picturebook is recognizable in what I have written.

For me the charm and the challenge of the picturebook arise directly out of its variety and versatility, its capacity for endless metamorphosis. We never quite know how the next generation of picturebooks will look. The capacity for genre incorporation will always ensure new words, new images and new combinations of word and image. The picturebook is thus ideally suited to the task of absorbing, reinterpreting and re-presenting the world to an audience for whom negotiating newness is a daily task. It is not an insignificant fact that the reading of picturebooks commonly takes place at the point where adult, child and the wider culture meet. The image of parent and child sharing a favourite picturebook is a key one, and it should remind us that in order to understand the book we need to understand its role in the complex interchange of gesture, language, ideas and images that go to make up the picturebook reading event. Formal accounts of the picturebook will, in the end, never be enough.

Perhaps this is the place to return to Barbara Bader and the words with which I opened this book. They make an equally good way of ending.

> A picturebook is text, illustrations, total design; an item of manufacture and a commercial product; a social, cultural, historical document; and, foremost, an experience for a child.
>
> As an art form it hinges on the interdependence of pictures and words, on the simultaneous display of two facing pages, and on the drama of the turning of the page.
>
> On its own terms its possibilities are limitless.
>
> (Prefatory note to Bader 1976:1)

Notes

1   The *Tactatus Logico-Philosophicus.*

2   In the account that follows I have drawn heavily upon certain chapters in Henry Le Roy Finch's *Wittgenstein* (Finch 1995).

3   The anthropologist and sociologist Pierre Bourdieu has made similar observations. He argues that ritualistic and customary human behaviour is organized and regulated by more or less stable dispositions to act in certain ways. These dispositions he refers to as 'habitus'. It is characteristic of the habitus that it is rooted in the body, in activity, in things people do. Habitus is engendered through involvement in the repeated patterns of life, patterns that can be observed, measured and recorded: characteristic postures, gestures, eye-movements, expressions, words, pauses, laughter, frowns, etc. However, this is not to be confused with behaviourist operant conditioning; belief is necessary to the formation of habitus in the sense that one has to belong, to submit willingly to the routine and the rituals. Bourdieu remarks, '... one cannot enter this magic circle by an instantaneous decision of the will, but only by birth, or by a slow process of co-option and initiation which is equivalent to a second birth' (Bourdieu 1992:68).

Developments in printing technology: bringing words and pictures together

Early techniques

Woodcuts

The bringing together of words and pictures on the same page has not been straightforward. The technologies required for printing verbal text and pictorial imagery have not always been compatible and at various periods during the development of the picturebook this incompatibility has kept the two media apart. From its beginnings in the workshops of Gutenberg and Caxton almost to the present day the printing of words has relied upon the design of the letters being raised in relief from the base of the printing block. The raised surface is inked and then pressed into the paper leaving behind the desired image. Other ways of printing letters and words have been devised, but the technologies of typecasting and printing first developed by Gutenberg in the middle of the fifteenth century were not seriously challenged for 400 years. Pictures on the other hand can be, and have been, printed in a number of different ways.

In the early days of the printed and illustrated book, most pictures were printed from woodcuts. These were well suited to the newly developed movable type as they could be fitted into the layout for a page, inked along with the letterpress and the two printed simultaneously. Woodcuts, however, have their limitations. They are cut from the plank side of a wooden block, the side that shows the line of the grain, and this makes them prone to splitting and warping. Furthermore, the technique of gouging away the unwanted wood so that the design appears in relief lends itself to the depiction of objects and figures in outline, rather like the images in a child's colouring book. More sophisticated effects of modelling and shading can be achieved but it took European artists of the stature of Albrecht Dürer, Albrecht Altdorfer and Hans Holbein the Younger to raise the technique of printing from woodcuts to a fine art. In Britain the woodcut remained a relatively crude and under-developed approach to print-making though it survived well enough as the favoured medium of chapbook and broadsheet printers.

Engraving on metal

Greater precision and sophistication could be achieved through engraving on copper, but to produce an image from an engraved metal plate requires a different kind of printing press from that used with letterpress. Engravings are produced by incising lines into the metal using a variety of sharpened tools. Ink is then pressed into the fine grooves and any surplus remaining on the surface of the plate wiped away. The image is then produced by passing both plate and paper through a much heavier press than that required for the printing of letterpress, so that the ink can be lifted from the grooves onto the paper. In terms of book production this meant that in order to have an engraving sited next to the text a page needed to be put through two different printing presses: a costly business. The alternatives were either to engrave text and illustration on the same plate (a simple enough process but one which loses the revolutionary flexibility of movable type) or to reserve illustrations for separate pages which could be bound in anywhere. Such a procedure was fine for the occasional illustration, but it clearly could not lead to the development of a composite form of text.

For a variety of reasons, not all of them deriving from the limitations of the available technology, early children's books often lacked illustration of any sort, although there were notable exceptions such as the celebrated *Orbis Sensualium Pictus* of Johann Comenius. This remarkable book, part Latin primer, part pictorial encyclopaedia and part instrument of social and educational reform, was first published in 1658 in Nuremberg and translated into English by Charles Hoole the following year. It purported to bring together the names and pictures of everything known to mankind from the materials and techniques of the stonemason to the varieties of 'Deformed and Monftrous People' and was illustrated throughout at every page-opening. (Interestingly, the illustrations for the first edition were printed from woodcuts but the translation made use of engravings causing Hoole much concern over the 'dearnesse of the book by reason of the brasse cuts in it' (quoted in Sadler 1968). The *Orbis Pictus* is often referred to as the first picturebook for children and it was clearly carefully designed so that at all points in the book related words and images were simultaneously present to the reader. Bettina Hurlimann maintains that in the *Orbis Pictus* '... the relationship between text and picture is so close that it is quite unthinkable that they were produced separately' (Hurlimann 1967:131). Not surprisingly, the work proved to be immensely popular and was translated and reprinted many times.

Wood engraving

Despite the immediate popularity and subsequent longevity of the *Orbis Pictus*, Comenius' example was not widely followed and it was not until the end of the eighteenth century that pictures became commonplace in books for the young.

The figure from this period who exercised the greatest influence upon the development of the printed illustration in Britain was undoubtedly Thomas Bewick. Bewick revolutionized the production of images from wooden blocks by working upon the end grain surface of the wood rather than the plank side. By using extremely hard and dense boxwood blocks he was able to achieve imagery of great delicacy through a process that came to be known as wood engraving. The term 'engraving' is misleading, however, for the technique is not an intaglio process like engraving upon metal, but is a relief process like the woodcut.

Bewick's approach came to be known as 'white line' engraving. The traditional woodcut block often resulted in images that were simply blank white spaces bounded by black lines. White line engraving meant that the image was coaxed from the void of the uncut block not by creating bounding lines but by producing shades and textures through a myriad of tiny white lines incised in the block. A direct result of this refinement was that it became possible for wood engravers to depict, relatively cheaply and easily, accurate renderings of gesture, posture, expression, etc. In fact, as Doonan (1989) points out, by the middle of the nineteenth century wood engraving had developed to great heights of realistic representation. Furthermore, Bewick approached wood engraving with a distinctly narrative sensibility (Alderson 1986). This can be seen most clearly in his 'tale-pieces', the little vignettes that he created to follow the depictions of animals and birds in his books *History of Quadrupeds* and *History of Birds*. In these little scenes he drew upon the landscape and figures of his native Northumberland to create little snapshots of life in action that seem to beg for explanation in the form of a story.

Wood engraving thus became a highly suitable medium for producing pictures that could be fully integrated with words into a truly composite text, and during the nineteenth century the processes involved were adapted and modified to accommodate the introduction of colour. By the 1830s a printer called George Baxter was producing coloured images by first of all printing the design from a metal key plate in a neutral tint and then applying the separate colours with a series of woodblocks. At first the process was expensive and was used only for work such as coloured frontispieces, but later in the century production costs were reduced and long print runs made colour illustrations commercially viable. The final step in the creation of a fully composite form of picturebook text was taken towards the end of the century when the printer Edmund Evans recognized the need for illustrators who were able to conceive of the books they worked on as integrated wholes. He recognized and fostered the talents of a number of illustrators, most famously, Walter Crane, Randolph Caldecott and Kate Greenaway. Crane was the first to work with Evans on new, improved versions of the simple form of nineteenth-century picturebook known as the toy book. These were so successful that he was quickly drawn into other related projects, designing wallpapers, tiles and furnishings. Crane was eventually unable to maintain his output of three toy books per year, and in 1878 Caldecott was persuaded to fill the gap. The result was a small body of work that set a standard in picturebook design and illustration that has rarely been surpassed.

By this reckoning we might put the age of the picturebook at something over 100 years, although such a method of dating hardly does justice to the full circumstances of the picturebook's development. What we can say with some confidence is that, despite their old-fashioned pseudo-eighteenth century air, Caldecott's toy books are genuine interweavings of words and pictures and as such they fully meet the most basic criterion for the picturebook. Caldecott's work exercised a powerful influence upon twentieth century illustrators such as Beatrix Potter and L. Leslie Brooke but by the end of the nineteenth century printing technology was undergoing rapid change and the refined wood engraving techniques developed by Evans and his fellow printers were soon to be superseded. In particular it was the application of photography to printing that undermined and gradually marginalized the wood engravers, and once more moved illustration away from the close integration of word and image.

Later developments

Photo-mechanical processes

From the beginning the effect of photography upon the printing industry was to assist in its mechanization. By the end of the 1860s photography was already being used to transfer drawings from paper to specially treated wood blocks ready for engraving. This simplified matters for the illustrator, as there was no longer any need to draw directly onto the block. It also enabled designs to be enlarged or reduced easily. Twenty years later photography was to mechanize the printing process further, and remove the need for the artisan-engraver entirely, when line-blocks became commercially viable. Line-blocks were created by photographically transferring drawings to specially treated zinc plates which eventually had the ground etched away with acid to leave behind images in relief of the original line drawings. These could then be printed at the same time as the letterpress. Aubrey Beardsley's distinctive black and white illustrations were produced in this way.

The line-block had limitations, however, for although it could reproduce the finest details in simple black and white, it was not able to render intermediate shades and tones. In order to reproduce such effects a further stage was introduced into the photo-mechanical process. The illustrator's original design, complete with gradations of tone, would be photographed through a finely ruled glass screen which broke it down into a series of tiny dots invisible to the naked eye. The resulting image was then transferred to a metal plate in much the same way as in the preparation of a line-block. Once printed, the image produced the illusion of graduated tones, the tiny dots being more or less densely clustered together according to the depth or lightness of the shading in the original picture. A further development of this *half-tone* process enabled pictures to be printed in colour. In the half-tone colour process the original artwork was not only photographed through a special screen, but also through coloured filters. This resulted in the production of three separate plates corresponding to the presence of the three primary colours in the original work. Each plate would be inked with the appropriate colour and the three then printed in succession, the superimposition resulting in a reproduction of the original colour scheme.

However, whereas the line-block, printing in solid black and white only, could transfer an image to many different kinds of paper, the half-tone process required a high finish, glossy surface for the tiny dots to print clearly without blurring. Once again, as with the incompatibility of letterpress and metal engraving, word and image were separated. Process work, as it became known, could result in very fine illustrations – and we particularly remember the work of artists such as Edmund Dulac and Arthur Rackham – but the technology was better suited to the production of expensive art books and gift books where the glossy illustrations were 'tipped in', that is, lightly glued onto mounting paper that was then bound into the finished product. Words and pictures could be printed together as they were in Beatrix Potter's books but her carefully crafted little books were very much the exception rather than the rule.

Lithography

The solution to the problem of how to integrate words and pictures easily and flexibly came from the development of another nineteenth-century printing technology: lithography. The process was actually discovered in the late eighteenth century by a German map inspector, Aloys Senefelder, but it was not until the 1800s that it was used commercially as a means of producing pictures for toy books and picturebooks. The process is *planographic* rather than relief or intaglio. This means that the printing surface is entirely flat rather than raised up from a base or incised into a plate. The technology involved rests upon the fact that grease and water repel each other. In its earliest and simplest form the image to be printed was drawn upon a smoothly ground block of limestone with oil-based ink or a greasy lithographic chalk (the literal meaning of lithography is 'drawing on stone'). Any pigment in the ink or chalk can be removed with a solvent leaving the grease behind in the stone. The stone is then wetted, the water dampening only the unmarked parts of the surface. Next the stone is inked, the oily printing ink adhering to the part of the stone marked with the design. The paper that is to receive the impression is laid onto the stone and then the whole assembly is passed through a lithographic press. For a multi-coloured image new stones would be prepared for the addition of each colour.

Fine art lithographs are still produced in this way but the basic technology – called 'chemical printing' by Senefelder – was developed and mechanized during the nineteenth century and used for many purposes including the creation of pictures and illustrations for children's books. The results were not always tasteful and many of the highly coloured, shiny 'chromolithographs' produced during the middle years of the century look garish and vulgar to a twenty-first century eye. In time, however, as the technology was refined and the hardware improved, illustrators and publishers began to see the range of possibilities that lithography made available. The heavy, cumbersome stones were replaced with metal plates, usually zinc in the early stages, and then by the end of the nineteenth century photography began to be used to transfer original drawings and paintings onto the metal plates which had been prepared with a light-sensitive coating. This made a wider range of media reproducible through printing. By the 1920s and 1930s a number of talented illustrators began to use photolithography to reproduce words and pictures together on the same page. William Nicholson's *Clever Bill* (1926) and *The Pirate Twins* (1929) were produced in this way, as were Jean de Brunhoff's *Babar* stories (begun 1931, 1934 in England) and Kathleen Hale's *Orlando* books (begun 1938).

Offset photolithography

The publication of Edward Ardizzone's *Little Tim and the Brave Sea Captain* in 1936 marked a further advance in that it was one of the first books to be produced by *offset* photolithography. In this version of the process the illustrator's design, along with the accompanying words, is no longer printed straight from the lithographic plate but is 'offset' (i.e. printed) to an intermediate plate, usually of rubber, called a 'blanket'. It is the blanket that is then used to print the final image onto the paper. The main advantage of offsetting is that the soft rubber blanket is able to conform to the surface to be printed much more intimately than a metal plate and this not only produces unrivalled print quality but also enables images composed in almost any medium to be transferred to almost any kind of paper and also to a wide variety of other materials such as metal and plastic.

Since offset photolithography produces excellent results, reproducing as closely as possible the original intentions of the illustrator who can work in whatever medium he or she desires, it is not surprising that it has become the dominant technology in the world of picturebook production. Modern picturebooks are printed on huge rotary presses that draw a continuous 'web' of paper from a reel through a succession of rollers. The printing plate, now usually made from a thin sheet of aluminium, is curved around one of these rollers but it does not come into direct contact with the paper passing through the press. It is damped, then inked by further sets of rollers and then, as it revolves, it passes on the image, or image plus text, to a rubber blanket roller which in turn transfers it to the paper. One set of rollers prints the top side of the paper and the same process occurs below as the paper passes through the press so that it is printed on both sides at the same time. Fast, efficient,

sensitive and flexible, the rotary offset litho press has transformed the production of the picturebook. Pictures and words can now be combined in more or
less any way that a book's designer might wish and that in turn raises all sorts of
possibilities and challenges for the reader.

Appendix 2

Gunther Kress and Theo van Leeuwen's *Grammar of Visual Design*, illustrated with examples from picturebook images

In 1996 Gunther Kress and Theo van Leeuwen published *Reading Images: the Grammar of Visual Design*. This book was an enlargement of an earlier work called simply *Reading Images* that had first appeared in 1990. Both books deal with the social semiotics of the visual image and differ mainly in the breadth and range of the examples to which the authors' analyses are applied. In the later book, many more different types of image were considered, but in neither work does the children's picturebook feature at all prominently. For this reason I have thought it worth illustrating some of the major features of Kress and van Leewuen's version of systemic functional grammar as an adjunct to the main text of this book. However, I have not aimed at complete coverage, partly because to do so would make this appendix unreasonably long and partly because a number of the processes described in *Reading Images* (1996) – for example, classificatory processes – seem less applicable to narrative picturebooks than do some others. I have not attempted to outline again the principles underlying systemic functional grammar and would refer readers back to the appropriate section in Chapter 7. For further clarification, as well as additional detail, Kress and van Leeuwen's work is itself admirably clear and could hardly be bettered. Needless to say, any confusions, misunderstandings and misinterpretations of the work are entirely my own responsibility. What follows here takes up from where the section on visual grammar left off in Chapter 7.

Three metafunctions

Kress and van Leeuwen's grammar of the visual image is organized under three headings. These are derived from the three 'metafunctions' underlying M. A. K. Halliday's systemic functional grammar of spoken and written language. The metafunctions are in essence the three very broad purposes that all language acts fulfil over and above the specific, localized functions of greeting, chastising, narrating, describing, entertaining, directing and so forth. The metafunctions are the *ideational* function, the *interpersonal* and the *textual*. The ideational concerns the ability of language to represent the external world and human consciousness. It is thus concerned with content and ideas and with how they are related. The following sentences taken from *Think of an Eel* are all concerned with providing information about states of affairs in the world and therefore reflect the ideational metafunction very clearly.

> Mudholes, burrows and cracks in the river bed are all homes for eels. ... In fresh water, the elvers grow bigger and turn into yellow eels ... eels feed mostly at night. ... An eel can live out of water for two days or longer ...

In Kress and van Leeuwen's adaptation of the ideational metafunction, participants may be depicted as interacting in some way, as in the example from *Granpa* analysed in Chapter 7, or they may be shown to be connected through some classification device such as a flow chart or taxonomic 'tree' structure. In ways such as this pictures and diagrams can show how people, objects and events in the world are related and organized.

The interpersonal metafunction concerns the dimension of language that enables the speaker, writer or image maker to interact and communicate with listeners, readers or viewers. It is the interpersonal that allows us to take on roles, to express and understand attitudes and feelings. For example, if I try to get my daughter to straighten up her bedroom by saying, 'Claire, I'd like you to tidy your room', the interpersonal function is realized in the use of the vocative, 'Claire'. If she then replies, 'I might do it this afternoon', the modal form 'might do it' conveys her attitude to the request and thus also reflects the interpersonal. In the case of images the interpersonal function can also be reflected through degrees of modality – in this case, the extent to which an image can be considered lifelike or reliable – and also through such features as whether a depicted participant, human or animal, meets our gaze or not. The chimpanzee in *Gorilla*, for example, looks back at us through the bars of its cage and seems to require some form of response. For this reason, Kress and van Leeuwen refer to such images as making a demand. In contrast, when participants look away, or seem oblivious to the reader's presence, they appear to offer themselves to the reader's gaze. *Demand* and *offer* are thus two contrasting ways in which the interpersonal function is realized in images.

The textual metafunction concerns the use of language to form internally coherent texts that relate in recognizable ways to the context in which and for which they were produced. Written and spoken texts are more than simply strings of unrelated sentences, and verbal language possesses a range of resources for ensuring a text's internal cohesion. For example, although we can readily understand the ideational content of the individual sentences extracted from *Think of an Eel* above, as a continuous passage of text it possesses no cohesion. Each sentence seems to stand alone, unconnected to the one before or after. The reason for this is that although they follow each other in the book, they are intended to be captions to pictures, not continuous prose. Were the sentences to be re-written as continuous prose the writer, Karen Wallace, would have made use of cohesive devices such as pronouns to refer back to participants already mentioned ('Eels feed mostly at night. *They* can live out of water for two days or longer ...'). Visual images too are held together and given coherence through compositional devices such as the polarities of top and bottom, left and right that were touched upon in Chapter 7.

The three metafunctions are not intended to be seen as acting independently of one other. Although they have been illustrated separately here, they interact and enmesh within whole texts and images to enable communication and to realize meaning. However, in expounding their adaptation of Hallidayan grammar, Kress and van Leeuwen take each metafunction in turn to show how images as well as speech and writing can submit to systemic functional analysis. In what follows I adopt the same approach to the analysis of picturebook images.

The ideational metafunction: narrative representations

According to Kress and van Leeuwen, images in their ideational aspect may be subdivided into *narrative* representations and *conceptual* representations. Narrative representations are those wherein participants act upon, or react to, each other in some way. They are representations where things happen, the happenings – the actions or reactions – being represented by vectors, strong directional and usually oblique thrusts that link participants together. Much of what the authors have to say about narrative representations was summarized earlier so I shall simply recap briefly here and add to that account those features not yet mentioned.

Action processes

So far we have referred to action processes and reaction processes and have briefly alluded to the possibility that such processes may be transactional or non-transactional. The isolated image of Granpa skipping depicts a *non-transactional action process* with Granpa as the sole actor. So does the image of 'Supergorilla' on the cinema screen in *Gorilla*. Aunt Bibba, on the other hand, the first visitor to knock at the door in *So Much*, is engaged upon a *transactional action process* for she reaches out in a gesture that turns her left arm into a clear vector aimed downwards towards the baby. We have also seen that sometimes a picture will represent an interaction rather than an action, the process being bi-directional and the participants taking the roles of actor and goal either simultaneously or sometimes – we might infer – sequentially. Thus the boy and the Man threaten each other at the same time and Uncle Didi from *So Much* makes to kiss his little nephew as the baby points with a delicate index finger.

Reaction processes

Whereas in the case of action processes participants need not be human or animal – they can indeed be entirely abstract, as in diagrams – in reaction processes, they must possess the faculty of sight, for in these processes vectors are produced by the gaze of the reactors. The traditions of anthropomorphism in picturebooks require us to extend the range of participants that can take the role of reactor, as toys and sometimes even such unlikely objects as steam trains and houses are brought to life in picturebooks and can be made to see. The essential point remains the same, though, whether the participant is Peter Rabbit, Thomas the Tank Engine or 'me and Loopy and Little Gee' from *The Park in the Dark*. Thus the girl watches her Granpa, and Hannah watches her father in *Gorilla*. These are *transactional reaction processes* as in both cases there is a phenomenon represented at the end of the vector produced by the eyeline: Granpa skips and Hannah's father sits working at his desk. However, when Nanny and Gran Gran arrive at the house in *So Much* they gaze adoringly and wave at something out of the frame. There is no represented phenomenon and so here we have a *non-transactional reaction process*. With such processes the reader must imagine what the participants are looking at and Kress and van Leeuwen point out that this fact can be used to manipulate reader reaction and interpretation. Sometimes picture editors on newspapers and magazines crop photographs to remove the object of a person's gaze and are then free to supply captions that mislead. However, in picturebooks such manipulation, where it exists, tends to be used for benign purposes such as to produce an air of mystery or tension such as when the three toys in *The Park in the Dark* first hear 'the THING' and glance upwards and right out of the page.

Speech and mental processes

In addition to action and reaction processes, Kress and van Leeuwen identify two further kinds: *speech* and *mental processes*. Speech and mental processes are represented in visual imagery by the speech bubble and the thought bubble respectively. Such devices are not uncommon in picturebooks although they tend to be restricted to images that are directly or indirectly drawn from the traditions of the comic strip and the cartoon. Speech processes are scattered liberally throughout *Have You Seen Who's Just Moved in Next Door to Us?* and a fine example appears at the very end of *Drop Dead* when the grandparents are reincarnated as battery hens and one scrawny chicken says to another, 'and who's idea was this?' In the case of both these processes the thinking or speaking participant is referred to as the *senser* rather that the actor or reactor.

Circumstances

Kress and van Leeuwen complete their account of the different forms of narrative representation with a consideration of *circumstances*. Participants appear and processes take place within settings and frequently come equipped with adjuncts such as artefacts, tools and minor figures that complete the meanings to be found in an image. Circumstances can thus be circumstances of *setting*, of *means* and of *accompaniment*. Setting is identified easily enough but it can be suggested in a number of different ways:

(i) major participants in the foreground may overlap scenes or objects in the background as when Granpa skips and his granddaughter watches in front of Granpa's house;

(ii) the setting is drawn or painted in less detail as when Raymond Briggs' Man stands on a rooftop silhouetted against the blurred townscape below and the hazy night sky behind;

(iii) the background is more muted in colour than the main participants as in the case of the baby in *So Much* with his red romper suit standing out against the greys, blacks and browns of his surroundings, and

(iv) the setting is lighter or darker than the foreground as when Hannah and the gorilla dance together in the darkened garden.

We could perhaps add as a fifth realization of setting the use of minimal props to metonymically suggest an absent background. Just as a chair and a table on a theatrical stage will stand in for the room that contains them but which is itself not represented, so Quentin Blake's dustbins, doors, chairs and pots and pans conjure up, in *All Join In*, a host of absent settings for his varied cast of characters. In fact, the most common means of realizing circumstances of setting in picturebooks is the simple overlapping of participants with backgrounds. In general there seems to be little interest on the part of illustrators in varying the means by which setting is created.

Various kinds of artefacts and tools are frequently present in action processes as *circumstances of means*. The boy threatens the Man *with* a telephone receiver and the Man threatens the boy *with* a match. The match and the receiver, of course, constitute the vectors at the heart of this particular bi-directional action process but there are no vectors linking hands with objects. The action processes are not directed towards the receiver and match but through them from one participant to the other. Sometimes, however, the means are realized not through discrete objects but through parts of the body as when the children's father in *Drop Dead* wrestles crocodiles *with his bare hands*.

Circumstances of accompaniment can be found in images where participants are clearly connected though not by any vector or eyeline. They are therefore not readily found in pictures depicting action or reaction processes but are much more likely to be present in images displaying a participant's characteristics or features. For this reason we are likely to find them in textbooks and non-fiction books where *analytical* images are more common (see 'Conceptual representations' on p. 151). Nonetheless, such circumstances can be found in picturebooks. In the second, monochrome picture in *Mr Gumpy's Outing* by John Burningham we see the main character standing on the riverbank in front of his boat. The boat is clearly not part of the setting as it overlaps Mr Gumpy

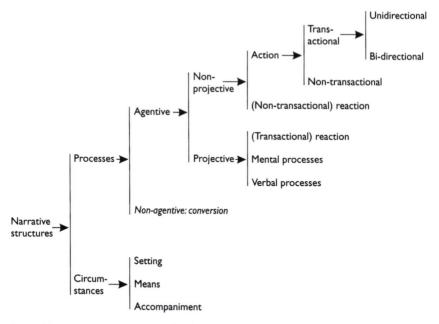

Figure 30 Narrative structures in visual communication

and not the other way around and nor is it a means to an end. There is no connecting vector or eyeline between Mr Gumpy and the boat so there are no action or reaction processes involved. The boat is a participant in the image but it lies before us inert, simply part of the scene. As the written text informs us, it is one of Mr Gumpy's possessions and the picture is there to show us what his boat looks like (it is a flat-bottomed punt rather than a rowing boat) and to establish his role as owner. Mr Gumpy simply stands *with* his boat. By way of contrast we can see in later pictures that Mr Gumpy is poling his punt along the river connected to it through vectors that establish action processes.

In analysing narrative representations in this way Kress and van Leeuwen reveal the pattern of choices that illustrators are compelled to make when they wish to represent characters and objects involved in scenes of action and reaction. The systemic nature of the grammar demands that if a particular choice is made then other choices must follow. If a transactional action process is to be depicted then it must be either unidirectional or bi-directional. If circumstances are to be added then they will be circumstances of setting and/or of means and/or of accompaniment. This system of choices – the system network – is represented diagrammatically in Figure 30. (Note that processes not described in the text are italicized in the diagram.)

The ideational metafunction: conceptual representations

Analytical structures

The key feature of narrative processes – the vector that links participants together in action and reaction structures – is missing from conceptual representations. At the beginning of Mr Gumpy's story, for example, when we first meet the character there is no discernible action or reaction represented (although strictly speaking Mr Gumpy 'carries a watering can'). He stands facing us and we are invited, with the words, 'This is Mr. Gumpy', to scrutinize his image. (In fact, the authors call such conceptual images 'a visual "this is" ' (Kress and van Leeuwen 1996:93).) He is posed rather like a dummy in a shop window or a model in a catalogue and so we view him not as an actor but as a *carrier* possessed of various *attributes* (watering can, wellington boots, jacket, wide-brimmed hat, etc.) This structure – carrier with attributes – Kress and van Leeuwen categorize as an *analytic conceptual structure*.

As in the case of narrative structures, conceptual representations need not involve people or animals and in certain kinds of books, usually do not. Maps are good examples of analytical conceptual structures as they tend to show whole regions or areas (Greenwich, London, Europe, the world) which act as carriers which are then analysable into different categories and levels of detail (streets, neighbourhoods, countries, populations, imports, physical features) which are the attributes. There is a small map in the top left-hand corner of page 8 of *Think of an Eel*. The map is not labelled but we could call it a map of the Atlantic Ocean. Only one region is marked on the map, the Sargasso Sea, the eels' spawning grounds (although the landmasses marking the boundaries of the ocean: North America, South America and Africa are also marked), so we could say that the Atlantic as represented here (carrier) is possessed of only one attribute (the Sargasso Sea). On another map of course the ocean could be represented as possessing many attributes, possibly not including the Sargasso. Such free-standing analytical images as Mr Gumpy and the map of the Atlantic Ocean are relatively rare in picturebooks, as the stories that most picturebooks tell require images of action and reaction for their telling. We do, however, find them embedded within more complex images (see section on 'Embedding' below).

The great majority of analytical processes are *spatial* in nature in that they draw attention to physical or spatial relations. Images such as time lines however, are attempts to represent *temporal* events. Kress and van Leeuwen consider time lines to lie somewhere between conceptual and narrative processes. The focus upon change over time suggests a leaning towards narrative but the absence of vectors – the key feature of narrative processes – and the emphasis upon a structure of fixed points and events, makes time lines far more analytical than narrative. Once again it is not surprising to find that such images are rare in picturebooks but there is a time line of sorts reproduced at the beginning and end of *Think of an Eel*. Most time lines are laid out horizontally, earlier stages or ages placed at the left, later ones at the right, but they need not be so arranged. The illustrations in *Think of an Eel* show the eel's development from the earliest stage to the mature creature in a series of unmarked steps proceeding diagonally from the top right of the page-opening to the bottom left. Despite the fact that the five separate stages are not labelled with captions or time markers, the image is neither narrative nor spatially analytical. There is perhaps a little ambiguity as the five eels are depicted naturalistically, swimming in parallel against an abstract, but recognizably watery background, but I think it is clear that the reader is not expected to assume a spatial relationship between the creatures. These are not five eels at various stages of development simultaneously swimming alongside one another in parallel. The relationship between them is a temporal one, albeit covert or implicit.

The gaps between each of the eels in this image are roughly the same, so, although the stages of development are represented in temporal sequence, there is no indication of the length of time it takes for each stage to develop into the next one. It is as if Stonehenge, St Paul's Cathedral, The Empire State Building, and the Greenwich Millennium Dome were all represented on the same architectural time line with equal gaps in between them. They would be represented *topologically* – that is, in the correct sequence – but not *topographically*. A topographical representation would be drawn 'to scale' with the time intervals correctly shown as part of the image, that is, with a proportionally bigger gap between Stonehenge and St Paul's Cathedral than between St Paul's and the Empire State Building.

Spatial analytical images can also be topological or topographical. The ones that we have considered so far have all been topographical, in other words they all represent accurately the way in which the attributes are represented in terms of relative size and location. Mr Gumpy's hat, jacket, trousers and watering can are all drawn to scale and arranged in appropriate order. Topological spatial images on the other hand show the logical relationships between a carrier's possessive attributes, in what order they appear and how they are connected, for example, but not how big they are or how far apart. The London Underground map is a good example of a topological spatial analytical structure. Not surprisingly such structures are hard to find in picturebooks and are more characteristic of diagrams than pictures.

There is more to analytical processes than is described here but the features that I have explained and illustrated are the ones that are most commonly found in narrative picturebooks. The system network for analytical conceptual structures is shown in Figure 31.

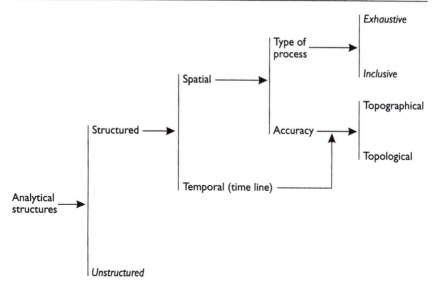

Figure 31 Analytical structures in visual communication.

Classificational structures

Classificational structures differ from analytical ones in that they represent participants as belonging to a class, or order, or category that distinguishes them from, and relates them to, other participants. Classification processes usually take the form of some kind of tree structure, or taxonomy with one or more superordinate participants related to a number of other, subordinate participants. The diagram represented in Figure 32 is a simple, single-levelled classificational structure.

We are unlikely to find free-standing examples of classificational image structures within narrative picturebooks. It is a little easier to find examples of *covert* taxonomies, that is, ones where only the subordinate participants are represented, the superordinate having been omitted or suppressed. We might just consider the rows of houses in *Have You Seen Who's Just Moved in Next Door to Us?* as having the form of a covert taxonomy. The houses are laid out

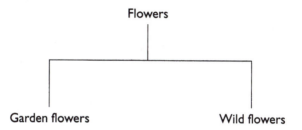

Figure 32 A simple classificatory tree structure.

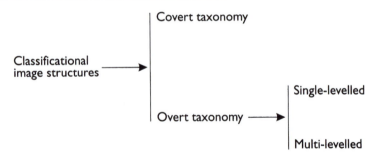

Figure 33 Classificational structures in visual communication.

before us along a horizontal axis and they are all depicted in front elevation and on the same scale just as they might be in a more 'scientific' or conceptual image. The superordinate that is suppressed here is the category of 'houses'. What we are presented with are the subordinate participants of 'the aliens' house', 'Frankenstein's house', 'King Kong's house', 'Superman's house' and so on. Within and around this structure are woven the micro-narratives, the action and reaction processes, that form the more prominent ideational features of the book. The pattern of choices available within classificational image structures is shown in Figure 33.

Embedding

So far I have discussed and illustrated a number of image processes in isolation, in particular those in the narrative realm – action, reaction, speech and mental processes and the kinds of circumstances that accompany them – but also some of those in the conceptual realm, in particular, classificatory and analytical processes. All are means by which the ideational function of image making is realized – in other words, how information about the world is structured and organized in pictures and other forms of visual representation. However, in pictures, as in spoken and written language, 'utterances' are rarely simple. Just as speakers and writers may create complex sentences involving embedded clauses with differing levels of subordination, so image makers frequently produce more or less complex image structures, and this is particularly true of the pictures in picturebooks.

We have already seen how, in Burningham's image of Granpa skipping, an action process can be combined with a reaction process to produce a complex visual 'statement'. We might find it hard to be sure which is the main and which the subsidiary 'clause', but the relationship between the two is clear. However, picturebooks can contain images that are much more complex than this, involving several layers of embedding and it is particularly interesting that such images readily combine narrative and conceptual structures. One further example might serve to demonstrate how these different kinds of processes can be pressed into service to further the picturebook maker's ends.

In *The Jolly Postman*, the picture of the postman with the Prince and his bride tells us much about the characters and their circumstances (see Figure 22). There are narrative structures at work here in the Prince's pouring of champagne for the suitably deferential mailman, the bottle and the Prince's arm forming a clear left to right and slightly downwards vector. This simple transactional action process is combined with transactional reaction processes as both men carefully watch the phenomenon: the postman's fizzing glass. To one side is another reaction process, this time with Cinderella as the reactor and the contents of the postman's letter as phenomenon. All of these narrative processes take place alongside appropriate circumstances of setting (the sideboard, flowers and telephone); of accompaniment (the vacuum cleaner and the suitcases); and of means (the champagne bottle). If we look for conceptual structures within the picture we will find no classification processes but can identify analytical processes in the images of Cinderella, the Prince and, in particular, the postman himself. Each of these figures can be considered to be analytical inasmuch as they are not only involved in narrative action and reaction but are also posed in such a manner that we can see at a glance what a fairy-tale prince and princess and old-fashioned bicycling postman actually look like. They therefore act as carriers with their apparel as attributes. This embedding of the conceptual (analytical) within the narrative (action and reaction) can perhaps best be understood if we once more transcode the depicted situation into verbal language. We might say 'the Prince pours champagne for the postman *who is dressed in a dark blue uniform, wears a postman's badge on his lapel and is holding his cap in his right hand*'. The figure of the postman thus provides us with non-narrative information as to what he looks like.

The interpersonal metafunction: representation and interaction

So far we have discussed the kinds of relationship that can exist between the participants in pictures, but there are in fact two kinds of participant present in the creation and reception of an image. These are the *interactive* participants – the producers of the image, the artists and designers, as well as the readers of the image who interpret the messages created by the producers – and the *represented* participants: the actors, reactors, and carriers that appear in the image. There are thus three kinds of relationship that can exist between these different kinds of participant.

(i)   Interactive participants communicate with each other through the medium of the image. In this relationship illustrators do something to, or for, their readers through their designs.

(ii)   Represented participants may be related to one another in a number of ways within an image and we have examined the structures of some of those relationships above.

(iii)   The reader as *interactive* participant is drawn into a relationship with the *represented* participants. In other words interactive participants will have attitudes towards and will make responses to the ideational aspects of images.

It is this third kind of relationship that we are concerned with in the next section.

Demand and offer

The social semiotic systems of image making offer the artist a range of resources for realizing this final kind of relationship. In terms of the three major metafunctions, images possess an *interpersonal* aspect. The interpersonal relationships formed under this aspect are clearly not of the same order as those formed between real, interactive participants. If a figure smiles at me out of a photograph I do not respond in quite the same way as if the same person were to stand in front of me and smile. The relationship implied by the represented smile is only a represented relationship and thus remains imaginary, but nonetheless the effects, in terms of the overall meaning we take from the image, are real enough. The image of the chimpanzee in *Gorilla* referred to already may affect us as readers quite powerfully not only because of its realism, its large size and closeness to the picture plane, but also because the creature gazes out at us. His gaze meets ours and he seems to watch us watching him. He seems to know that he is being looked at. Furthermore, his flat stare has a slightly melancholy edge and the firm set of his mouth and hand gesture give him a sad but resigned expression. When we meet his gaze, as we must, we are likely to recognize these characteristic markers of patience and stoicism in the face of adversity, and it is this that determines the nature of our response.

As I have already noted, Kress and van Leeuwen call this kind of image a *demand*. Characters that look out of pictures at the viewer looking in seem to address the viewer directly and call for some kind of response. Other kinds of images where the eyes of participants are averted from those of the viewer are called *offers*. The participants in such images seem to present themselves for the viewer's inspection. With an offer image we are invited to scrutinize whatever is represented as a dispassionate observer without being drawn into a quasi-personal relationship. If we turn the page in *Gorilla*, for example, we find a small, square picture showing Hannah and the gorilla, backs to the viewer, buying cinema tickets from a box-office attendant whose eyes are cast down towards her hands. The contrast with the preceding illustration could not be stronger. Here the small frame, surrounded by a large expanse of white page, accentuates the impression of looking in on a scene that is being played out for our scrutiny. The participants interact with each other but are 'unaware' of our presence.

Many picturebooks avoid demand images and it is easy to see why, at least in those books that tell straightforward stories. The moment that a participant turns to face the reader then the narrative spell is broken and the boundary separating (imaginary) characters from (real) readers is breached. (For a fuller discussion of 'boundary breaking' in picturebooks, along with some other practices that disturb storytelling norms, see Chapter 6.) A good example of the effect produced by this particular kind of boundary breaking can be found in *Oops!* by Colin McNaughton. This book tells the story of the young Preston Pig who time after time narrowly escapes the greedy jaws of a caricatured Mr Wolf. On one of the early pages the Wolf turns his gaze outwards from the book, shrugs his shoulders, raises both palms and addresses the reader directly. 'Don't look at me like that,' he begs and goes on to justify his existence in stories like the one that the reader is currently reading.

Framing and social distance

The way participants within an image are framed can also make a difference to a picture's interpersonal dimension. For example, if we look again at the picture of the chimpanzee from *Gorilla* we can see that framing the animal's face in close up, or what a film director might call a 'tight close shot' has produced the effect of close proximity. If the animal were to be present in front of us at the same distance we would be very close indeed. We would be so close that not only would we be able to make out the details of skin texture and hair that Anthony Browne has so carefully rendered, but also to put our arms around the creature and no doubt smell it too! In our everyday interactions with others we would only allow this degree of proximity to our closest intimates, our wives, husbands, partners, children and so on. Kress and van Leeuwen, following Edward Hall (1966), call this 'close personal distance'. The effect of framing the chimpanzee in this way is thus to coerce the reader into entering an imaginary relationship of empathy and sympathy that parallels the real relationship one might have with an intimate in the same circumstances. Had Browne depicted the chimpanzee at a greater distance, say far enough away to see the whole figure and its surroundings (that is at 'far social distance': see Table 1 below) we would feel much less involved with the animal's plight. Table 1 shows a scale of social distance that Kress and van Leeuwen adapted from Hall (1966) which gives some idea of the effects produced by varying the degree of reader–character proximity. (Note that judgements of social distance such as this are inevitably culture-specific.)

Table 1 Markers and effects of social distance (based on Hall 1966).

Social distance	Defining characteristics and visual field	Typical practical effects
Close personal distance	Could hold or grasp other person. Only face visible	Only intimates allowed this close
Far personal distance	Space between one arm outstretched and two arms outstretched. Head and shoulders visible	The distance at which 'subjects of personal interests and involvements' discussed
Close social distance	Beyond the touching range of close social distance. Whole figure visible	Impersonal business transacted
Far social distance	Distance to which people move when asked to 'stand away so that I can look at you'. Whole figure visible plus surrounding space	Formal and impersonal business and social transactions
Public distance	Anything beyond far social distance	Distance between strangers who are to remain strangers

There is thus an intimate relationship between the extent of the visual field in an image in relation to a particular represented participant and the degrees of intimacy, empathy and formality that we imaginatively extend towards them. The figures in *Have You Seen Who's Just Moved in Next Door to Us?* are represented at public distance and this keeps our relationship with them very much at arm's length: we are to laugh at them, not empathize with them. In contrast, the front cover of *The Little Boat* depicts the boat's owner in close up as head and shoulders only, and this draws us imaginatively closer to him; for adult readers, this could be a child of their own, and for child readers this could be a close friend.

Perspective and subjective and objective images

Images not only draw viewers into more or less close contact with the represented participants, but they are also often constructed so that the participants are viewed, both literally and metaphorically, from a particular angle. When we use the phrase 'point of view' about a picture, or for that matter a story, we refer to the way that the position from which we view events has been constructed for us by the way the picture or story has been put together. In painting, the system of perspective is the most powerful means by which point of view is created. When we view pictures in perspective we not only look at the picture from our actual position in front of it, we seem to look into it from the position occupied by the original viewer of the scene, the painter or illustrator. This in turn allows the image, or rather the image maker, to manipulate our subjectivity, to make us see things in a particular way, to 'subject' us to the order of things as represented. For this reason Kress and van Leeuwen refer to such images as *subjective*. Once again, they draw us into a particular relation to the represented participants.

Not all pictures, however, are constructed along such lines. Pre-Renaissance frescoes and Byzantine mosaics, for example, often present the viewer with a more objective image, one that displays everything that there is to be known about the participants, or at least everything that the image maker considered to be important or relevant. When standing in front of such works our point of view is not determined for us by the work itself. Figures are painted against a flat gold ground rather than a landscape or architectural setting receding into the distance, and the illusion of depth is further frustrated by the lack of modelling and shading. In the absence of any constructed point of view we look at such images from where we stand for, as the authors put it, 'Objective images ... disregard the viewer. They say, as it were: "I am this way, regardless of who or where or when you are" ' (Kress and van Leeuwen 1996:137).

In the picturebook, although drawing and painting in perspective is still probably the dominant mode, it is not hard to find examples that exploit other representational forms. Fiona French pastiches art styles and manners from different ages and cultures, and Gerald McDermott's *Arrow to the Sun* employs a resolutely flat, two-dimensional manner derived from the artworks and cultural artefacts of native Americans. Caricature, cartoons and the comic have had a huge influence upon the development of the picturebook and their lack of respect for post-Renaissance representational conventions can be found everywhere in the picturebook. In the sample of books that I have been drawing upon Babette Cole, Colin McNaughton and Janet Ahlberg use perspective as and when it suits them but they are not expressly concerned to render every image naturalistically. In fact, the variety of images within a single book – vignettes and monochrome sketches as well as full colour plates and double page spread bleeds – often allow objective and subjective imagery to be found between the same covers. In *Drop Dead*, for example, Babette Cole does not seem to be overly concerned with constructing the reader's point of view through perspective. She frequently uses washes of colour to produce semi-abstract backgrounds that are only notional deserts or skies, and she sometimes treats solid, three-dimensional forms, such as the tower-block with the party on the roof, in an objective full-frontal manner that reduces it to a patterned rectangle. On the other hand, she renders the children's school in textbook perspective. This overall lack of concern for the reader's point of view and the general leaning towards objectivity suits her purpose well for – as with Colin McNaughton's creations – we are expected to laugh at these people

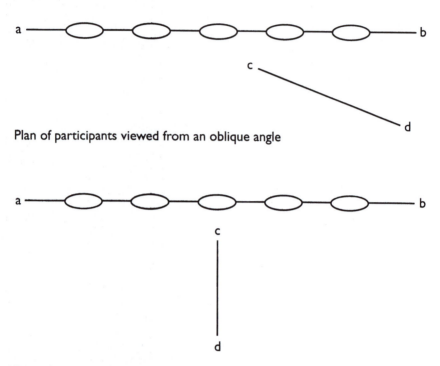

Plan of participants viewed from an oblique angle

Plan of participants viewed from an frontal angle

Figure 34 Oblique and frontal horizontal angles.

and the situations they find themselves in. Both the story and the pictures that form part of its text are non-naturalistic, extravagant and ridiculous.

Horizontal and vertical angles

When images are rendered in perspective we can examine how as a viewer we have been aligned with the represented participants, both horizontally and vertically. In the case of the horizontal angle we can draw a distinction between pictures that have participants arranged more or less obliquely in relation to the viewpoint, and those where the viewer confronts participants front on. The diagrams in Figure 34 show the difference between these two positions. Line AB represents an array of participants, for example a group of people being photographed, and line CD the direction from which the participants are viewed (that is, the position from which the photograph is taken).

Kress and van Leeuwen argue that when we are positioned to view participants frontally we are much more likely to feel some involvement with them.

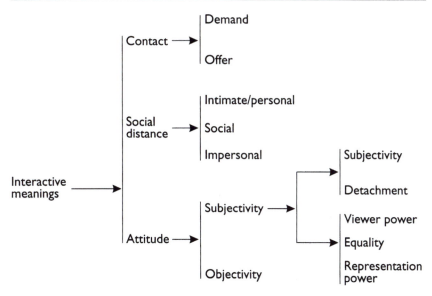

Figure 35 Interactive meanings in images.

We sense that 'these are people like us'. In contrast, participants viewed obliquely are likely to feel somewhat alien to us, we look at them 'askance', or 'from the sidelines'. Kress and van Leeuwen illustrate this difference with a group of photographs of Australian aborigines, some outside their homes, and some as children in school. They claim that the horizontal angle persuades us to feel a sense of involvement with, or similarity to, the white mission school teachers who are photographed frontally and a sense of detachment from the aborigines who are viewed at a sharp angle.

In picturebooks there seem to be few clear examples of figures, or groups of participants viewed from the sidelines and I suspect that this is not a visual structure that picturebook makers find useful. We rarely find figures lined up in simple groups and ranks and when we do they are usually 'facing the camera' as they are on the cover of *All Join In*. Just occasionally, however, it is possible to find an example of a skewed angle, usually in a book that deals with dramatic transformations or very deliberate manipulations of the reader's viewpoint. Such an image occurs at the turning point of Chris Van Allsburg's *The Wretched Stone*.

In this story, the crew of a sailing ship has been transformed by the wretched stone of the title into ape-like beasts. The Captain's discovery of this metamorphosis is illustrated by a picture that shows the creatures in a group intently watching the glowing stone which is out of the frame to the right. Although the crew are the clear focus of the picture they are sited to the far right of the double page spread and observed from a sharply skewed angle as if to distance the reader from the disconcertingly hybrid beings that the men have become.

When the point of view is manipulated upwards or downwards along a vertical axis we experience something like an increase or diminution of power over the represented participants. We can be positioned so that we literally, and thus metaphorically too, look down upon, or up to, participants in the story. In *The Park in the Dark*, shortly after the three toys pass through the park gates, we seem to see them from high above amongst the branches of the gnarled and twisted trees. Later in the book we look up from the point of view of the toys towards the frightening 'THING', the commuter train that drives them back home. Similarly, in *The Man*, the reader is sometimes positioned at the same level as the tiny figure looking up towards a foreshortened boy, especially when the former is pleading with the latter or trying to wheedle some favour out of him. The system network for the interactional aspects of the interpersonal metafunction is shown in Figure 35.

The interpersonal metafunction: modality

Modality in words and pictures

Modality in language concerns the extent to which we consider the things we say or hear, read or write, are true and reliable. When we read the opening lines of *Gorilla* ('Hannah loved Gorillas') or *Rosie's Walk* ('Rosie the hen went for a walk') we find no doubt or hesitation expressed about what the participants in each case felt or did. In *The Jolly Postman*, on the other hand, the narrator does not seem quite so confident about the absolute truth value of the events he is about to relate: 'Once upon a bicycle,/So *they say*,/A Jolly Postman came one day ...' (my emphasis). The phrase 'So they say' has the effect of distancing the narrator from what he is saying. An element of doubt is introduced into the proceedings from the very start, as if the narrator were to plead, 'this may not actually be what happened, it is only what I have heard.' Later in *Gorilla*, when the toy has metamorphosed into an apparently real animal, we hear a similar note of caution and hesitation when it first addresses Hannah: 'Hannah was frightened. "Don't be frightened, Hannah," said the gorilla, "I won't hurt you. *I just wondered if you'd like to go* to the zoo"' (my emphasis). The statements and commands that make up the first part of this passage are unequivocal about the state of affairs ('I won't hurt you'), but the invitation to the zoo is far more tentative. Without it the invitation, 'would you like to go to the zoo?' would sound much stronger. But even in this contracted form the invitation is still not maximally positive. 'Would you like to go to the zoo?' is much weaker than, say, 'Let's go to the zoo'. It is more akin to 'Shall we go to the zoo?' a question which clearly reveals the tentativeness of the suggestion.

In social semiotic terms, the openings of *Gorilla* and *Rosie's Walk*, as well as the opening of the gorilla's first words up to '... won't hurt you', can be said to possess *high modality*. The opening of *The Jolly Postman*, on the other hand, and the second part of the gorilla's speech possess relatively *low modality*. In speech and writing this sliding scale of 'truth' or 'factualness' or 'credibility' is realized through the system of modal auxiliary verbs such as 'may', 'might', 'could' and 'shall'; through the use of adjectives and adverbs such as 'probable', 'probably', 'possible' and 'possibly'; and through constructions like 'so they say'.

Pictures and other kinds of visual images also possess degrees of modality, although the ways in which the 'truth value' of visual 'statements' is represented are peculiar to the visual mode. Part of the interpersonal metafunction of images consists in suggesting to viewers that what they see is more or less true to life. We might, for example, contrast a photograph of a tree with a hasty sketch of the same tree. We know that neither image is a real tree – we recognize them both as representations – but we would not hesitate to indicate the photograph as being the more lifelike and thus as possessing the higher modality. Because we generally find it fairly easy to identify which is the more lifelike of a pair of images we might be tempted to think the modality of visual images simply a matter of resemblance. Thus the more an image resembles whatever it is an image of the higher modality it should have. However, Kress and van Leeuwen are careful to point out that modality is always modality within a cultural system and that the lifelike can only ever be lifelike in relation to a culturally saturated view of what counts as real.

An extreme example of the way in which the modality of images depends upon the cultural context is the case of the scientific diagram. Such diagrams (for example, electrical or electronic circuits) are never represented naturalistically as if seen in perspective from a single point of view. Such an approach tends to foreground the surface appearance of specific things, the fleeting and ephemeral nature of the visible world, whereas the circuit diagram – an assemblage of lines and symbols – aims to represent a state of affairs beyond or behind the visible. Truth to reality here, and therefore high modality, depends upon a stripping away of unimportant detail and a clear and unambiguous marshalling of a restricted range of signifiers. Colour, shading, modelling, perspective: none of these contribute to high modality in the diagram, but all are modality markers in pictures.

If we confine ourselves to a consideration of pictures, then colour, shading, modelling, etc. all become important for they all contribute to creating a sense of visual realism. This realism, however, is still not dependent upon a naïve resemblance of image and object for our sense of what is naturalistically real in pictures has been heavily influenced by our experiences of colour photographs. At the beginning of the twenty-first century we see pictures as naturalistically real, and hence possessed of high modality, the closer they approximate to the images produced by 35mm colour photography. As a result we tend to think of images with more saturated colour and finer and sharper detail than the average colour photograph as hyper-real and thus possessed of lower modality, or truth-to-life. Indeed, it is the existence of a photographic standard for what is to count as realistic, a standard that has in-built technological limitations, that has made art movements such as hyper-realism possible.

Very few picturebook artists aim for anything like photographic naturalism in their illustrations and deploy the characteristic markers of modality in many different ways, frequently combining indicators of high and low modality in the same image. For example, in many of his illustrations Anthony Browne tends to employ intensely saturated colours (deep intense reds, greens, blues, etc.) with high levels of colour differentiation (many different colours rather than a restricted palette) but very little colour modulation (lawns are almost flat expanses of green, skies almost flat expanses of blue). The saturation is too intense for naturalism and therefore lowers the modality of his images. The differentiation is closer to a naturalistic range, but the modulation is at the lower end of the scale, which again lowers the modality. However, in some images he comes much closer to high modality naturalism. The image of the chimpanzee in *Gorilla* that we have already discussed owes its relatively naturalistic, photographic quality to its rather muted, modulated colours, its attention to detail, its representation of the play of light over the creature's face, and its varying degrees of brightness.

Helen Oxenbury's illustrations for *So Much* also show clearly how illustrators can vary the modality of their images. Three different kinds of picture are represented in this book: full-colour painterly illustrations of the baby's relatives, equally painterly images of the gathering family in muted shades of brown, cream and black, and monochrome sketches in black, white and shades of grey. The drawing in each type of illustration is equally accomplished and attentive to the details of illumination, brightness and depth. What makes them vary in terms of their modality, or lifelikeness, is the degree to which colour is present or absent. This does not mean that the full-colour illustrations are automatically the most true to life for it may be the case that they are too saturated and therefore beyond the photographic norm. Individual readers might have different views about which illustrations – the colourful ones or the muted ones – most closely approach the condition of high modality.

The textual metafunction: composition

So far we have considered two of the fundamental functions of the language of images: to display the nature of things and events in the world and in human consciousness (realized through the image's represented participants), and to enable the writer or illustrator to interact and communicate with his or her audience (realized through the represented participants' effects upon the interactive participants). The third metafunction, the textual, concerns the language's resources for organizing the represented participants, the processes in which they are involved and the interpersonal features so that they cohere to form a composition that is in itself meaningful. Kress and van Leeuwen's discussion of 'The meaning of composition' (their Chapter 6) ranges across the placement of elements in various zones of the image: top and bottom, left and right, centre and margin; the salience, or visual importance of the various elements; and some further aspects of framing. Here I shall illustrate the textual metafunction, as it appears in some picturebook images, mainly through a consideration of the meaning values accorded to top and bottom, left and right.

In Chapter 7, I briefly mentioned the work of William Moebius on the codes of left and right, top and bottom. He ascribes to these zones a sense of high self-esteem or social status (top); low self-esteem, low spirits or low status (bottom); relative security (left); and relative risk (right). Kress and van Leeuwen describe these positions rather differently, although there are obvious connections between the two accounts. In *Reading Images*, the top and bottom of an image, or visual display, are considered to represent the realms of the ideal and the real respectively. In the image of 'Supergorilla', for example, the picture on the screen clearly represents an idealized version of reality while the audience are 'grounded' below in the auditorium. Likewise the front cover of *The Man* represents the character's nameless yearning through having him stand on a rooftop looking up into the sky in the upper portion of the picture. His feet however are firmly planted on the ridge-tiles, linking him to the difficult real world of human beings below.

Of course, not all images make such obvious and prominent use of the vertical axis and not all picturebook pictures are structured in such a way that a clear top and bottom can be located. The polarity of left and right, however, is much more significant for a form that relies heavily upon left to right reading conventions and upon the regular rhythm of the turned page. Borrowing once again from Halliday's functional grammar, Kress and van Leeuwen argue that the informational value of the right and the left zones of an image are associated with 'the given' and 'the new' respectively. In other words we tend to see participants and events on the left-hand side of a visual display as something already known and understood whereas whatever takes place on the right-hand side is something we are drawn to see as a novel state of affairs. This coding system is central to the effectiveness of *The Little Boat*. All of the illustrations are stretched horizontally to emphasize the left-right axis and almost every image places objects and scenes recalling the shore from which the little boat sets sail to the left, while the open sea – representing constant change and movement – is always to the right. Towards the end of the book we come to see the ocean as the 'given', that which is taken for granted and understood. 'Newness', then, comes to be represented by first of all the exotic boats of the native fishermen (the largest, and therefore most salient of which, is placed to the right) and then on the final page, the palm-fringed beach of yellow sand.

Salience, or the visual prominence and significance of participants, cuts across these orderings of information into zones. In one image it may be that processes and participants represented in the realm of the ideal are the most salient simply because they are larger, more brightly lit or represented in the foreground. Such is the case with Supergorilla. His brightness and boldness mean that he is clearly intended to be the focus of our attention (and therefore

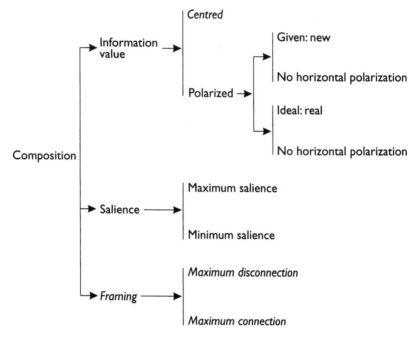

Figure 36 The meaning of composition.

represents something charged with meaning – the mysterious, powerful and transforming effect of gorillas upon mere human beings?). The watchers in the audience below, represented as simple white curves in the darkness, have their modality reduced to such a point that they become insignificant both visually and in terms of their information value. In *The Little Boat*, the boat itself is sometimes the most salient feature and sometimes the least. Compare the image of the boat drifting away from the legs of the children at play on the beach with the picture two pages further on of it dwarfed by the cliff-like stern of a huge supertanker. In the former the tiny scrap of polystyrene stands out through its position in the foreground of the image and through its whiteness. It is positioned to the right while the children's legs are over to the left, so we are alerted to the fact that a change in state is about to take place for the boat. It is also positioned very low down while the legs of the children at play are up above (there is not much headroom in these pages so the children disappear upwards out of the image and Benson demarcates top and bottom with the line where 'the sea meets the land'). So, not only is change imminent, but this is going to be the new 'reality' for the little boat down below while the children remain above and behind in their unknowing and innocent, ideal world of play. In contrast, the much longer perspective on the supertanker reduces the boat to an insignificant piece of flotsan.

Figure 36 summarizes the distinctions made in this section.

Finally, it must be noted that Kress and van Leeuwen apply these compositional analyses across whole page layouts – text and pictures together – as well as individual images. It is their belief that efforts must be made to find a common language within which the effects of words and images can be described. Such a project is clearly of great relevance for the study of the picturebook but there is no space to elaborate upon it here. I suggest that readers interested in whether such a way of proceeding might illuminate individual picturebooks should turn first to the relevant pages in Kress and van Leewuen 1996 (181–229), and then try for themselves to unpack how the best picturebook makers and designers organize their pages.

Glossary

Bleed; bled to the edges Pictures 'bleed' when they are extended to the very edges of the page with no framing of any kind. They may bleed to all four edges or to only one, two or three.

Cross-hatching Patches or clusters of short parallel lines (*see* **hatching**) that are crossed through with lines in a different direction used to darken areas in a picture or to model three-dimensional forms.

Discourse; form of discourse In linguistics, discourse is any stretch of language larger than a sentence. In recent years the term has developed wider meanings and has come to refer to forms of language and their associated social practices. Sermons, lectures, poems, sports commentaries, pop songs and political speeches are thus all forms of discourse.

Double page spread The complete visual display created when a picturebook is opened out flat showing the left- and right-hand pages side by side. The term is used interchangeably with **page-opening**.

Emergent reader A young, inexperienced reader who possesses some of the knowledge required by fully competent readers and who is capable of reader-like behaviour (e.g. holding a book correctly and turning the pages). Emergent readers still require a great deal of support from parents and other care-givers in their efforts to understand the words and images in a picturebook.

Endpapers The papers, or pages, visible immediately inside the front and back covers of a book. In a picturebook the endpapers may be plain or they may display designs that are germane to the text proper. It is always worth looking closely at images displayed on the endpapers as they frequently contain information and/or images useful in the interpretation of the story.

Genre A type or kind of literary text bound by rules or conventions (e.g. thriller, detective story, science fiction, school story). Latterly the term has been extended to cover non-literary forms that are also bound by conventions that determine structural features and language choices.

Gutter The groove created in an open book where left- and right-hand pages meet at the spine. In a conventional verbal text the gutter merely separates blocks of text which we read sequentially, first the left and then the right. In a picturebook however, pictures can be made to extend across the gutter, sometimes requiring the reader to look across both pages of a page-opening before moving down to the next part of the text rather than reading the left page first and then the right (see *Drop Dead*). The gutter can be used to demarcate different textual realms or narrative strands as it is in *Time to Get Out of the Bath, Shirley*.

Hatching Patches or clusters of short parallel lines used to darken areas in a picture or to model three-dimensional forms (*see* **Cross-hatching**).

Hue A technical term for colour. Red, green, yellow, etc. are all hues.

Intaglio (printing) Forms of printing that require the design to be incised into a metal plate. Ink is forced into the grooves and the plate cleaned to remove any surplus. The paper to be printed is usually damped and then lain on top of the plate. A thick felt blanket is placed on top of the paper and the whole assembly passed through a heavy press that lifts the ink out of the grooves and onto the paper. Engraving and etching are typical intaglio processes.

Interanimation The process by which, in composite texts such as picturebooks, comics and graphic novels, the words and images mutually influence one another so that the meaning of the words is understood in the light of what the pictures show, and vice versa.

Landscape (format) Books or images in landscape format are rectangular with the longer edges running horizontally. Landscape format picturebooks create space for illustrators and designers to spread a single image, or position multiple images, across the page or page-opening.

Letterpress The printing of text from letter forms in relief. Letterpress originated in the middle of the fifteenth century with the invention of movable metal type, and for almost five hundred years was the main mass printing process.

Lithography Literally, 'drawing on stone'. A **planographic** method of printing which exploits the incompatibility of oil and water. The text or image to be printed is drawn upon a smooth, flat lithographic stone, usually limestone, with a greasy medium such as oil crayon. The stone is wetted and then inked, the printing ink adhering only to the greasy marks. Paper is lain on the stone which is then pulled through a lithographic press.

Chromolithography A form of lithography used in the nineteenth century to create multi-coloured images. The overlaying of different coloured inks gave chromolithographs a glossy, sticky appearance.

Offset lithography A later development of the lithographic process which involved the transferring of the image from the lithographic plate to an intermediate, rubber 'blanket' and then from the blanket to the paper. Offsetting results in better print quality and a wider range of applications for the process, e.g. printing on plastics and metal.

Modulation (of colour, line)   The varying of colour or line so that an image is not composed solely of flat, unchanging areas of colour and/or a uniform thickness and delicacy of line.

Movable   A generic term for picturebooks that contain moving parts. These may include, amongst many other processes, scenes or figures that stand up when the book is opened out flat at a particular page; figures or objects that appear and disappear or otherwise move when tabs are pulled; and pictures that can be made to dissolve and metamorphose into something else.

Page-opening   The complete visual display created when a picturebook is opened out flat showing the left- and right-hand pages side by side. The term is used interchangeably with **double page spread**.

Planographic (printing)   Forms of printing where the design is transferred from one flat surface, e.g. a lithographic stone, to another flat surface such as paper.

Point of view   The term used to describe the 'position' that readers and viewers are placed in by texts and images and from which they perceive the represented persons, objects and events. Linear perspective in pictures places viewers in the position of the artist so that they see only what the artist has seen or imagined seeing. In stories, point of view usually combines the impressions provided by whoever narrates the events (who speaks in the story?) with those provided by whoever perceives the events (who sees in the story?). Point of view always affects readers' attitudes towards, and understanding of, texts they read and images they look at.

Portrait (format)   Books or images in portrait format are rectangular with the longer edges running vertically.

Recto   The surface of a page that appears on the right-hand side of a **page-opening**. The surface that is revealed on the left when the page is turned over is the **verso**.

Register   The term used to describe variation in language use according to social context. We use different registers – that is, we adapt our use of language – according to what the subject matter is, whether we are speaking or writing, and also the person or persons with whom we are communicating.

Salience   In pictures salience refers to the importance or prominence of particular objects or persons within the image. The salience of a particular feature is enhanced by being, amongst other things, strongly coloured and/or brightly lit and/or close to the foreground and/or sharply focussed. Other factors can be important too. Human figures, because of their importance to us, tend to possess higher salience – other things being equal – than inanimate objects.

Synergy   *The Shorter Oxford Dictionary* defines synergy as: 'the production of two or more agents, substances, etc., of a combined effect greater then the sum of their separate effects.' Synergy in the picturebook, therefore, is the outcome of the **interanimation** of words and pictures.

Text-type   The term is used in this book interchangeably with **genre**. A text-type is thus a form of text governed by conventions that are shared and implicitly understood by both writers and readers.

Verso   The reverse or underside of the page on the right-hand side of a **page-opening**. The verso appears when this page is turned.

Vignette   A miniature illustration, usually unframed and with little or no background, placed alongside or near a passage of text, often in the corner of a page. See many of the pages of *The Jolly Postman*.

Woodblock (printing); woodcut   Wood block printing is one of the oldest printing processes, predating letterpress. The image to be printed is created by carving away unwanted material from the smooth plank side of a piece of wood leaving behind the image as a linear design. Because they are both relief processes, woodblocks and letterpress can be printed together at the same time.

Wood engraving   Despite its name, wood engraving is not an intaglio process like engraving on metal but is a relief process like **woodblock printing**. The difference between the processes lies in the materials used and the way the design is created from the original wooden block. In wood engraving hard boxwood blocks are used and the end grain surface worked upon rather than the plank side. Rather than cut away unwanted wood, the wood engraver builds up the image through incising lines into the block which eventually will become the white lines and spaces that are not registered in the final print.

Bibliography

Abish, W. (1974) *Alphabetical Africa*, New York: New Directions Publishing.

Agosto, D.E. (1999) 'One and inseparable: interdependent storytelling in picturebooks', *Children's Literature in Education* 30(4): 267–80.

Alderson, B. (1973) *Looking at Picture Books*, London: The National Book League and Bocardo Press.

Alderson, B. (1986) *Sing a Song for Sixpence: The English Picture Book Tradition and Randolph Caldecott*, Cambridge: Cambridge University Press in Association with the British Library.

Arnheim, R. (1974) *Art and Visual Perception: a Psychology of the Creative Eye*, London: University of California Press.

Bader, B. (1976) *American Picture Books from Noah's Ark to the Beast Within*, New York: Macmillan.

Bakhtin, M. M. (1981) *The Dialogic Imagination: Four Essays*, M. Holquist (ed.) trans. C. Emerson and M. Holquist, Austin: University of Texas Press.

—— (1984) *Problems of Dostoevsky's Poetics*, trans. C. Emerson, Manchester: Manchester University Press.

—— (1986) *Speech Genres and other Late Essays*, C. Emerson and M. Holquist (eds) trans. V. W. McGee, Austin: University of Texas Press.

Barth, J. (1969) *Lost in the Funhouse*, London: Secker & Warburg.

—— (1982) *Sabbatical*, London: Secker & Warburg.

Barthelme, D. (1976) *City Life*, New York, Pocket Books.

—— (1979) *Great Days*, New York: Farrar Strauss Giroux.

Barthes, R. (1986) 'Rhetoric of the image', in R. Barthes *The Responsibility of Forms, Critical Essays on Music, Art, and Representation*, trans. R. Howard, Oxford: Basil Blackwell.

Barton, D. (1994) *Literacy: an Introduction to the Ecology of Written Language*, Oxford: Blackwell.

Bateson, G. (1973) *Steps to an Ecology of Mind: Collected Essays in Anthropology, Psychiatry, Evoloution, and Epistemology*, London: Paladin Books.

Bourdieu, P. (1992) *The Logic of Practice*, trans. R. Nice, Cambridge: Polity Press.

Brautigan, R. (1976) *The Hawkline Monster: a Gothic Western*, London: Pan

Burdon, V. (1996) unpublished case study.

Burns, A (1969) *Babel*, London: Calder & Boyars.

Burroughs, W. (1985) *Exterminator!*, New York: Penguin.

Calvino, I. (1981) *If on a Winter's Night a Traveller*, London: Secker & Warburg.

Chukovsky, K. (1968) *From Two to Five*. revised edn., trans. and ed. M. Morton, Berkeley and London: University of California Press.

Coover, R. (1969) *Pricksongs and Descants*, London: Pan.

Cortázar, J. (1968) *End of the Game and Other Stories*, trans. P. Blackburn, London: Collins and Harvill Press.

Crago, M. (1979) 'Incompletely shown objects in picture books: one child's response', *Children's Literature in Education*, 10(3): 151–7.

Craig, G. (1976) 'Reading: who is doing what to Whom?', in G. Josipovici *The Modern English Novel: The Reader, the Writer and the Work*, London: Open Books.

Dondis, D.A. (1973) *A Primer of Visual Literacy*, Cambridge MA: MIT Press

Doonan, J. (1989) 'Realism and surrealism in wonderland: John Tenniel and Anthony Browne', *Signal* 58: 9–30.

—— (1993) *Looking at Pictures in Picture Books*, Stroud: Thimble Press.

Drabble, M. (1969) *The Waterfall*, London: Weidenfeld & Nicolson.

Egoff, S., Stubbs, G. T., Ashley, L. F. and Sutton, W. (eds) (1996) *Only Connect: Readings on Children's Literature*, 3rd edn, Toronto: Oxford University Press.

Federman, R. (1971) *Double or Nothing*, Chicago: Swallow Press.

Finch, H. L. (1995) *Wittgenstein*, Shaftesbury, Dorset: Element Books.

Gibson, J. (1986) *The Ecological Approach to Visual Perception*, Hillsdale, NJ: Lawrence Erlbaum Associates.

Golden, J. M. (1990) *The Narrative Symbol in Childhood Literature: Explorations in the Construction of Text*, Berlin: Mouton.

Hall, E. (1966) *The Hidden Dimension*, New York: Doubleday.

Halliday, M. A. K. (1978) *Language as Social Semiotic: the Social Interpretation of Language and Meaning*, London: Edward Arnold.

—— (1985) *An Introduction to Functional Grammar*, London: Edward Arnold.

Hassan, I. (1986) 'Pluralism in postmodern perspective', *Critical Inquiry* 12(3): 503–20.

Hurlimann, B. (1967) *Three Centuries of Children's Books in Europe*, trans. and ed. B. Alderson, London: Oxford University Press.

Irving, J. (1978) *The World According to Garp*, London: Victor Gollancz.

Kress, G. and van Leeuwen, T. (1996) *Reading Images: the Grammar of Visual Design*, London: Routledge.

Kuhn, T. S. (1996) *The Structure of Scientific Revolutions*, Chicago: Chicago University Press.

Lanes, S. (1980) *The Art of Maurice Sendak*, London: The Bodley Head.

Lewis, D. (1995) 'The picture book: a form awaiting its history', *Signal* 77, 99–112.

Lodge, D. (1980) *How Far Can You Go?* Harmondsworth: Penguin.

Lorraine, W. (1977) 'An interview with Maurice Sendak', in S. Egoff, G.T. Stubbs and L. Ashley (eds) (1980) *Only Connect: Readings on Children's Literature*, 2nd edn, Toronto: Oxford University Press.

Lyon, D. (1994) *Postmodernity*, Buckingham: Open University Press.

Lyotard, J. (1984) *The Postmodern Condition: a Report on Knowledge*, trans. G. Bennington and B. Massumi, Manchester: Manchester University Press.

Major, C. (1975) *Emergency Exit*, New York: Fiction Collective.

Marantz, S. S. and Marantz, K. A. (1988) *The Art of Children's Picture Books: a Selective Reference Guide*, New York and London: Garland Publishing.

Meek, M. (1992) 'Children reading – now', in M. Styles, E. Bearne and V. Watson (eds) (1992) *After Alice*, London: Cassell.

Mitchell, W. J. T. (1987) *Iconology: Image, Text, Ideology*, Chicago: Chicago University Press.

Moebius, W. (1986) 'Introduction to picturebook codes' in P. Hunt (1990) *Children's Literature: the Development of Criticism*, London: Routledge.

Moss, E. (1990) 'A certain particularity: an interview with Janet and Allan Ahlberg', *Signal* 61: 20–26.

—— (1973) 'Chiyoko Nakatami', *Signal* 12: 135–8.

Moss, G. (1992) ' "My Teddy Bear Can Fly": postmodernizing the picture book' in P. Hunt (ed.) *Literature for Children: contemporary criticism*, London: Routledge.

Nabokov, V. (1969) *Ada or Ardor*, London: Pan.

Nikolajeva, M and Scott, C. (2000) 'The dynamics of picturebook communication', *Children's Literature in Education* 31(4):225–39.

—— (forthcoming) *How Picturebooks Work*, Garland Press

Nodelman, P. (1988) *Words about Pictures: The Narrative Art of Children's Picture Books*, Athens, Georgia: University of Georgia Press.

Pullman, P. (1989) 'Invisible pictures', *Signal* 60: 160–86.

—— (1993) 'Words and pictures: an examination of comic strip technique', in K. Barker (ed) (1993) *Graphic Account*, Newcastle-under-Lyme: The Library Association Youth Libraries Group.

Pynchon, T. (1975) *Gravity's Rainbow*, London: Pan.

Rorty, R. (1989) *Contingency, Irony and Solidarity*, Cambridge: Cambridge University Press.

Sadler, J. E. (1968) 'Introduction' to J.A. Comenius (1659) *Orbis Pictus*, a facsimile of the first English edition, London, Oxford University Press.

Schwarcz, J. H. (1982) *Ways of the Illustrator: Visual Communication in Children's Literature*, Chicago: American Library Association.

Sipe, L. R. (1998) 'How picture books work: a semiotically framed theory of text-picture relationships', *Children's Literature in Education* 29(2): 97–108.

Snow, C. E. and Goldfield, B. A. (1983) 'Turn the page please: situation specific language learning', *Journal of Child Language* 10(3): 551–69.

—— and Ninio, A. (1986) 'The contracts of literacy: what children learn from learning to read books', in W. Teale and E. Sulzby. (eds) (1986) *Emergent Literacy*, New Jersey: Ablex.

Sorrentino, G. (1980) *Mulligan Stew*, London: Marion Boyars.

Stewart, S. (1984) *On Longing: Narratives of the Miniature, the Gigantic, the Souvenir, the Collection*, Baltimore: Johns Hopkins University Press.

Styles, M. (1996) 'Inside the tunnel: a radical kind of reading – picture books, pupils and post-modernism' in V. Watson and M. Styles (eds) *Talking Pictures: Pictorial Texts and Young Readers*, London: Hodder and Stoughton.

Teale, W. and Sulzby, E. (eds) (1986) *Emergent Literacy*, New Jersey: Ablex.

Unsworth, L. 'Exploring multi-modal meaning-making in literature for children' in L. Unsworth (forthcoming) *Teaching Multiple Literacies Across the Curriculum*, Milton Keynes: Open University Press.

Vidal, G. (1969) *Myra Breckinridge*, London: Panther.

Volosinov, V. N. (1976) 'Discourse in life and discourse in art', in V.N. Volosinov *Freudianism: a Marxist Critique*, trans. I. R. Titunik, New York: Academic Press.

Vonnegut, K. (1959) *The Sirens of Titan*, London: Hodder.

—— (1979) *Slaughterhouse-Five*, London: Triad/Granada.

Vygotsky, L. S. (1978) *Mind in Society*, M. Cole, V. John-Steiner, S. Scribner, and E. Suberman (eds) Cambridge Mass: Harvard University Press.

Waugh, P. (1984) *Metafiction: the Theory and Practice of Self-conscious Fiction*, London: Methuen.

Williams, G. (1996) 'Reading and literacy' in P. Hunt (ed.) *The International Companion Encyclopedia of Children's Literature*, London: Routledge.

—— (1998) 'Children entering literate worlds: perspectives from the study of textual practices', in F. Christie and R. Misson (eds) (1998) *Literacy and Schooling*, London: Routledge.

Wittgenstein, L. (1968) *Philosophical Investigations*, trans. G. E. M. Anscombe, Oxford: Basil Blackwell.

Picturebook bibliography

Each Peach Pear Plum by Allan Ahlberg illustrated by Janet Ahlberg, Viking, 1978

The Worm Book by Allan Ahlberg illustrated by Janet Ahlberg, Granada, 1979

Peepo by Allan Ahlberg illustrated by Janet Ahlberg, Viking, 1981

The Baby's Catalogue by Allan Ahlberg illustrated by Janet Ahlberg, Kestrel, 1982

Yum Yum by Allan Ahlberg illustrated by Janet Ahlberg, Viking, 1984

Playmates by Allan Ahlberg illustrated by Janet Ahlberg, Viking, 1984

The Jolly Postman or Other People's Letters by Allan Ahlberg illustrated by Janet Ahlberg, Heinemann, 1986

The Jolly Christmas Postman by Allan Ahlberg illustrated by Janet Ahlberg, Heinemann, 1991

The Jolly Pocket Postman by Allan Ahlberg illustrated by Janet Ahlberg, Heinemann, 1995

The Mysteries of Harris Burdick by Chris Van Allsburg, Houghton Mifflin, 1984

The Wretched Stone by Chris Van Allsburg, Houghton Mifflin, 1991

Anno's Aesop by Mitsumasa Anno, Reinhardt Books in association with Viking, 1990

Little Tim and the Brave Sea Captain by Edward Ardizzone, Oxford University Press, 1936

Zoom by Istvan Banyai, Viking, 1998

Benjamin's Book by Alan Baker, André Deutsch, 1982

Mrs Armitage on Wheels by Quentin Blake, Jonathan Cape, 1987

All Join In by Quentin Blake, Jonathan Cape, 1990

Clown by Quentin Blake, Jonathan Cape, 1995

The Snowman by Raymond Briggs, Hamish Hamilton, 1978

When the Wind Blows by Raymond Briggs, Hamish Hamilton, 1982

The Tin-Pot Foreign General and the Old Iron Woman by Raymond Briggs, Hamish Hamilton, 1984

The Man by Raymond Briggs, Julia MacRae, 1992

Ethel & Ernest by Raymond Briggs, Jonathan Cape, 1998

Bear Hunt by Anthony Browne, Hamish Hamilton, 1979

Hansel and Gretel by Anthony Browne, Julia MacRae, 1981

Gorilla by Anthony Browne, Walker Books, 1983

Voices in the Park by Anthony Browne, Doubleday, 1998

Mr Gumpy's Outing by John Burningham, Jonathan Cape, 1970

Come Away From the Water, Shirley by John Burningham, Jonathan Cape, 1977

Time to Get Out of the Bath, Shirley by John Burningham, Jonathan Cape, 1978

Would You Rather ... by John Burningham, Jonathan Cape, 1978

Granpa by John Burningham, Jonathan Cape, 1984

Where's Julius? by John Burningham, Jonathan Cape, 1986

John Patrick Norman McHennessy, the Boy Who Was Always Late by John Burningham, Jonathan Cape, 1987

Making Faces by Nick Butterworth, Walker Books, 1993

Aladdin by Errol Le Cain, Faber & Faber, 1981

Hey Diddle Diddle and *Baby Bunting* by Randolph Caldecott, first published George Routledge & Son, [1882]; New Orchard Editions, 1988

The Very Hungry Caterpillar by Eric Carle, 1970

Princess Smartypants by Babette Cole, Hamish Hamilton, 1986

Drop Dead by Babette Cole, Jonathan Cape, 1996

So Much by Trish Cooke illustrated by Helen Oxenbury, Walker Books, 1994

Simon's Book by Henrik Drescher, André Deutsch, 1984

Tom's Pirate Ship by Philippe Dupasquier, Andersen, 1993

The Story of a Little Mouse Trapped in a Book by Monique Felix, Moonlight Publishing, 1981

Way Home by Libby Hathorn illustrated by Gregory Rogers, Andersen Press, 1994

The Little Boat by Kathy Henderson illustrated by Patrick Benson, Walker Books, 1995

How Tom Beat Captain Najork and his Hired Sportsmen by Russell Hoban illustrated by Quentin Blake, Jonathan Cape, 1974

Alfie Gets in First by Shirley Hughes, The Bodley Head, 1981

Rosie's Walk by Pat Hutchins, The Bodley Head, 1970

Tidy Titch by Pat Hutchins, Julia MacRae, 1991

Where, Oh Where, is Kipper's Bear? by Mick Inkpen, Hodder and Stoughton, 1994

The Snowy Day by Ezra Jack Keats, The Bodley Head, 1967

Pinkerton, Behave! by Steven Kellogg, Dial Press, 1979

The Book Mice by Tony Knowles, Evans, 1980

Black and White by David Macaulay, Houghton Mifflin, 1990

Lady Muck by William Mayne illustrated by Jonathan Heale, Heinemann, 1997

Arrow to the Sun by Gerald McDermott, Puffin, 1977

Have you Seen Who's Just Moved in Next Door to Us? by Colin McNaughton, Walker Books, 1991

Who's That Banging on the Ceiling? by Colin McNaughton, Walker Books, 1992

Oops! by Colin McNaughton, Andersen Press, 1996

Goal! by Colin McNaughton, Andersen Press, 1997

The Paperbag Princess by Robert Munsch, Little Hippo, 1999

On the Way Home by Jill Murphy, MacMillan, 1982

Clever Bill by William Nicholson, Heinemann, 1926

The Pirate Twins by William Nicholson, Faber and Faber, 1929

Angry Arthur by Hiawyn Oram illustrated by Satoshi Kitamura, Andersen Press, 1982

Sunshine by Jan Ormerod, Kestrel Books, 1981

The Dancing Class by Helen Oxenbury, Walker Books, 1983

Say Cheese! by David Pelham , Jonathan Cape, 1998

Haunted House by Jan Pienkowski, Heinemann, 1979

Robot by Jan Pienkowski, Heinemann, 1981

The Tale of Peter Rabbit by Beatrix Potter, Frederick Warne, 1902

Nothing Ever Happens on My Block by Ellen Raskin, Athenium, 1966

Where is Monkey? by Dieter Schubert, Hutchinson, 1987

The True Story of the Three Little Pigs by John Scieszka illustrated by Lane Smith, Viking, 1989

The Stinky Cheese Man and Other Fairly Stupid Tales by John Scieszka illustrated by Lane Smith, Viking, 1992

Where the Wild Things Are by Maurice Sendak, The Bodley Head, 1967

How Dogs Really Work by Alan Snow, HarperCollins, 1993

Sylvester and the Magic Pebble by William Steig, Simon & Schuster, 1969

The Three Little Wolves and the Big Bad Pig by Eugene Trivivas illustrated by Helen Oxenbury, Heinemann, 1993

Can't You Sleep Little Bear? by Martin Waddell illustrated by Barbara Firth, Walker Books, 1988

The Park in the Dark by Martin Waddell illustrated by Barbara Firth, Walker Books, 1989

Think of an Eel by Karen Wallace, Walker Books, 1993

How Do I Put it On? by Shigeo Watanabe and Yasuo Ohtomo, The Bodley Head, 1979

Index